Sacred Queer Stories

Sacred Queer Stories

Ugandan LGBTQ+ Refugee Lives and the Bible

Adriaan van Klinken and Johanna Stiebert
with Sebyala Brian and Fredrick Hudson

JAMES CURREY

James Currey
is an imprint of
Boydell & Brewer Ltd
PO Box 9, Woodbridge
Suffolk IP12 3DF (GB)
www.jamescurrey.com
and of
Boydell & Brewer Inc.
668 Mt Hope Avenue
Rochester, NY 14620–2731 (US)
www.boydellandbrewer.com

The publisher has no responsibility for the continued existence or accuracy of URLs for
external or third-party internet websites referred to in this book, and does not guarantee
that any content on such websites is, or will remain, accurate or appropriate

British Library Cataloguing in Publication Data
A catalogue record for this book is available from the British Library

ISBN 978-1-84701-283-8 (James Currey hardback)
ISBN 978-1-84701-367-5 (James Currey paperback)

Contents

Illustrations

Images © The Nature Network, Nairobi

Full credit details are provided in the captions to the images in the text. The editors, contributors and publisher are grateful to all the institutions and persons for permission to reproduce the materials in which they hold copyright. Every effort has been made to trace the copyright holders; apologies are offered for any omission, and the publisher will be pleased to add any necessary acknowledgement in subsequent editions.

Notes on Authors and Contributors

Sebyala Brian (also known as Raymond Brian and as Mother Nature) is an LGBTQ+ community advocate from Uganda. They are co-founder of The Nature Network, a community-based organisation of LGBTQ+ refugees in Nairobi, Kenya, and served as its Executive Director until their resettlement in the US in June 2020. They were a local research coordinator of the Sacred Queer Stories project.

Fredrick Hudson is a Ugandan LGBTQ+ refugee community activist based in Kenya. He currently serves as Executive Director of The Nature Network, a community-based organisation of LGBTQ+ refugees in Nairobi. He was a local research coordinator of the Sacred Queer Stories project.

Tom Rogers Muyunga-Mukasa originates from Uganda and now resides in the United States, where he is a Political Science Major with a bias in medical/health/social justice at St Mary's College in California. Tom is a refugee community health and development activist, an advocate for LGBTQ+ persons, and a co-founding member of The Nature Network.

Stella Nyanzi is a radical queer feminist activist and medical anthropologist with a doctoral degree from the London School of Hygiene and Tropical Medicine. She has twenty years of academic research and publishing experience focused on the study of human sexualities in Uganda and The Gambia.

Johanna Stiebert is Professor of Hebrew Bible at the University of Leeds (UK). Her work focuses on ideological- and gender-critical readings and applications of Hebrew Bible texts. She co-edited, together with Musa W. Dube, *The Bible, Centres and Margins: Dialogues Between Postcolonial African and British Biblical Scholars* (T&T Clark, 2018). Her most recent monograph is *Rape Myths, the Bible, and #MeToo* (Routledge Focus, 2020).

Adriaan van Klinken is Professor of Religion and African Studies at the University of Leeds (UK) and Extraordinary Professor at the Desmond Tutu Centre for Religion and Social Justice, University of the Western Cape (South Africa). His work focuses on issues of religion, gender, and sexuality in contemporary Africa. Among his recent publications is the monograph *Kenyan, Christian, Queer: Religion, LGBT Activism, and Arts of Resistance in Africa* (Penn State University Press, 2019).

Glossary and Abbreviations

AHA	Anti-Homosexuality Act (Uganda, 2014)
AHB	Anti-Homosexuality Bill
CAC	Cosmopolitan Affirming Church (an LGBTQ+ inclusive church in Nairobi)
CBO	Community-based organisation
CBS	Contextual Bible Study (a liberatory method of socially engaged biblical scholars and theologians reading the Bible with ordinary readers)
HIAS	Hebrew Immigrant Aid Society (a Jewish American non-profit organisation that provides humanitarian aid and assistance to refugees)
Kakuma	UNHCR-run refugee camp in Turkana County, north-western Kenya
LGBTQ+	Lesbian, Gay, Bisexual, Transgender, Queer, and others
RAS	Refugee Affairs Secretariat (a Kenyan government agency)
TNN	The Nature Network (a community-based organisation of Ugandan LGBTQ+ refugees based in Matasia, at the outskirts of Nairobi)
UN	United Nations
UNHCR	United Nations High Commissioner for Refugees (the UN Refugee Agency)

Acknowledgement

This publication is an output of a research project funded under the British Academy/Leverhulme Trust Small Research Grant scheme (grant no. SRG1819\190405). The grant was derived from the British Academy's partnership with the Department for Business, Energy, and Industrial Strategy, and with the Marc Fitch Fund.

Foreword

Sacred Queer Stories – a Gift to Queer African Studies

Sacred Queer Stories is an important collation of improbable combinations in a world of dichotomies. It is about the possibility of paradoxes. Combining the affirmative roles of religion (specifically Christianity and Islam) with non-heteronormative sexual orientations and non-binary gender identities, within the context of Ugandan LGBTQ+ people of refugee status is a brilliant achievement. Many of the individuals whose stories are narrated and shared in this collection were forced to flee from their home country, Uganda, because of political persecution arising out of widespread homophobia propagated by Christians in the loosely organised anti-gay movement. Religious bigotry and homophobia were socially engineered into the legislature and executive arms of the state, to the effect of tabling, processing, and enacting a private member's Bill of Parliament called the Anti-Homosexuality Bill (2009). The public processes and public discourses emerging from this Bill had dire consequences for the private everyday lives of people with non-heteronormative sexual orientations and non-binary gender identities. The most dangerous consequence was the proposal of the death penalty for people convicted with some forms of homosexual behaviour. However, there were several other harmful proposed penalties including life imprisonment, prison sentences, and monetary fines.

Considering that religion – in particular, Christianity – was among the foundational premises of their persecution which led to fleeing from Uganda, seeking for asylum and eventual refugee status in Kenya, it is remarkable that these Ugandan LGBTQ+ people generally held onto Christian scripture and ethos to make meaning of their lives. Although Christianity was responsible for their political persecution, dislocation, loss of citizenship and ejection from their home country Uganda, it is a wonderful paradox that they continued to find inspiration from Christian scripture and particular Bible stories. This point is made even stronger because, instead of abandoning religious scripture in the midst of facing further marginalisation while in their second country and awaiting resettlement to a third country of refuge, these LGBTQ+ people still spoke fondly of the Bible stories. It is almost a miracle of faith that these individuals turned to the very scriptural text used to justify their homophobic persecution to innovatively draw resilience from specific Bible stories. This is a brilliant agentic subversion of the source of their persecution.

For queer African scholars, such as myself, this book is a welcome rare gem because it exemplifies a successful queer and queering project. The book represents African queerness and queer African-ness in tripartite form. First, there is the unapologetic queerness of non-normative sexualities and non-conforming gender identities. In the process of reading the book, I was deeply honoured to discover that Ugandan LGBTQ+ refugees with whom I had previously interacted during my own academic ethnographic research and LGBTQ+ activism prior to their exodus from Uganda, remembered and wrote about me in their life stories shared in this book. Second, the individual stories and collective descriptions of the community of queer refugees explore and shore up alternative forms of kinship and belonging outside normative patriarchal or matriarchal kinship structures in Africa. The queering of kinship is cast into sharp relief in the book. Third, the book presents the queerness of statelessness, and irregular citizenship status of refugees prior to obtaining documented status but after departure from home. The story contributors and authors of this book must be celebrated for capturing a marginalised, silenced, and invisibilised population group that is in transit; all its ambiguities and complexities permanently brought to the fore by being located indelibly on the pages of this book.

In as far as the collection successfully destabilises the rigid binary separation between the sacred on the one hand, and the queer – non-heteronormative sexualities and non-conforming gender identities – on the other hand, it is a powerful contribution to Queer African studies. Moreover, *Sacred Queer Stories* draws from African Religion, African Theology, and African Philosophy to simultaneously queer the sacred, and to make sacred the queer. Complicating, obscuring, and troubling the seemingly neat dichotomy between the sacred and the queer is at once a successful queering project that more closely reflects the complexities of human experience. To quote from the book:

> Indeed, they have actively engaged in reading the Bible through the lens of their own perspectives and experiences. The resulting queer interpretations of the Bible adopt a variety of methods and strategies which represent an act of appreciating and reclaiming the Bible – a process of

'taking back the word' – by people who on the basis of their sexuality and gender identity have often been preached against (and worse) from the same book.

Twelve personal stories of Ugandan LGBTQ+ refugees form Part I of the book. This is a generous and rare gift to Ugandans, Kenyans, Africans, and humans – whether scholars, policy-makers or designers of service delivery and programmes, because these twelve personal stories fill a gap in knowledge about the queerness and liminality of lives in transit as refugees. There is scanty knowledge about the lives of forced migrants during the period after the exodus from their home country and resettlement into the third country of asylum. Often living undetected below the radar as undocumented or unregistered migrants, stateless individuals, or urban refugees, many people who flee from their home countries are inaccessible and untraceable – making it difficult (almost impossible) to document and conduct research about them. For me, as a scholar of queer African studies focused on ethnographies in Uganda and The Gambia, these stories fill a big gap in the archive of knowledge about Africa's queer folk. A missing piece of the archive is reclaimed, retold, and reinserted back to us Queer African scholars, through this book. A component of the queer African archive that is lost through exodus is now found and narrated back to us. Sustained access to forced migrants awaiting resettlement requires innovative, flexible, bold, and highly adoptable research methods. The authors generously share the methodology and processes of inter-reading life stories and Bible stories. Indeed, as the Introduction to the volume states, 'this is the first collection of Ugandan LGBTQ+ refugee stories to be published'.

The acknowledgement of co-authors Sebyala (Raymond) Brian and Frederick Hudson is politically important towards redressing the imbalance of power in asymmetrical partnerships of knowledge creation between academics based in the northern hemisphere and local interlocutors located in the study communities of the southern hemisphere. The two lead authors are widely published academics at the University of Leeds. While Adriaan van Klinken is Professor of Religion and African Studies, Johanna Stiebert is Professor of Hebrew Bible. During the research partnership on which the book is based, Sebyala Brian and Frederick Hudson were Ugandan LGBTQ+ refugees and community advocates living in Kenya. The asymmetrical power relations in this research partnership are evident in the comparison between the permanence of tenure in a leading university of the United Kingdom and the highly transient role of being LGBTQ+ community advocates for a refugee community-based organisation – The Nature Network (TNN). Rather than conceal their contribution in an obscure footnote, the two lead authors acknowledge their Ugandan refugee counterparts as co-authors. Furthermore, in order to allay any assumptions that this is tokenist authorship, the lead authors explain that 'Sebyala [Raymond] Brian and Frederick Hudson, served as invaluable research assistants, coordinating much of the on-the-ground work, facilitating the workshops, conducting most of the individual interviews, and translating some of them from Luganda to English'.

The conscious and deliberate decision to democratise knowledge generation is further implemented through the use of autobiographical storytelling in which the personal narratives of Ugandan LGBTQ+ refugees form the core of the first part of the book. The readers can hear first-account narratives of a highly invisibilised, historically silenced, and often marginalised group of people. The giving of voice back to queer asylum seekers waiting for uncertain outcomes of a long resettlement process indeed (re)humanises people who have been dehumanised for both their non-heteronormative sexual orientations and non-conforming gender identities, as well as their marginality in terms of citizenship and belonging. The personal narratives sketch the dysfunctions to life prior to the flight from Uganda, the challenges and opportunities during refugee status determination and asylum seeking in Kenya, and eventual hopes of a better life after resettlement into a third country. These personal stories smash the long overdue silence and absence of queer African asylum seekers produced in the dark crucible of Uganda's anti-homosexual legislation-making. The research subjects thereby cease to be objects under the microscopic gaze of outsiders and rather transform into powerful agentic co-creators of queer African knowledge. This methodological decision is very affirming and empowering.

The centrality of the community-based organisation – The Nature Network (TNN) – to the (re)telling of the sacred queer stories cannot be over-emphasised. Defined as, 'a Kenya-based transgender-led refugee support safe space', TNN's impact, effects, results, productions, and outpourings are evident in the pages of this volume. Indeed, the key methods of research and knowledge generation relied upon in this book draw from the strengths of TNN's own organisational methods, ethos, and praxis. Individual in-depth interviews, focus group discussions to internalise Bible scripts, drama productions combined with poetry, and reinterpretation are built on TNN's creative work and its commitment to produce 'art with a vision'. The centrality of storytelling to the book is re-echoed from the importance of stories to the collective existence of TNN. The regular Christian meetings, fellowship, and communing of members of TNN's safe space draw from the biblical practice of collective spirituality. Thus, this research was greatly shaped, informed and dependent on TNN's character. It was perhaps easier to methodologically call on the research participants to dramatise the Bible scripts using contemporary interpretations, because drama, acting, and role-playing are central to the existence of TNN. Queer appropriation of the Bible through drama and poetry illustrates how the Bible can be an integral component of subversive political processes that facilitate articulating queer realities and identities.

Drawing on community-based theatre for development, the drama performances used two Bible stories (Daniel in the lions' den, and Jesus with the adulterous woman) to retell the stories of Ugandan LGBTQ+ refugees. Likewise, the two poems in the book combine Bible stories with the everyday realities of these Ugandan LGBTQ+ refugees. Thus, the title of the book, *Sacred Queer Stories: Ugandan LGBTQ+ Refugee Lives and the Bible*, arises from the dialogical reading of stories from life and the Bible. Re-storying was a group process that involved reading the selected Bible stories and then retelling and dramatising the contents of the story in their own contemporary context. The passing of the Anti-Homosexuality Bill and the phobia it unleashed onto the LGBTQ+ community is mapped onto the throwing of Daniel into the lions' den. Likewise, the effects of the 'indecency between males' arising from the Kenyan Penal Code is mapped onto the Bible story of Jesus with the woman caught in adultery. This inter-reading perhaps offers the foundations of developing a queer African biblical hermeneutics as has been developed in the contexts of HIV/AIDS, feminism, and liberation in diverse African settings.

The book formally starts the journey to redress the scarcity of African queer interpretations of the Bible, a sacred book that has mainly been used as a tool of condemnation and judgement of people with non-heteronormative sexual orientations and non-binary gender identities.

Stella Nyanzi, Nairobi – Kenya[1]

---

[1] I started writing this foreword in November 2020, when I was in Uganda. And then in January 2021, I fled from Uganda because of political persecution. I completed writing the foreword in February 2021 when I was another Ugandan asylum seeker in Kenya.

Introduction

How impressionable and vulnerable we are in the face of a story. ...
Stories matter. Many stories matter. Stories have been used to dispossess and to malign. But stories can also be used to empower, and
to humanize. Stories can break the dignity of a people. But stories
can also repair that broken dignity. ... When we reject the single
story, when we realize that there is never a single story about any
place, we regain a kind of paradise.

Chimamanda Ngozi Adichie[1]

About life stories and Bible stories

This is a book about stories. To be precise, it is about two categories of
stories: life stories and Bible stories. It explores the creative process of
putting particular life stories – of Ugandan LGBTQ+[2] (mostly gay and
transgender) refugees – in conversation with select biblical stories – stories

[1] Chimamanda Ngozi Adichie, 'The Danger of a Single Story', TED Global 2009,
www.ted.com/talks/chimamanda_ngozi_adichie_the_danger_of_a_single_
story (accessed 16 December 2020).

[2] Lesbian, Gay, Bisexual, Transgender, Queer, and others. In this book we use
the LGBTQ+ acronym as an open-ended term for a variety of non-heteronormative sexual and gender expressions (when participants used a different version of this acronym, such as LGBTI with the I of intersex, we have
respected that). As will become clear throughout this book, in the context of
our study, the categories L, G, B, T, and Q are relatively fluid and ambiguous. We did not add the I of intersex, because none of our participants explicitly identified with that term. We acknowledge the West-centric origins of
LGBTQ+ terminology, and their limitations in African contexts. However,
our participants, like many sexual and gender non-conforming activists and
communities across Africa, have adopted this language. Although the word
kuchu has been used by Ugandan LGBTQ+ people to identify themselves, it
was not widely used among our participants.

that the refugees themselves identified as inspiring and as speaking to their life experiences. This process of dialogue, or inter-reading as we call it, between life stories and Bible stories engenders a new body of stories, which we describe as sacred queer stories. In fact, we take each of the three bodies of stories that are central in this book to be *both* sacred and queer. This may be puzzling to some readers.

Obviously, the life stories of LGBTQ+ people are queer – queer as referring to perspectives that do not conform to, but challenge and subvert the norms of gender and sexuality in society. As the life stories presented in this book demonstrate, such non-conformance comes at a great personal cost. Many African societies, including Uganda, in recent decades have witnessed heated public debates about issues of homosexuality and LGBTQ+ rights, and increasing levels of socio-political homophobia, or 'anti-queer animus'.[3] In Uganda, this culminated in the passing of the infamous Anti-Homosexuality Act (early 2014). Although only short-lived, the Act and the underlying politicisation of homosexuality created a social and political climate in which many LGBTQ+ people no longer felt safe. Hundreds left (and continue to leave) the country for neighbouring Kenya, registering as refugees and entering a process of resettlement in a third country, through the United Nations refugee agency (UNHCR).[4] This resettlement process is notoriously slow, and, in the meantime, they experience further marginalisation in Kenya, because of their refugee status *and* their sexuality. Demonstrating resilience and inventiveness, many of the refugees have organised themselves in grassroots community-based organisations, in order to collectively procure such basic necessities as accommodation and food. One of these organisations, called The Nature Network, has been the key partner in generating the research that inspired and resulted in this book. The life stories of these refugees are queer, not only in the sense that they narrate non-normative sexualities (queer in a sexual sense), but also in how they narrate alternative forms of kinship and belonging (queer in a social sense), and in how they reflect the ambiguity and complexity of location, as their lives are in transit (queer in a spatial sense). But how are these queer life stories also sacred?

[3] Patrick Awondo, Peter Geschiere, and Graeme Reid, 'Homophobic Africa? Toward A More Nuanced View', *African Studies Review*, 55:3 (2012), 145–168; Ryan R. Thoreson, 'Troubling the Waters of a "Wave of Homophobia": Political Economies of Anti-queer Animus in Sub-Saharan Africa', *Sexualities*, 17:1–2 (2014), 23–42.

[4] Gitta Zomorodi, 'Responding to LGBT Forced Migration in East Africa', *Forced Migration Review*, 52 (2016), 91–93.

The term 'sacred' usually comes as part of a binary, its opposite term being 'profane'. This dichotomy is strongly rooted in the sociology of religion and in social theory more generally, often in parallel with other binary frames, such as 'religious and secular', 'worldly and otherworldly', 'spiritual and material', and so on. Now, in African contexts these dichotomies are problematic because traditionally, as the Kenyan scholar of religion John Mbiti reminds us in his classic *African Religions and Philosophy*, indigenous religions 'permeate all the departments of life, there is no formal distinction between the sacred and the secular, between the religious and non-religious, between the spiritual and the material areas of life'.[5] Mbiti, like the Tanzanian scholar Laurenti Magesa in his recent book *What Is Not Sacred?*, suggests that in African religious worldviews, there is a sacred realm encompassing all of reality and life.[6] 'To African peoples this is a deeply religious universe ... and human life is a religious experience of that universe. So, African people can find or attribute religious meaning to the whole of existence.'[7]

One might take issue with the somewhat monolithic and a-historical account of African religiosity offered by scholars such as Mbiti and Magesa. In contemporary African societies, religion is a diverse and complex phenomenon; colonialism, modernity, Christianisation, and Islamisation have profoundly affected the ways in which people experience the sacred or spiritual nature of life. But the basic point that a dichotomy of profane versus sacred is problematic, and that anything *can* be sacred, still holds true (and is also increasingly recognised in more recent Western sociological writing).[8]

The people whose stories are told in this book are not necessarily deeply religious in the sense of fervently participating in activities such as prayer and worship (although several are), but they do demonstrate a natural religiosity integrated with their daily lives. The above-mentioned lack of formal distinctions between the sacred and profane chimes in with queer theory, which is all about interrogating and destabilising binary schemes of analysis, by highlighting their ambiguity, complexity, and fluidity. Specifically, in relation to sexuality and the body, queer religious

---

[5] John Mbiti, *African Religions and Philosophy*, 2nd edn (London: Heinemann, 1990), 2.

[6] Laurenti Magesa, *What Is Not Sacred? African Spirituality* (Maryknoll: Orbis, 2013).

[7] Mbiti, *African Religions and Philosophy*, 73.

[8] E.g. see Gordon Lynch, *The Sacred in the Modern World: A Cultural Sociological Approach* (Oxford: Oxford University Press, 2012).

thought has questioned the widespread assumption that these belong to the sphere of the profane and has highlighted the ways in which they can and do in fact emerge as sites of the sacred.[9] In this book we use 'sacred' as an open-ended term referring to the various ways in which, through storytelling, lives are signified and given meaning. The bottom line is the humanistic principle that human life has intrinsic value. For many of the people featured in this book this is a religious idea: human life is sacred, because it is created by God. The life stories featured here are powerful, precisely because they come from a group of people suffering from dehumanisation. Through telling the stories of their lives they affirm and reclaim their fundamental human dignity and value: that is, they narrate and thereby assert the sacredness of their lives. To the extent that their stories reflect narratively on questions of faith and the divine – the relationship to and understanding of God – they can also be read as narrative queer theologies. In the words of queer theologian Chris Greenough, these life stories come to 'complement scripture as sacred stories'.[10]

So, the life stories of LGBTQ+ people featured in this book are *both* queer and sacred. But what about Bible stories? Obviously, Bible stories are sacred: they are part of a book that Christians and (as far as the first Testament is concerned) Jews consider as holy scripture.[11] Certainly, for the Ugandan LGBTQ+ refugees who participated in the project underlying this book, the Bible holds high esteem. Most of them are Christian, a few of them Muslim, but all of them approached the Bible as a sacred text, a text with religious authority, a text through which they could discern the voice of God speaking to them and to their lives. This was most clearly expressed that moment, at the beginning of one of our focus group discussions, when some participants raised their hands and insisted that the session should be opened with prayer – something everyone agreed to. Subsequently, all sessions were opened, and closed, with prayer. This anecdote illustrates the status of the Bible in contemporary Africa: it is not just a highly popular text that is widely read, but also a book that is assigned authority and holds sacred status. So, Bible stories are sacred, yet why would they also be queer?

[9] E.g. see Marvin M. Ellison and Kelly Brown (eds), *Sexuality and the Sacred: Sources for Theological Reflection*, 2nd edn (Louisville: Westminster John Knox Press, 2010).

[10] Chris Greenough, *Queer Theologies: The Basics* (London and New York: Routledge 2020), 132.

[11] The Hebrew Bible is the first part of the Christian Bible, which Christians usually refer to as the Old Testament.

Referring to the history and ongoing realities of Christian-inspired colonialism, racism, patriarchy, and other forms of oppression, Kenyan theologian Nyambura Njoroge has asked whether the Bible is actually a curse or a blessing to Africa.[12] We will return to this question in the Conclusion of this book. At this point, we simply echo Njoroge's critical question because the Bible in Africa, like in other parts of the world, often serves to fuel homophobia and maintain the status quo of heteronormativity: 'It is Adam and Eve, not Adam and Steve'; 'Homosexuality is an abomination'; 'Sodom and Gomorrah were destroyed because of this sin'. However, in spite of this dominant usage, many same-sex loving people, in Africa and elsewhere, continue to read this book, often taking it to be God's Word, and getting encouragement and inspiration from it. Indeed, they have actively engaged in reading the Bible through the lens of their own perspectives and experiences. The resulting queer interpretations of the Bible adopt a variety of methods and strategies, which represent an act of appropriating and reclaiming the Bible – a process of 'taking back the Word'[13] – by people who, on the basis of their sexuality and gender identity, have often been preached against (and worse) from the same book.

One additional way of making sense of this is to point out that the sacred texts of the Bible are queer – in the sense that the Bible, too, is in many ways about non-conformance and about challenging and subverting, including challenging and subverting norms of gender and sexuality. As the queer biblical scholar Ken Stone puts it, 'the attempt to ground heteronormativity in appeals to biblical literature may prove to be less secure, less "straight"-forward, or less inevitable than many of those who make such appeals imagine'.[14] *The Queer Bible Commentary* also identifies queer characters and stories throughout the Bible. So, not only the interpretive lens but, arguably, the Bible itself, and hence its stories, too, are queer.[15]

---

[12] Nyambura J. Njoroge, 'The Bible and African Christianity: A Curse or a Blessing?' in Musa W. Dube (ed.), *Other Ways of Reading: African Women and the Bible (Atlanta: Society of Biblical Literature*, 2001), 207–236.

[13] Robert Goss and Mona West (eds), *Take Back the Word: A Queer Reading of the Bible* (Cleveland: Pilgrim Press 2000).

[14] Ken Stone, 'Queer Reading between Bible and Film: Paris is Burning and the "Legendary Houses" of David and Saul', in Teresa J. Hornsby and Ken Stone (eds), *Bible Trouble: Queer Reading at the Boundaries of Biblical Scholarship* (Atlanta: Society of Biblical Literature, 2011), 95.

[15] Deryn Guest, Robert E. Goss, Mona West and Thomas Bohache (eds), *The Queer Bible Commentary* (London: SCM, 2006).

Alongside the Bible being a queer text, the Bible is also a distinctively African text in essential respects. Not only is sub-Saharan Africa home to one in four of the world's Christians, with the fastest-growing Christian populations, but the Bible is also populated by African characters and locations. Notable among African places are Mitzrayim (Egypt) and Cush (identified with Ethiopia and Sudan) and, among people, Asenath, mother of two heads of the tribes of Israel, the Queen of Sheba, the Prophet Zephaniah, and the Ethiopian eunuch, to name just a few.[16] Via Coptic Christianity in Egypt, and Tewahedo Orthodox Christianity in Ethiopia, the Bible also has a reception history on the African continent starting early in the Common Era and continuing up to today.[17] Rastafarianism has invoked these traditions to emphasise and enhance the Africanness of the Bible.

It is through dialogue and interaction between LGBTQ+ life stories and biblical stories that new sacred queer stories emerge. As the queer religion scholar Melissa Wilcox puts it, 'personal stories react to and interact with sacred stories, but they also create them. ... When they have divine or sacred authority personal stories can make, unmake, and remake the sacred world.'[18] That is what the project underlying this book seeks to facilitate: a narrative process of sacred queer world-making through a creative interaction between the life stories of Ugandan LGBTQ+ refugees, and selected Bible stories. As such, this book both exemplifies and enhances the narrative turn in the study of religion and theology. This turn is based, in the words of theologian Ruard Ganzevoort, on the critical observation that

> human beings tell – indeed: live – stories that invite and serve them to see the world in a certain way and act accordingly. And they do so in close interaction with the stories of a religious tradition that offer possible worlds, created through narrative and portrayed in stories and symbols, rituals and moral guidelines.[19]

[16] David T. Adamo, *Africa and Africans in the Old Testament* (Eugene: Wipf and Stock, 2001); Tokunboh Adeyemo (ed.), *Africa Bible Commentary* (Nairobi: WordAlive Publishers; Grand Rapids: Zondervan, 2006).

[17] Gerald O. West and Musa W. Dube (eds), *The Bible in Africa: Transactions, Trajectories and Trends* (Leiden: Brill, 1998).

[18] Melissa M. Wilcox, *Queer Religiosities: An Introduction to Transgender and Queer Studies in Religion* (Lanham: Rowman & Littlefield 2020), 55.

[19] R. Ruard Ganzevoort, 'Introduction: Religious Stories We Live By', in R. Ruard Ganzevoort, Maaike de Haardt and Michael Scherer-Rath (eds), *Religious Stories We Live By: Narrative Approaches in Theology and Religious Studies* (Leiden: Brill, 2014), 1.

The present book advances this turn by demonstrating how the interaction between life stories and religious (in this case, biblical) stories can be actively stimulated in creative activist-scholarly work with vulnerable and marginalised communities, such as the LGBTQ+ refugees featured in these pages. It further foregrounds and examines the potential and significance of this narrative Bible-centred approach for LGBTQ+ activism and queer scholarship in an African context.

It has been observed that queer studies in religion and theology are an overwhelmingly Euro-American enterprise.[20] This book contributes to an emerging interest in queer theologies and religiosities in global contexts, which decentre the white Western body as the main subject of queer theorising, putting the bodies and perspectives of people of colour centre stage.[21] Its narrative methodology also counters the way in which Western queer studies often appears to privilege dense, rather inaccessible theorising, instead embracing storytelling as a valid strategy to bring in alternative, hitherto marginalised perspectives from what liberation theologian Gustavo Gutiérrez has called 'the underside of history'.[22]

As far as the study of Christianity is concerned, this book acknowledges that Africa has become a major part of contemporary world Christianity. At the same time it draws critical attention to those communities that tend to be overlooked in the prevalent accounts of African Christianities. Indeed, the voices and experiences of Ugandan LGBTQ+ refugees centred in this book provide a unique East African insight into Christianity as a 'lived religion in transgressive form', and they allow for a queering of the discourse about African Christianity.[23] Paraphrasing the question posed by the eminent scholar of world Christianity, Lamin Sanneh, 'Whose religion is Christianity?', one could ask: Whose book is the Bible? The answer being that, indeed, the Bible, like Christianity, is not exclusively Western, but also African. It is so, in a way that does not exclude, but

---

[20] See chapter 3 in Susannah Cornwall, *Controversies in Queer Theology* (London: SCM Press, 2011).

[21] For an overview of this trend, see chapter 3 in Greenough, *Queer Theologies*. For examples from Asia and Latin America, see Robert Shore-Goss and Joseph N. Goh (eds), *Unlocking Orthodoxies for Inclusive Theologies: Queer Alternatives* (London and New York: Routledge, 2020).

[22] Gustavo Gutiérrez, *The Power of the Poor in History* (Eugene: Wipf and Stock, 2004), chapter 7.

[23] Kathleen T. Talvacchia, Michael F. Pettinger, Mark Larrimore (eds), *Queer Christianities: Lived Religion in Transgressive Forms* (New York: New York University Press, 2015).

firmly extends to African LGBTQ+ communities.[24] As the South African Archbishop Desmond Tutu observes, in contemporary Africa (but not only there) too many LGBTQ+ people 'have been hurt and traumatised – treated as outcasts – because of the way the Bible has been interpreted'; in that context it is 'time for healing' as LGBTQ+ people journey with the Bible themselves.[25]

African LGBTQ+ life stories

An in-depth discussion of the rationale for, and methodology of, our process of inter-reading Ugandan LGBTQ+ life stories and Bible stories is presented in the chapter that opens Part II of this book. That chapter is followed by two in-depth accounts of this process, its outcomes and effects, focusing on the story of Daniel in the lions' den, and of Jesus and the woman caught in adultery, respectively. However, preceding that, Part I of the book presents twelve personal stories of Ugandan LGBTQ+ refugees, which need some introduction and contextualisation.

These stories are part of, and contribute to, a recently emerging body of African LGBTQ+ life narratives, published in a range of collections from across the continent.[26] Together with other forms of cultural production such as films, these collections of non-fiction life stories add to the building of queer African archives. The queer African archive, as Kenyan

---

[24] Lamin Sanneh, *Whose Religion Is Christianity? The Gospel Beyond the West* (Grand Rapids: William B. Eerdmans, 2003).

[25] Desmond Tutu, 'Foreword', in *The Bible and Homosexuality* (Cape Town: Inclusive and Affirming Ministries, 2008), iv.

[26] Unoma Azuah (ed.), *Blessed Body: The Secret Lives of Nigerian Lesbian, Gay, Bisexual and Transgender* (Jackson: Cooking Pot Publishing, 2016); Jude Dibia and Olumide F. Makanjuola (eds), *Queer Men's Narratives* (Abuja: Cassava Republic, 2020); Pepe Hendricks (ed.), *Hijab: Unveiling Queer Muslim Lives* (Cape Town: The Inner Circle, 2009); Zelly Lisanework (ed.), *Tikur Eugeda: Queer Stories from Ethiopia* (Addis Ababa: House of Guramayle, 2019); John Marnell, *Seeking Sanctuary: Stories of Sexuality, Faith and Migration* (Johannesburg: Wits University Press, 2021); Azeenarh Mohammed, Chitra Nagarajan and Rafeeat Aliyu (eds), *She Called Me Woman: Nigeria's Queer Women Speak* (Abuja: Cassava Republic, 2018); Kevin Mwachiro (ed.), *Invisible: Stories from Kenya's Queer Community* (Nairobi: Goethe Institut, 2013); *Stories of Our Lives* (Nairobi: The Nest Collective, 2015); Makhosazana Xaba and Crystal Biruk (eds), *Proudly Malawian: Life Stories from Lesbian and Gender-Nonconforming Individuals* (Johannesburg: GALA, 2016).

queer studies scholar Keguro Macharia critically points out, consists of 'names, faces and stories [that] form an archive of disposability'; it is 'an archive that is not admitted into official view, an archive whose presence undoes much of what we might mean by archive'.[27] The recent efforts of activists and scholars to dis-close the names, faces, and stories of African LGBTQ+ persons and communities, by documenting queer African pasts and presents, seek to interrogate this historical and contemporary disposability and marginality of those bodies and lives considered to be sexually and gender deviant. Thus, Kevin Mwachiro aptly titles his collection *Invisible*; yet by sharing stories from Kenya's queer community he renders the lives of LGBTQ+ Kenyans visible. Unoma Azuah's collection of narratives of the 'secret lives' of Nigerian LGBTQ+ persons is poignantly called *Blessed Body*, suggesting that self-narration is key to reclaiming queer bodies as blessed. As the editors of another recent collection from Kenya put it, through telling their stories LGBTQ+ people challenge the popular representations about them, and instead 'the self-representing queer Kenyan grants the reader permission to explore private and intimate worlds – WHERE THE VAGARIES OF QUEER PUBLICNESS, SILENCE, INTIMACY, MILITANCY AND LOVE HAPPENS'.[28] Reviewing recent projects of African LGBTQ+ autobiographical storytelling, the Kenyan queer studies scholar Eddie Ombagi captures the significance of such work by stating that, as an 'important narrative archive [they] engage not only against dominant narratives but also actively unmask the hidden narratives and voice the silent ones.'[29]

Thus, the stories presented in Part I of this book are part of an existing genre and body of literature. Yet they also add something new to it: as far as we know, this is the first collection of Ugandan LGBTQ+ refugee stories to be published.[30] The stories contribute to the building of queer African archives by providing insight into the life experiences of a specific African queer constituency: those LGBTQ+ people from Uganda who,

---

[27] Keguro Macharia, 'Archive and Method in Queer African Studies', *Agenda*, 29:1 (2015), 140.

[28] *Stories of Our Lives*, xiii (small caps original).

[29] Eddie Ombagi, '"Stories We Tell": Queer Narratives in Kenya', *Social Dynamics*, 45:3 (2019), 422. For a discussion of the political and theological significance of such queer storytelling, see chapter 3 in Adriaan van Klinken, *Kenyan, Christian, Queer: Religion, LGBT Activism, and Arts of Resistance in Africa* (University Park: Penn State University Press, 2019).

[30] But see the photobook by Jake Naughton and Jacob Kushner, *This is How the Heart Beats: LGBTQ East Africa* (New York: The New Press, 2020).

because of their sexuality, decided to leave their country, and are in the process of leaving the continent. They are the victims of what the Ugandan author Deborah Kintu describes as the 'Ugandan morality crusade'.[31] Yet their stories transcend the narrative of victimhood in which they are usually captured, as they reflect a remarkable level of agency, courage, resilience, and creativity. In the words of the Kenyan scholar Damaris Parsitau, storytelling can transform victimhood into 'creative resistance'.[32] As mentioned earlier, life storytelling is a humanising process and therefore has humanistic value. Perhaps this is particularly true for the stories of refugees. As the anthropologist Michael Jackson points out,

> Migrant narratives are, in many ways, allegories of human existence, in which the hope that our lives may be made more abundant, for ourselves and those we love, constantly comes up against the limits of what we may achieve and the despair into which we may be plunged when we find ourselves unable to achieve that state of well-being and flourishing that Aristotle called *Eudaimonia* [human flourishing].[33]

The stories presented in this book illustrate this point; yet, as much as they narrate the struggle for a life of dignity and flourishing, and the limits to achieve that, overall they remain surprisingly hopeful. This, perhaps, reflects the particular status and situation of these refugees: in a process of resettlement to a third country, which maintains their hope that even if the past in Uganda, and the present in Kenya, are tough, a promising future might be awaiting them.

The research project of which this book is the outcome was a collaboration between the two lead authors, and the earlier mentioned community-based organisation, The Nature Network (TNN). Two TNN leaders, Sebyala Brian[34] and Fredrick Hudson, served as invaluable research assistants, coordinating much of the on-the-ground work, facilitating the workshops,

---

[31] Deborah Kintu, *The Ugandan Morality Crusade: The Brutal Campaign against Homosexuality and Pornography under Yoweri Museveni* (Jefferson: McFarland, 2017).

[32] Damaris Parsitau, 'From Victimhood to Creative Resistance: The Book that Tells Stories and Signals Other Ways of Being', *Religious Studies Review*, 46:3, 337–339.

[33] Michael Jackson, *The Politics of Storytelling: Variations on a Theme by Hannah Arendt*, 2nd edn (Copenhagen: Museum Musculanum Press, 2013), 6.

[34] Sebyala Brian is their official name. They usually go under the names Raymond Brian, which is used throughout this book, and are also known as Mother Nature.

conducting most of the individual interviews, and translating some of them from Luganda into English. For this crucial work in the process of producing the knowledge presented here they are acknowledged as co-authors of this book. The project was set up in two stages: first, individual life story interviews, and second, group work and creative drama focused on select Bible stories. Here, we will briefly discuss the first stage; details about the second stage can be found in the opening chapter of Part II.

Individual interviews were carried out with participants, exploring their life experiences, especially in relation to their sexuality, refugee status, and faith. The interviews, conducted in the period September–October 2019, focused on participants' past experiences in Uganda, their present situation in Kenya, and their hopes and plans for the future. Adriaan and Johanna provided interview training to Raymond and Hudson, and conducted test interviews with them. Raymond and Hudson then carried out the majority of the twelve individual interviews, for which they had selected participants from the TNN community and the wider network of Ugandan refugees in Nairobi. They transcribed the audio-recorded interviews and translated two of the interviews from Luganda into English (Stories 3 and 12). Adriaan and Johanna then carried out light-touch editing to improve readability. As part of this process, the voice of the interviewer was removed from the text in order to make the interviews read as personal stories. Some explanatory footnotes have been added for clarification purposes. The resulting stories and the chosen titles – brief quotations from the interviews – were shared with the participants for approval. The names with which participants identify in the stories are self-chosen, sometimes being pseudonyms, sometimes nicknames, sometimes actual names.

The twelve participants of the first stage are mostly in their early twenties, with a few in their thirties and one in the early forties. They mostly identify as gay men, some of them as trans women, and one as a trans man. These categories themselves are, in fact, somewhat fluid: an interviewee would frequently use more than one term to describe their sexuality and gender, interchangeably referring to themselves as gay, trans, non-binary, and/or gender-fluid. With regard to religious identity, most of them identified as Christian, and one as Muslim; two interviewees had converted from Islam to Christianity while growing up. Although we did not seek to select a representative sample, with these characteristics the twelve participants present a reasonable cross-section of the Ugandan LGBTQ+ refugee community in Nairobi, which predominantly consists of gay men.[35] The

---

[35] Zomorodi, 'Responding to LGBT Forced Migration', 91.

second stage of the process included a wider variety of participants from across the LGBTQ+ spectrum, including several trans women, a few lesbian women, and some bisexual men, but with gay men in the majority. The total number of participants in the second stage was considerably larger – a total of over thirty.

One of the questions in the individual interviews was about the interviewee's favourite story from the Bible (or in the case of the Muslim participant, the Qur'an), and how that story speaks to their life experiences. This resulted in a list of biblical texts that are part of what can be conceptualised as a 'queer biblical archive'. Out of this list, two stories were selected that were each mentioned more than once, and that in our assessment would work well for the second stage of the project. These stories were Daniel in the lions' den, from the Old Testament, and Jesus and the woman caught in adultery, from the New Testament. Thus, in the second stage, two focus group discussions were organised, each focusing on one of the two Bible stories. These discussion sessions centred on a group process in which participants would collectively engage in a close reading of the Bible story, identify the main characters and events, and link these to characters and events in their own life situations as Ugandan LGBTQ+ refugees. After discussing this in small groups, information was then shared in the plenary group. This exchange moved on to the next part, where the group was asked to develop and perform a script for a drama play that placed the Bible story into their own context and experiences.

Ugandan LGBTQ+ refugees

There may have been earlier relocations of Ugandan LGBTQ+ folk to Kenya, but the first group that officially registered as refugees reportedly crossed the border with Kenya early 2011.[36] This was just a year after the introduction of the Anti-Homosexuality Bill, in October 2009, by Ugandan MP David Bahati. The initial version of the bill included a death penalty clause for 'aggravated homosexuality', leading the bill to be dubbed the 'Kill the Gays Bill' in Western media. Introduced as a private member's bill by Bahati (with apparent support of some US conservative evangelical figures[37]), the government under the leadership of President Yoweri Museveni (in power since 1986) initially appeared

---

[36] Isaac Otidi Amuke, 'Facing the Mediterranean', in *The Gerald Kraak Anthology: African Perspectives on Gender, Social Justice and Sexuality*; Vol. II *As You Like It* (Auckland Park: Jacana Media, 2018), 2.

[37] Kapya Kaoma, *Christianity, Globalization, and Protective Homophobia:*

rather hesitant to endorse it. Among other reasons, this had to do with mounting international pressure, including threats from several North American and European governments to cut development aid to Uganda if the bill would pass. The bill was shelved a few times, but then reappeared in parliamentary debate. Although the death penalty was dropped from a later version, its remaining clauses still had profound legal implications and a severe impact on human rights of sexual minorities, which the Ugandan legal scholar Sylvia Tamale has helpfully analysed.[38] The bill was finally passed by the Ugandan parliament on 20 December 2013 and signed into law by President Museveni on 24 February 2014. Perhaps as an anti-climax of this process of years, within six months after its passing, the Anti-Homosexuality Act was nullified by the Constitutional Court on procedural grounds (it had been passed through parliament without the required quorum). Although there have been frequent rumours that it will be reintroduced, so far this has not happened.

The historical and socio-political dynamics of which the Anti-Homosexuality Bill was part, and the various discourses of culture, religion, and nationalism surrounding it, have been analysed and discussed in depth by a number of scholars.[39] The Ugandan scholars Stella Nyanzi and Andrew Karamagi, for instance, argue that 'the anti-homosexuality law became a paradoxical symbol for nationalism, sovereignty, economic autonomy, Africanness, traditional culture, Christian conservatism, progressiveness, propriety, defiant sexualities, foreign intervention, and neo-imperialism'.[40] Other scholars have explored the geo-political dynamics that put the

---

Democratic Contestation of Sexuality in Sub-Saharan Africa (New York: Palgrave Macmillan, 2018), 60–63.

[38] See Sylvia Tamale, 'A Human Rights Impact Assessment of the Ugandan Anti-homosexuality Bill 2009', *The Equal Rights Review*, 4 (2009), 49–57.

[39] E.g. see Barbara Bompani and Caroline Valois, 'Sexualizing Politics: The Anti-Homosexuality Bill, Party-politics and the New Political Dispensation in Uganda', *Critical African Studies*, 9:1 (2017), 52–70; Stella Nyanzi, 'Dismantling Reified African Culture through Localised Homosexualities in Uganda', *Culture, Health and Sexuality*, 15:8 (2013), 952–967; Emma Paszat, 'Why "Uganda's Anti-Homosexuality Bill"? Rethinking the "Coherent" State', *Third World Quarterly*, 38:9 (2017), 2027–2044; Amar Wahab, '"Homosexuality/Homophobia Is Un-African"? Un-Mapping Transnational Discourses in the Context of Uganda's Anti-Homosexuality Bill/Act', *Journal of Homosexuality*, 63:5 (2016), 685–718.

[40] Stella Nyanzi and Andrew Karamagi, 'The Social-political Dynamics of the Anti-Homosexuality Legislation in Uganda', *Agenda*, 29:1 (2015), 24.

Ugandan case at the centre of global conversations about LGBTQ+ rights and contemporary sexual politics in a postcolonial world.[41]

Although the Anti-Homosexuality Act was nullified in 2014, homosexuality continues to be deeply politicised, and the social and political climate is still filled with strong anti-LGBTQ+ sensitivities. Up to today, politicians, clergy, and other opinion leaders continue to insert homophobic hate speech into the public domain, and police continue to harass members of the LGBTQ+ community. In the light of this intense, ongoing politicisation of homosexuality, Uganda became known in Western media narratives as possibly the world's 'worst place to be gay'. This framing has rightly been critiqued for its homogenising depiction and colonialist undertones, associating Africa with backwards conservative politics as opposed to a liberal and progressive West.[42] In fact, there still is a relatively strong and well-organised LGBTQ+ community in Uganda, with several LGBTQ+ organisations operating in the country, and even with occasional queer Pride protests taking place (although frequently disrupted by the police).[43] Online spaces also allow for new ways of activism, mobilisation, and visibility.[44] Nevertheless, in the years leading up to the passing of the Anti-Homosexuality Bill and also after its nullification, many LGBTQ+ Ugandans felt that their home country was no longer safe. One human rights organisation reported the risks as follows:

> Openly LGBT Ugandans confront stigma, discrimination, legal restrictions, harassment, intimidation, violence and death threats. They are often denied access to healthcare and HIV services. ... LGBT people also encounter restrictions on their freedom of speech, movement and actions. Ugandan families have been known to discriminate against and disown

[41] Rahul Rao, *Out of Time: The Queer Politics of Postcoloniality* (New York: Oxford University Press, 2020); S. M. Rodriguez, *The Economies of Queer Inclusion: Transnational Organizing for LGBTI Rights in Uganda* (Lanham: Lexington Books, 2019).

[42] Kwame Edwin Otu, 'LGBT Human Rights Expeditions in Homophobic Safaris: Racialized Neoliberalism and Post-Traumatic White Disorder in the BBC's *The World's Worst Place to Be Gay*', *Critical Ethnic Studies*, 3:2 (2017), 126–150.

[43] Stella Nyanzi, 'Queer Pride and Protest: A Reading of the Bodies at Uganda's First Gay Beach Pride', *Signs: Journal of Women in Culture and Society*, 40:1 (2014), 36–40.

[44] Austin Bryan, 'Kuchu Activism, Queer Sex-work and "Lavender Marriages," in Uganda's Virtual LGBT Safe(r) Spaces', *Journal of Eastern African Studies*, 13:1 (2019), 90–105.

LGBT family members whose sexual orientation or gender identities (SOGI) are exposed.[45]

Numerous cases of police and mob violence against LGBTQ+ people have been documented.[46] It is against the background of this hostile environment that many decided to leave the country in search for a safer and better future. Neighbouring Kenya was deemed the best option, in spite of having its own colonial laws criminalising 'carnal knowledge against the order of nature' still in place.[47] This LGBTQ+ migration from Uganda to Kenya fits into a longer history, as 'Kenya and Uganda have had an unofficial pact of providing a passageway for each other's escapees'.[48]

Although the first refugees moved to Kenya in 2011, the stream became much bigger after the passing of the bill in late 2013. Reportedly, over 400 Ugandans sought safety in Kenya in the period from January 2014 to February 2015 alone.[49] The Ugandans, who are by far the majority of LGBTQ+ refugees in Kenya, were joined by others also claiming asylum on the basis of their sexuality from countries such as Rwanda and Sudan. In his well-researched journalistic report, the Kenyan writer Isaac Otidi Amuke offers an in-depth narrative account of the phenomenon. He documents how the United Nations refugee agency (UNHCR) initially assumed that it was dealing with 'a small and manageable group'.[50] Acknowledging the particular risks to this group – both in Uganda, and in Kenya – the UNHCR decided to prioritise their case load, to provide financial support, and to speed up resettlement in third countries.[51] The UNHCR-run Kakuma refugee camp, in Turkana County, north-western

---

[45] Saurav J. Thapa, 'LGBT Uganda Today: Continuing Danger Despite Nullification of Anti-Homosexuality Act', *Human Rights Campaign: Global Spotlights*, September 2015, http://assets2.hrc.org/files/assets/resources/Global_Spotlight_Uganda__designed_version__September_25__2015.pdf (accessed 16 December 2020), 1.

[46] E.g. see the 'Uganda Report of Violations Based on Gender Identity and Sexual Orientation', The Consortium on Monitoring Violations Based on Sex Determination, Gender Identity and Sexual Orientation, September 2015, https://outrightinternational.org/sites/default/files/15_02_22_lgbt_violations_report_2015_final.pdf (accessed 16 December 2020).

[47] Kenyan Penal Code, art. 162.

[48] Amuke, 'Facing the Mediterranean', 1.

[49] Zomorodi, 'Responding to LGBT Forced Migration', 91.

[50] Amuke, 'Facing the Mediterranean', 5.

[51] According to UNHCR policies, third country resettlement is one of the durable solutions (alongside voluntary repatriation and local integration) for

Kenya, which at that time accommodated over 150,000 refugees from neighbouring countries, such as South Sudan and Somalia, was not considered a safe space for LGBTQ+ refugees.[52] Consequently, they were mostly accommodated in Nairobi. However, the assumption that this was a small and manageable group proved wrong, and the decision to prioritise them backfired: 'Before long, word got back to Kampala that there was a direct passage either to Europe or America if one pitched at the UNHCR in Nairobi or Kakuma citing persecution based on sexuality. It was said that there would even be financial assistance as one awaited resettlement.'[53] Groups of refugees started arriving, all claiming to be persecuted on the basis of their sexuality. Soon, doubts emerged about the truth of these claims, which often were difficult to verify, and there were concerns about human smuggling and asylum fraud.[54]

By the end of 2014, UNHCR reconsidered its decision to prioritise the Ugandan LGBTQ+ caseload and decided to treat them like any other refugees. This meant that they lost financial support (after the first three months upon their arrival), that the asylum application process took much longer (up to several years), and that resettlement to third countries was no longer guaranteed. Around the same time, the Kenyan authorities, under the pretext of an anti-terrorism campaign, introduced a policy to remove all refugees from the urban areas and to relocate them in the official

---

refugees who fled their home country. LGBTQ+ refugees tend to be resettled in Western Europe, North America, and Australia.

[52] Kakuma is the site of a vast UNHCR refugee camp, first established in 1992. It was initially established to host refugees who had fled the war in Sudan but is now populated by tens of thousands from many parts of the continent. Situated in one of Kenya's poorest regions, there are not only tensions with the local community of Kakuma town but considerable tensions and outbreaks of violence within the camp. Malnutrition and outbreaks of diseases cause ongoing problems, as do hopelessness and desperation, as refugees linger in Kakuma camp in difficult, crowded conditions for indeterminate periods of time. LGBTQ+ refugees (including several who participated in this project) report that Kakuma is a place of queer-phobia and violence. For instance, see Namupa Shivute, 'UNHCR's Kakuma Camp is No Refuge', 25 February 2020, https://gal-dem.com/kakuma-lgbtqi-refugee-unhcr-kenya-queerphobia (accessed 22 April 2020). In April 2021, a Ugandan refugee died in a Nairobi hospital from his burn wounds, a month after a petrol bomb attack on him and fellow LGBTQ+ refugees in Kakuma. The tragic events have spurred new calls for evacuating these refugees from the camp.

[53] Amuke, 'Facing the Mediterranean', 5.

[54] Zomorodi, 'Responding to LGBT Forced Migration', 92.

camps, such as Kakuma.[55] Those LGBTQ+ refugees who end up in the camps are provided with basic necessities, such as shelter and food, but they often experience stigmatisation, exclusion, and violence from other camp residents and, as some of the stories in Part I testify, also from the camp security and police.[56]

The refugees who decide to stay in Nairobi, on the other hand, have an ambiguous legal status and thus are extra vulnerable to abuse and mistreatment by landlords, the police, state authorities, and so on. Not being allowed to engage in formal employment, they depend on support from NGOs such as the Hebrew Immigrant Aid Society (HIAS) and try to make a living in the informal sector, including sex work. In recent years, there have been numerous protests of groups of LGBTQ+ refugees at the UNHCR premises in Nairobi as well as in Kakuma, against what they consider inhumane treatment. In 2019, tens of Nairobi-based protesters were arrested and spent a few weeks in prison, only to be released after they had been able to secure a considerable amount of bail money from donors. In response to the protests, UNHCR and HIAS point to the procedures they are bound by, and to the limited resources available. These organisations suggest that the refugees are impatient and unrealistic in their expectations.[57] As Gitta Zomorodi captures the situation: 'The migrants had high expectations of their helpers and, as refugee processing times lengthened, the challenge became how to support a group so focused on resettlement to become self-sustaining.'[58]

Instead of a fast-track gateway to Europe or North America, for many refugees Kenya has turned out to be a land of drawn-out hardship where they find themselves stuck, struggling to survive, while nervously awaiting the uncertain outcome of the very slow process of asylum and resettlement. Several of the participants in the project of this book have been in Kenya for a period of four to five years. In addition to the economic challenges, the refugees also struggle socially, as they usually don't speak Swahili or any of Kenya's local languages[59] and they find it difficult to

---

[55] This is known as the encampment policy. See 'Refugee Law and Policy: Kenya', Library of Congress, www.loc.gov/law/help/refugee-law/kenya.php#_ftn69 (accessed 16 December 2020).

[56] Kate Pinnock, 'UNHCR and LGBTI Refugees in Kenya: The Limits of "Protection"', *Disasters*, 22 May 2020.

[57] Amuke, 'Facing the Mediterranean', 15–16.

[58] Zomorodi, 'Responding to LGBT Forced Migration', 92.

[59] Most Ugandan refugees do speak English, which is widely spoken in Kenyan urban centres. Yet still they report experiencing considerable language

build connections with the Kenyan LGBTQ+ community. For the latter, supporting the Ugandan refugees has not always been a priority; instead, they reportedly 'feared that providing services to a population in Kenya possibly illegally could endanger their work, and worried that heightened attention to the LGBTQ+ community more generally could jeopardise the gains made by the Kenyan LGBTQ+ movement'.[60]

As a result of the hardship, many refugees face serious mental illness and despair. In April 2020, the refugee community in Nairobi was shocked by the news that one of their own had committed suicide on UNHCR premises. Because of the very difficult situation in Kenya, some of the refugees have returned to Uganda. Many others have decided to stay in Kenya, and new ones keep arriving (although in much smaller numbers now than some years ago). They are encouraged by the stories of those who have made it and who are now resettled in countries in North America, Europe, and Australia. Those still in Kenya, in the words of Amuke, are 'living in limbo' while 'holding out for what is possible'.[61] In the meantime, they have sought to organise themselves, in response to the earlier-identified challenge, to become self-sustaining.

In the Nairobi area, several organisations exist in which groups of refugees have joined hands to collectively provide accommodation and other basic necessities and to engage in self-support and -empowerment. Self-sustainability appears to be still some way off, as they continue to rely heavily on donor support (from humanitarian aid organisations such as HIAS, from resettled refugees, and from friends and other contacts both in Kenya and abroad); yet they have demonstrated inventiveness in setting up income-generating projects, from handcraft, to creative arts, to farming. In addition to economic support, as community-based organisations these groups play also other vital roles – most basically, they provide community, social support systems, or, as discussed below, a 'family' space.

The Nature Network

This book is deeply indebted to the work of The Nature Network (TNN), one of the community-based organisations of LGBTQ+ refugees in Nairobi. One of the authors, Adriaan, was introduced to TNN in 2015, when conducting research in an LGBTQ+ Christian church in Nairobi

---

barriers; not being able to speak Swahili or local languages immediately reveals their non-Kenyan identity.

[60] Zomorodi, 'Responding to LGBT Forced Migration', 92.

[61] Amuke, 'Facing the Mediterranean', 15–16.

(Cosmopolitan Affirming Church, or CAC), which was frequented by a number of Ugandan refugees. Via them, he learned more about the situation these refugees found themselves in and about the severe challenges they faced. He befriended several of them and would catch up with them during subsequent visits. In February 2016, he was invited to attend the official launch of TNN, and two years later, together with CAC leaders, to be part of a church service hosted by the organisation.

Although officially launched as The Nature Network on 27 February 2016, the birth of the organisation should be dated to 2014. A Ugandan priest, temporarily based in Nairobi, had rented a house in the far outskirts of the Nairobi urban area, to accommodate refugees from his home country who had fled to Kenya in search of a safer environment and a more secure future.[62] It was then called Ark Commune, a name that alludes to the biblical ark of Noah and symbolises sanctuary. A year or so later, the priest returned to Uganda and was unable to continue his support. One resident of the house, Raymond Brian, gradually took over the leadership of the organisation. With mentorship from a former refugee, Tom Rogers Muyunga-Mukasa,[63] they developed it into an organisation that specifically (but not exclusively) caters for, and is led by, transgender persons.[64] Raymond variably identifies as a gay man and a trans woman, and is also known as 'Mother Nature'.[65] Hence, the new name 'The Nature Network' was adopted for the organisation. At the time of the research that resulted in this book (2019–2020), Raymond was still in charge of TNN, serving as executive director. Their resettlement to the US had been postponed because of the COVID-19 pandemic outbreak in 2020, but finally took place in June of that year. Raymond was assisted by a leadership team, which included Hudson, who served as treasurer and, after Raymond's departure, took over as executive director of TNN. The two of them together served as local research coordinators in the project that culminated in this book.

---

[62] See Kyle's story (no. 3) in Part I for a narrative testimony of the priest's support.

[63] Tom Rogers Muyunga-Mukasa was part of the first wave of Ugandan refugees who fled to Kenya. He resettled to the United States in 2012. At the time of this research, he was back in Nairobi to support the work of TNN, and he was one of the facilitators of the focus group discussions. He stars as the president in the dramatisation based on Daniel 6 (see Chapter 2 in Part II of this book) and contributed two poems to this book (also included in Part II).

[64] In this context, 'transgender' appears to be a loose term including effeminate gay men, non-binary, gender-fluid and trans persons.

[65] See their story in Part I.

The Nature Network is based in Matasia, a semi-urban town in the beautifully lush Ngong hills of Kajiado County, which neighbours Nairobi County. From Nairobi city centre, the distance to Matasia is about 20 miles, and depending on traffic it can easily take one hour to drive there by car, and two hours or more when travelling by *matatu* (Kenya's crowded public minibuses that serve as public transport). The community house offers residence to a fluctuating number of people – ranging between about fifteen and thirty. Some stay for several years, while others come and go. Most of them are registered as refugees in Kenya, and in the process of resettlement to a third country through the UNHCR. Some residents who participated in this project have been resettled in the meantime. As becomes clear from several of the stories presented in Part I, for many residents TNN is a family. Many of them have been ostracised by their biological families back home in Uganda but have found a new family in the TNN community. As community members write on the TNN blog: 'We love the family created at The Nature Network. It is a nurturing safe space. … We are so proud to have it, for it represents the best family ever in our lives.'[66]

Clearly, this community presents a case of 'queer kinship' *avant la lettre*, providing a space of belonging, a space to feel at home, for people whose lives are in transit.[67] It does so under the warm and inspiring leadership of Mother Nature, who likes to refer to themself as 'the bearded mother', and whose stunning pictures decorate the living room. During our first project visit in September 2019, a flipchart paper was mounted on the wall, with a quote from Mother Nature: 'Blood does not make family. Those are relatives. Family are those with whom you share your good, bad, and ugly, and still love one another in the end. Those are ones you select yourself.' The quote illustrates the key point about queer kinship as captured in the title of anthropologist Kath Weston's classic study, *Families We Choose*.[68] However, the case of TNN also complicates this notion of queer family

66 The Nature Network, 'Could This Be The Love You Get From Your Bio-logical Parents?', 29 October 2019, https://thenaturenetworkgroup.blogs-pot.com/2019/10/could-this-be-love-you-get-from-your.html (accessed 16 December 2020).

67 Queer kinship is a concept for close familial and communal networks not based on biological ties. See Robert E. Goss and Amy Adams Squire Strong-heart (eds), *Our Families, Our Values: Snapshots of Queer Kinship* (Bing-hamton: The Haworth Press, 1997).

68 Kath Weston, *Families We Choose: Lesbians, Gays, Kinship*, rev. edn (New York: Columbia University Press, 1997).

based on voluntary choice, because the context in which this alternative queer family is established is one of forced migration to a foreign land and the related experience of social and economic marginalisation. Indeed, many of the stories that follow in Part I testify to the pain and trauma that comes with being excluded from the biological family back in Uganda, and losing touch with parents and siblings.

Like many families, TNN is a place of security, affection, and love, but also sometimes of tensions and disagreements. There are rules – which are not always kept – and there are roles. The rota with daily housekeeping chores is mounted on the wall in the spacious lounge. Every week, there is a house meeting where issues of concern are discussed, activities are planned, and the budget is reviewed. Everyone living here is supposed to make a financial contribution to the monthly budget for rent and food, which is difficult, as refugees are not able to secure a work permit in Kenya and thus to generate a basic or regular income. As narrated in some of the stories, for several of the refugees, sex work is the only way to make some money for daily survival. The Nature Network has developed some income-generating activities but remains reliant on support from donors – both former residents who now have been successfully resettled, and other friends of the community.

The community house in Matasia is located just off the main road. The little road leading to the premises is untarmacked, potholed, and bumpy, impassable for regular cars. The entrance has a large, green, metal gate, with a little pedestrian doorway at its centre. Behind the gate is a spacious, grassy yard. There is often a washing line stretching across it. A couple of chickens wander about, and vegetables are grown in a corner. Steps lead up to the house via a terrace. On first view the house looks quite grand. The central room you enter first, where gatherings and communal meals and workshops take place, is of a generous size. There is a big table, a large screen, a stack of many chairs. The room was big enough to accommodate our focus group sessions, close to thirty attenders, and to serve as the setting of the drama performances. Yet although the house is nice and spacious and has electricity and Wi-Fi (if the bills have been paid on time), it is far from luxurious. When entering into the warren of rooms towards the back, one realises that the first impression of largesse is deceptive, especially when taking into account that each room is shared by several residents – sometimes up to five. There is no running water; all water comes from an outside pump, and containers full of water are found in the kitchen and bathroom. Some parts of the house are clearly damp, and in some places there is no ceiling – only a view of the beams of the roof. There is overdue maintenance, and the only way in which the house remains liveable is through ongoing effort and persistence. Yet this state of the house, and its remote distance, is why the rent is relatively low and thus affordable.

The slogan of TNN is 'art with a vision', which refers to the initial focus on community empowerment through creative arts. As Tigan, one of the community members since the early days, narrates in his story in Part I, TNN 'started as a joke', when Raymond and others began mimicking Ugandan TV personalities. From there, it developed: 'We started doing all kinds of creative things. And people started talking about it, it became a thing.' A concrete output of this is a TV show, initially called 'Nature Show', and later renamed, with a somewhat different format, as 'The Couch'. Live-streamed on the TNN Facebook page, in this talk show Raymond and other community members serve as hosts, offering a mix of entertainment, commentary, and information on a wide range of issues such as LGBTQ+ culture, lifestyle, and fashion, spirituality and faith, relationships, sexual health, refugee life, and the resettlement process. It is broadcast somewhat irregularly: at the time of writing 'The Couch' has twenty-one episodes available on its Facebook page, the latest one from 3 March 2020.[69] In addition to this show, TNN also engages in the production of cultural dance and drama. For instance, at the launch of Adriaan's book *Kenyan, Christian, Queer*, at the British Institute for Eastern Africa in Nairobi in September 2019, TNN performed two dances and a drama sketch. The initial idea was to perform dance and drama at events as a way of income generation, but the number of bookings remains low. Therefore, TNN engaged also in other income-generating activities, such as poultry and rabbit farming.

The organisation also developed a programme of activities concerned with TB (tuberculosis), HIV (human immunodeficiency virus) and sexual health more generally, educating and sensitising the refugee community in Nairobi and beyond. They successfully secured some funding from relevant donors in the public health sector, on an ad hoc basis. Their work in this area is informed by the awareness that sexual minorities, in particular men who engage in sexual relationships with other men, sex workers and refugees, are among the recognised high-risk populations for HIV. Not only are they more likely to engage in sexual practices that put them at risk, they also are more vulnerable to concurrent endemic scourges (notably TB and malaria), and they often struggle to access HIV testing

[69] See Nature Network Facebook page, www.facebook.com/pg/kenaturenetwork/videos (accessed 16 December 2020).

services and antiretroviral treatment due to stigma and discrimination. While none of the life storytellers in Part I of this book disclose their HIV status, it is obvious from their stories that they are very much aware of the realities of the epidemic and the risks they face. Tigan refers to a fellow refugee from Uganda who contracted HIV, probably through sex work, and who, without any other way to support himself, returned home to die (Story 2). Several other storytellers, too, describe sex work as the 'only means of survival' (Story 9, Shamuran), alongside the ways they have been exploited as sex workers (Story 2, Tigan; Story 3, Kyle). Henry even mentions directly the risk of contracting HIV and other sexually transmittable diseases (Story 5). Out of the awareness of the risks of HIV, TNN actively engages in HIV prevention and education campaigns, sensitising members of the LGBTQ+ refugee community, supporting those who live with HIV to take their medication, and addressing HIV-related stigma in the community. During our visit in September 2019, the living room of the TNN house in Matasia was decorated with posters on the walls, with hand-written slogans such as, 'Am HIV Positive & Am Human', and 'HIV is a Virus, but Stigma is the Deadly Disease'.

In early 2020, with the outbreak of the COVID-19 pandemic in Kenya, TNN built on its experience with health awareness to educate refugees on this new virus and the risks involved. Alongside all these activities, TNN supports refugees in the asylum application and resettlement process, engages in advocacy for the refugee community, builds networks with other refugee organisations as well as Kenyan LGBTQ+ organisations, liaises with bodies such as UNHCR, and so on. All of this is captured in the mission statement that describes TNN as 'a Kenya-based transgender-led refugee support safe space', that seeks to foster 'healing, agency, autonomy, self-belief, self-determination and self-preservation', and aims at the 'continued humanization of refugees' and at 'protection of rights and dignity of refugees irrespective of status'.[70]

Although not formally a faith-based organisation, religion is naturally integrated into the life and work of TNN. The religious demographics of Uganda are reflected in the community of LGBTQ+ refugees: by far the majority is Christian, of diverse denominations (mostly Anglican, Catholic, and Pentecostal-Charismatic), with a minority of Muslims.[71] In

---

[70] The Nature Network, 'Nature Network – a Profile', 9 April 2020, https://thenaturenetworkgroup.blogspot.com/2020/04/nature-network-profile.html (accessed 16 December 2020).

[71] Recent reliable statistics are not available, but to give an indication: according to the 2014 population census of Uganda, 39% of the population is

the same way as many LGBTQ+ Ugandans have been ostracised by their families and have found a new family in the community of TNN, they have also generally experienced ostracism from faith communities, with TNN offering an alternative space to express their religiosity. As one community member writes on the TNN blog:

> At The Nature Network, we dance until our bones crack. We sing until our voices are hoarse. We laugh until we are breathless. We love life and are grateful to God. We are a social support community. We are affirming Lesbian, Gay, Transgender, Intersex, Bisexual, Queer, and Questioning. We pray, play, and pay it forward together.[72]

Because of negative experiences with organised religion, most members rarely attend church services or prayers at the mosque. The aforementioned LGBTQ+ church, CAC, is based in downtown Nairobi, which is too far away for TNN members to attend regularly. However, the observation of the scholar of African sexualities, Marc Epprecht, that LGBTQ+ people in Africa generally are 'proudly, happily and deeply religious', certainly applies to Ugandan refugees as well.[73] The Nature Network provides a space to collectively express this religiosity. The weekly house meetings include prayers and religious reflection, until recently led by a resident pastor (who resettled to Canada the day after he was interviewed for this book – see Keeya, Story 12). Frequently, on Sunday afternoons, there is a gathering for religious worship, also attended by other members from the LGBTQ+ refugee community. Although Christian language and forms dominate this space, it is remarkable at the same time how inclusive it is. Muslim members are naturally included, are invited to share about their faith, and welcomed to participate in prayers. Thus, although religion is integrated in TNN family life, it does not become dogmatic but occurs in an atmosphere of respect, inclusivity, and togetherness.

Catholic, 32% Anglican, 11% Pentecostal/evangelical, and 14% Muslim. See National Population and Housing Census 2014 – Main Report (Kampala: Uganda Bureau of Statistics, 2016), 19.

[72] The Nature Network, 'Homosexuality, Religiosity and the Beauty of All Creatures; A Transgender Group's Take', 2 July 2017, https://thenaturenetworkgroup.blogspot.com/2017/07/homosexuality-religiosity-and-beauty-of.html (accessed 16 December 2020).

[73] Marc Epprecht, *Sexuality and Social Justice in Africa: Rethinking Homophobia and Forging Resistance* (London: Zed Books, 2013), 66.

This book

The project underlying this book was developed together with TNN leaders and was designed to capitalise on the organisation's existing expertise, interests, activities, and networks. The focus on storytelling converges with the TNN aim of providing a space of healing and agency, or of 'dignity-affirmation and self-esteem enhancement among LGBTIQQ refugees'.[74] The use of drama builds on the organisation's creative work and its commitment to produce 'art with a vision'. The engagement with Bible stories is natural for a community where faith is integrated in its activities. Thus, in Part I, we present the life stories of twelve of the participating refugees, while Part II offers a detailed account of the inter-reading of their life experiences with two Bible stories.

Acknowledging first, the importance of life storytelling as an activist and academic method when working with marginalised groups such as LGBTQ+ refugees, and second, the status of the Bible as a popular and influential religious text of East Africa, this book explores a two-fold question: how do Ugandan LGBTQ+ refugee life stories and biblical stories speak to each other, and how can the Bible be creatively appropriated to signify African queer lives? As such, this book contributes to two fields of study. The first is the growing body of literature about LGBTQ+ and queer identities, communities, and politics in contemporary Africa.[75] Recent work has engaged religion, and specifically Christianity, as a site of African LGBTQ+ activism and empowerment.[76] Building on that, we specifically foreground the potential of the Bible as a resource for African queer self-narration. The second is scholarship on the status of the Bible in African contexts, and on local biblical interpretations and appropriations.[77] Some valuable research has been done into the use of the Bible to legitimate homophobia in contemporary Africa.[78] Complementing that,

---

[74] The Nature Network, 'Nature Network – a Profile', 9 April 2020, https://thenaturenetworkgroup.blogspot.com/2020/04/nature-network-profile.html (accessed 16 December 2020).

[75] Sokari Ekine and Hakima Abbas (eds), *Queer African Reader* (Dar es Salaam: Pambazuka Press, 2013); Zethu Matebeni, Surya Monro and Vasu Reddy (eds), *Queer in Africa: LGBTQI Identities, Citizenship, and Activism* (London and New York: Routledge, 2018).

[76] E.g. see van Klinken, *Kenyan, Christian, Queer.*

[77] West and Dube, *The Bible in Africa*; Gerald O. West, *The Stolen Bible: From Tool of Imperialism to African Icon* (Leiden: Brill, 2016).

[78] E.g. see Masiiwa R. Gunda, *The Bible and Homosexuality in Zimbabwe: A Socio-historical Analysis of the Political, Cultural and Christian Arguments*

our suggestion is to foreground the reading of biblical texts from the per-spective of African queer experiences. In the introductory chapter to Part II, we make further efforts to embed this book in these literatures and to outline its contribution. Before doing so, we will present the life stories of twelve of our participants, to amplify their voices and foreground their experiences.

in the Homosexual Public Debate with Special Reference to the Use of the Bible (Bamberg: Bamberg University Press, 2010).

PART I

Ugandan LGBTQ+ Refugee Life Stories

It's my nature, this is who I am

Based on a life story interview with Raymond Brian, aka Mother Nature
(15 September 2019)

I am in Nairobi, Kenya and I'm a refugee right now. I work with The Nature Network: that's a group of LGBTI Ugandan refugees and asylum seekers, who are talented in different arts. I am transgender, I am gay. I keep myself as a gay man but I feel like a transgender person. Just because of where we are right now, I can't express all my feelings to the wider community. The community where we are right now is not ok with transgender persons yet. I would love to be there as a transgender person.

I am one of the founders of The Nature Network. It started when we were just mimicking TV presenters, radio presenters. We have a WhatsApp group where we do audio-radio presentations, we do vlogs, we post them on Facebook and our YouTube channel, on Twitter and Instagram. So, through these, we pass on information about our life as LGBTI people, so that people get to know who we are and what we go through, and that we are not so different from other people.

Here in Matasia, we have a number of people in the house. We are currently sixteen and we all contribute. Everyone contributes a certain amount, so that we can pay the rent, utility bills, so we can buy food as a family, because we take ourselves as a family. We are fellow refugees, mostly Ugandans, though we are not limited by nationalities but by who can go by our rules as The Nature Network.

We used to get some funding from different funders: we got a grant from International AIDS Alliance, which changed its name to Frontline AIDS now. It used to support us, because we had people living with HIV with us. We are still having them in our house but, you know, funds are always limited to three months or four months. Still, we are having some income-generating activities. We used to have poultry, do photography and videography, whereby we get hired on some occasions, mostly from the gay-friendly communities here in Kenya, and some churches. We actually had an opportunity to get a contract from Global Platform Kenya (Action Aid Kenya): it was about documenting a project of an alliance between religious leaders and LGBTI activists.

We also used to get some little contribution from well-wishers, friends who were resettled and those who get interested in the work we do – though it's not on a daily basis, or monthly basis, but here and there. Most of our members are unable to get jobs and so they are involved in sex work, I am sorry to say. But they need to survive, because as an organisation we can't afford to provide everything, or even spoon-feed anyone, because if you spoon-feed everyone you will make them lazy and they won't go anywhere.

I am Mother Nature. Here at Matasia I take myself as a mother. We also have an aunt. We are like a family, so we take up these responsibilities like what a mother does: sometimes we have counselling, bedroom talk sessions with our auntie, we have our uncle, we have our pastor.

Way back when I was still a kid in primary school, year 2 or 3, I was aged 7 or 6, when I used to go to school, people used to abuse and insult me, calling me names like girl-boy, because I was so girly, they couldn't identify whether I was a boy or girl – only by my name they could tell. I went back home, reported to my mum that at school they abused me, because how I am acting like a girl, yet I am a boy. What she told me was, 'No, that's your nature; that's how you are; a girl is also good and girls are beautiful.' She didn't know about sexuality and she further said, 'that's how you are: I can't take you back to my womb and I can't say to God, "why did you give me this child?"' You know, and from there that's where I got the name 'Nature' and I then started telling people who used to insult me, 'that's my nature!'

It was mostly boys who abused me, because I used to associate mostly with the girls. The boys were always complaining that I am in the company of girls: 'you are a girl-boy!' But the girls were so welcoming, because we used to like the same things, like playing the round game, skipping, making dolls, the games for the girls. Those are the moments I really remember, which always come into my mind and keep me going with my nature.

But it got more complicated, because I used to fight inside me when I was growing up – at around the age of 11, 12, 13, when I started going to high school, getting real feelings. When I was younger, I just felt comfortable playing with the girls. I continued staying in the company of the girls but getting attracted to boys. It really used to drive me crazy; like, am I really normal? Why am I attracted to boys?

I didn't know anyone who was like me. I had to pretend a lot. Whenever I would share a bed with a fellow boy or cousin, I would feel attracted to them but with my cousin-sisters, or other girls: nothing. I would feel nothing. It used to torture me so much! Even dressing! I used to want to be in dresses and when I was in a dress I used to feel fine and I could walk around but when I would put on trousers or shorts, I couldn't feel comfortable. It tortured me so much and *no one* could understand but would rather insult me, that I am a boy putting on girls' clothes.

In class, giving an answer when a teacher asked questions, I used to feel so nervous, I couldn't raise my hand, because when I would speak, people would shout at me, calling me a girl-boy, because my voice was so soft, like a girl. Those moments tortured me so much. But again, when I was growing up – by then it was 2010, 2011 – I went to high school where I started to see people who are like me, in a bar we used to go to. A friend of mine took me to a place where there were many people who were like me: trans women. But then we didn't understand that they, we, were trans women.

When I first went to that bar, oh my God! Oh my God!! I felt like Jesus has risen! You know, somewhere you feel so at home; somewhere you don't want to leave. I used to leave school and go seek their company. We used to share a lot, talk about relationship issues, and some could open up that they have boyfriends. At first it used to shock me how freely they said it! I had a boy I was crushing on but I never told him. In most of my conversations I used to say that I am crushing on a girl, yet it was a boy I was referring to.

Time came when my feelings were getting stronger for this boy. There's a day I fell sick at school and I don't know if it was hysteria. Going to the hospital they could not find anything. Mum used to ask, 'What's wrong with you? You are only ever sick when at school but when you come back home, you get ok!' But she couldn't really know what I was going through.

There was a day I went to church. My auntie was a born-again Christian and I stayed with her for quite a long time, so we used to go to church with her. I also had another auntie who was a pastor. So there's a time we went to my other auntie's church (the pastor's), and I had bangles on my hands. When she saw me, she was like, 'oh my God: remove those bangles! You are a boy. You are not supposed to put on those bangles!' From then on, I never wanted to go to church ever again. So in the other church where we used to go, there were boys who were playing the piano. I really liked to play the piano but these feelings wouldn't let me, because I got feelings for another boy. The last one I had feelings for, I never told him and it tortured me so much. So, in the church we used to have night prayers. We used to have youth meetings and rehearsals, conferences, and seminars; so we sometimes used to sleep at church with the boys and I would feel attracted to them. In the night I'd pray and pray, asking God, 'what is this happening to me?' because of how church talks about it. They used to talk about it in church so much, when the Anti-Homosexuality Bill was introduced in parliament in 2009 in Uganda. These pastors used to talk about it as a curse, that a man cannot fall in love with a man.

I used to pray not to love boys. I love God so much, so whenever I could go to church or when alone, I used to pray to God to help me get out the demon in me, because of the way they used to talk about it. I was fasting, praying every day for this – but then I would see a fellow boy and get attracted, but the girls: no. And there was a time I was like, 'let me be with these girls all the time so that I will change.' But nothing changed. I was like, 'I wish these people could know how I am feeling'. Before even knowing this other group of people, the LGBTI community, they used to talk about gay people in a bad way: that a man cannot fall in love with another man; it was written in the Bible, and that's why Sodom and Gomorrah were burnt.[1] It was a lot. We think church is the best place to be but then you can't handle church, because of the hate.

I also couldn't go into church with my earrings. Back then, they used to kidnap kids for ritual sacrifice in Uganda and there was a saying that when a kid is circumcised or pierced they would not kidnap him or her for ritual sacrifice. So mum pierced one of my ears. I presumed it to be a style, or a trend. I wasn't comfortable with only one piercing, so I pierced the second ear as well. And they were like, 'oh my God! No man can pierce the ears! No man can have long hair, or you are not a man. If you are not man enough, you are a homosexual. Homosexual people are the ones who do that stuff.' You know, when you put on any clothing and it's so fitting and tight they would also say you are homosexual. Culture states that a man is supposed to marry a woman, not a fellow man, so it was so challenging when they talked about culture when we were growing up.

By then, in 2011, I discovered myself. I joined groups where we were of the same sexuality, and I joined the Faculty of Law, Gender, and Sexuality at Makerere University. Working with Dr Stella Nyanzi, I learned more about religion, law, gender, and sexuality in a research project we did at

---

[1] The biblical story of the judgement of Sodom and Gomorrah (Genesis 18–19) is often linked to the practice of homosexuality in these cities, an association that is reflected in the word 'sodomy'. For a critical historical reconstruction of this trope, see Mark Jordan, *The Invention of Sodomy in Christian Theology* (Chicago: University of Chicago Press, 1997). For an alternative reading of the passage in a contemporary African Christian context, see Masiiwa Ragies Gunda, 'Jesus Christ, Homosexuality and Masculinity in African Christianity: Reading Luke 10:1–12', *Exchange*, 42:1 (2013), 16–33.

Makerere University. It opened my ears so very much. I learned more about culture, Buganda culture, including about homosexuality. I learned that King Mwanga used to practise homosexuality and that's why the Uganda martyrs were killed, because they refused to do what he wanted them to do for him.[2] So I was like, 'I'm a Muganda and they say that Buganda culture doesn't allow homosexuality, but yet I'm hearing it was practised way back!' It became so confusing and challenging to me, even how they talk about it in church.

For me, it's my perspective that the Bible was written *by someone* and it can be used in different ways. It's a good book and I am not against it. It's so good, because it nurtures us. There are so many things from the Bible that make us to be good: like, it teaches about respect, forgiving, it teaches about different things which are so good; and yet, it's the same thing people use to hate and preach against others. So, sometimes I get confused of the Bible, though I stand on my nature.

The Bible, it's condemning and loving at the same time. And when you come to culture, there's also love and condemnation. So I am Nature and I have the Bible. And I ask myself, 'Who put me in my mother's womb?' It was God: we have never seen him but I believe he is there. I'm not against the laws, but what if the person who wrote the Bible was created by God and that person doesn't have my feelings? Because I used to fight inside me, spiritually, psychologically, emotionally. When I got to discover more about my feelings in 2011, when I found this company of trans women, whenever I could go where they are, I could feel I am home.

There was a scenario when I was living with my auntie, whereby she never let us associate with girls. Whenever she was going for a burial, or visiting people, the girls would be taken away to my grandmother's house and then they'd bring the boys over. And I was always like, 'why is this happening?!' When they brought boys over I would feel so good – but my aunt thought she was preventing us from getting intimate with the girls.

[2] King (*kabaka*) Mwanga II ruled in the late 19th century, when the British colonisers and missionaries arrived. He is at the centre of the story about the Ugandan martyrs: a group of 45 young men who were pages in the royal court. Following their conversion to Christianity, the *Kabaka* instructed them to be killed. One of the suggested reasons is that the pages, after their conversion, did no longer want to engage in same-sex sexual practices with the king. For an overview of this history and its complex role in the contemporary politics of homosexuality in Uganda, see Rahul Rao, 'Re-membering Mwanga: Same-sex Intimacy, Memory and Belonging in Postcolonial Uganda', *Journal of Eastern African Studies*, 9:1 (2015), 1–19.

And yet, some of us were actually attracted to the boys instead. Sometimes when I was praying, I used to ask, 'Why bring boys this side and why are the girls taken away when I could actually get intimate with some of the boys?' I was kind of blaming my auntie for what she was doing, but the moments when I could get a chance and share with others, I would also feel better and gain some confidence, and feel empowered.

Some of the people who we used to live with were educated: counsellors, doctors. When I used to see different people of different education, religion, I was like, 'Oh, wow! It's all about feelings not about what you see.' Because there were people who were feminine but not gay, and those who were gay but very manly and married to women, because some were forced by their families to marry women and have kids. This is because culture says that you need to have a kid by a certain age, a sort of legacy to leave behind when you die.

As for my legacy, I don't know what God prepared for me – but I will wait for what God has prepared for me, because even if I wanted to leave a child behind, or do what other people want me to do: I may find, mum wants something, dad wants something, your sister also wants something. I would love to have a child. I would *love* to have a child. But again, when it comes to sleeping with girls, I don't have the feelings and when you think of artificial insemination, it's way too expensive for me, so it brings lots of questions to me.

Right now, I have a legacy which is there and which I will leave behind: like helping people, being good to people, saving someone by sharing what I am going through. In instances when you meet someone and they tell you that the video you did inspired or changed them, I feel like I have done something, even if indirectly, in the community. In my community back home, we used to get invited for workshops and conferences where we talked about ourselves, story sharing. We started an organisation called Youth on Rock Foundation and we used to perform in modelling, singing, dancing, acting. It was mostly about our sexuality.

It was by chance that Dr Stella Nyanzi was working on a certain project at Makerere University and she came to our organisation to do interviews. She gave me a camera to take pics, because I asked to help her. The next day she was calling me to ask me if I could help her, and I agreed, because I was flexible and open to learning. I didn't know how to even use a camera or do any research! We used to go to conferences and she used to tell me that I need to come out to take field work notes. So, I'd go with her, I'd take pictures as she was interviewing, and I'd study the environment and listen too. I'd write down everything I hear and it had to add up so that it makes sense. You know these stories, there's something they build: you start it from down there and it ends up with something big. I used to report everything in the notes and I built up skills.

With Dr Stella I got more and more experience from being a field work officer and I started doing interviews. I didn't go to university. I stopped in high school because of school fees issues, so it was so hard. But I used to pray that if someone else has done this, then it means I can do it too! Whenever I used to pray to God, I used to pray for wisdom from God. I told God, 'you knew me even before anyone knew me; you knew me from my mother's womb, and I am gay and I can't go back: could you just pave a way for me and make a way for me where there is no way?' What surprised me so much is that on that team from the university, I remained, only me, who continued working even after the project ended. There were people with degrees who we were doing research with. But I was flexible. I had no contract and I was just helping with doing different stuff and I got some little payment, like a stipend, allowances. And I got empowered. So the project research was ending and contracts were not being renewed but Dr Stella called me to help her on other occasions. She taught me a lot about trust: that I don't have to steal people's money; I don't have to steal peoples' property. I am not saying I used to do that – but as she was nurturing me to be the person I am right now, she used to tell me a lot. Then she went for a different project in South Africa and I didn't know what to do.

I went to work as a peer educator in Mulago Hospital in Uganda with people most at risk of getting infected with HIV. I used to visit sex workers, male and female, and I got to know and meet some doctors. They got interested in what I was doing. Let me say, I was favoured and I used to work without any academic documents, any papers (like from the university) but I think being genuine, being transparent, people will always like you, however much you may be gay. Because for me, I believe in myself, however much I am gay I can do this, I can help out. I used to take chances, even right now where I am in Kenya it's about taking chances and risks. Some people hate others, not knowing what they go through, like people judge and hate sex workers, but they don't really know what those sex workers go through, why they ended up on the streets, why I ended up as a gay person.

Do they think people want to go into bad things? Be, as they call it, demonic? Would I choose to go into demonic things?! People *don't know* and they lack knowledge. But I was so open to learning and I went so deep, the extra mile, to understand myself and discover myself. It took me long to accept myself, where I fall, my identity. My boyfriend, with whom I was in a long-distance relationship, when I told him that I was gay and that I loved him, he was like 'Oh my God! You are so open to people!' And he said that I should not tell anyone, that I will be beaten, or killed. And I was like, 'I don't go around telling everyone I see, because I also love my life.' I have to be protective but again, it's me and it's not them: they don't feel what I feel. Even if you love me, you can't feel what I feel; even if you are my mother, sister, brother, boyfriend or girlfriend.

I sit down with my children here[3] and I wish they could share also with their [biological] parents, instead of the parents neglecting them, because of culture, the Bible. The Bible didn't bear them, the culture didn't either! They are from your womb so if you get time, listen to them. These people are so talented; we are so talented; we do different stuff, more than those people who call themselves holy and straight, and who claim they're going to heaven. You find some musicians are gay but they can't come out; some pastors are gay but they can't come out! But these people still do a good job.

When I was working with Dr Stella, we used to do so much on law, gender, and sexuality in the LGBTI community. Now, when the Anti-Homosexuality Bill was brought to parliament, it was passed, and then it was nullified in 2014. It was passed in February and it was nullified, I think in August. I don't remember the exact month but it was in 2014. So, in August they celebrated Pride. The first was in 2012 or 2013. We were there. We enjoyed it so much! It was fun. But some of our friends were arrested, because they were dragging.[4] We were dragging: I was cross-dressing and I had makeup on. I love makeup so much!

So, then I was put in the newspapers. In the first, it was in the middle (inside) so people couldn't recognise me that much. But when the Bill was nullified, we went to celebrate and there were some journalists who were there and they were taking pictures. They were like, 'we are taking pics for our own reporting' and that it won't be published anywhere. It was ok; I was so free. They took pictures as I posed, with makeup, lipstick, bangles, you know, it was so fun!

The following day, it was Saturday and then Sunday. On Monday my friends started calling me, 'Raymond: your face has been put on the front page of the paper and the words that are written there are "we are back".' Oh my GOD! For me, I was a bit ok: I had been through sharing sessions, so I had gotten that confidence, accepting myself. But the problem was with the people I was living with, they couldn't accept me. They were gay; they were the same: but they were not open. It frightened them.

---

[3] Having identified themself as a mother in The Nature Network family, Raymond here refers to other TNN residents as their children.

[4] Dressed in drag.

So, I am on the front page of newspapers, and the community was like 'We know this one! We have seen this one!' It all happened abruptly. I couldn't go where my friends were, because the community was so bitter! The community turned on me. My uncle called my dad, saying, 'You know your boy has been put in newspapers and that he is the leader of homosexuals in Uganda?' They also wrote there that a homosexual is 'a male who plays a female role in bed'. My mum, brothers and sisters were like, 'You have shamed us.' Mum is a Muslim; dad is a Christian. How could they go back to church? My sister was like, 'you have been telling us that you are working at the university on law, gender, and sexuality! You have been lying to us; you are just messing with our mind, yet you are a gay. You are doing homosexuality!' Even my boyfriend – I had a boyfriend by then – wasn't ok, because he was not open. He felt tortured. Instead of worrying about myself, I was worried more about what my boyfriend was going through at that time.

I felt so bad and uncomfortable, I couldn't stay in Uganda. But the good thing I appreciate is Dr Stella: she did a wonderful job, and my sister Keem, she's a trans person. Dr Stella took me to her village during this time. Dr Stella told me maybe Uganda isn't comfortable, because the law doesn't allow homosexuality. The community might do mob justice on me, because I had many times been beaten. I felt tired of life but in me I was like, 'God loves me; God has a reason why.'

People talk bad about gay people but I have seen good ones. Being gay is just sexuality. There are some heterosexual people who rape kids, you know, they kill. As for me, I am with my fellow man and we have consented. I am against those who rape, those who steal, blackmail others, torture other people. Also, we are *of the same*, regardless of the sexuality, but we cannot *be the same:* that's why God created us, some black, some white, some lame, but God doesn't make mistakes. We're *all* human beings; we breathe in oxygen – even the pastors, or doctors. All our blood is red; just our skin colour is different. That brings the diversity that, actually makes God! That's nature: be who you are, because rich or poor, you still die. Rich or poor, you can get a kid. I can still get artificial insemination with my boyfriend and have a kid!

Back in Uganda, I used to love art. That's why, when I got a chance of starting The Nature Network, I came through art. I want to shine. That keeps me strong. That's why our thing at The Nature Network is all about art: we tell stories, and we tell people we're not going to shy away from what we are. We go to different workshops and we share! As a mother, I know and I feel like a mother. I feel like a woman in me, however much you may think I'm not. I nurtured these mothers' kids whom they neglected, here in Kenya. I have stayed in Kenya for five years, because I came in 2015. But people who have passed through my arms are very many; in my, or our, Network there are very many.

Some of the pastors, they go to Mass, but when they come to the pulpit, they start to torture others; they start talking trash, and they start speaking negativity. I am gay but I am doing a wonderful job in the community, where others who are straight do not. It's just God who pushes things. I personally, I can't say that I know what's next. If you look for protection anywhere, you can get anything: you can be beaten, you can die. When I'm going to that side, to another country, to be resettled, I'm not saying it is heaven! For me, God is protecting us: the Lord who is protecting the lame is the one who is protecting the gay people. So, for me, however much I am having a dream of going somewhere, I believe I'm going to change the nation. That's my voice, I like being the voice of the voiceless. Even when praying, I'm like, 'God, use me as the voice, let people see change! Give me wisdom! Even if you don't give me money, give me wisdom!' With wisdom, I can make a chance of getting that money: not like saying, 'Oh God, give me money, I am gay, I can't do this, I can't do that.'

Okay, I won't say that I am into the Bible, because those people who use the Bible to hate people make me hate the Bible. But I believe. So, in the Bible, there is a story of David and Goliath. Goliath was so big, so he thought he could beat everyone, he could put everyone down. But for me, I am David: a little, small person but I am using what I have to go and talk to the world, to talk to people that have not come to fight. I listen because David used to listen. But for me, with the little I have, I pray to God to give me wisdom, to understand; I will go, move to places where you who think that you're holy, you cannot reach. David used just a stone because it's what he had, while Goliath had arrows; he had everything protecting him and he had fought many. But for me, what I'm having is my nature, my creativity, the way I talk, respect, the way I care for people, the way I care about myself – and that can help me fight. I mean, not even fighting: to tell people. I've moved places in Kenya, I've seen God protecting me: so, if you tell me that you're gay and the Lord doesn't like you, I am here and I've nurtured many people. We can't work but we get food. Why is the Lord seeing us and providing? Because we use the little skills we have to target the biggest. David used just a stone to kill Goliath.

For me, that's where I stand: as the Network, as Nature, as Raymond. And I can achieve what I achieve, using my skills, my techniques. I shouldn't have to fight for my rights: you should accept me. No, no, no, we just sit at the table and I can talk to you. If you understand me, great; if you don't, it's okay. I live, you live. I do something, I feed myself, I'm not lazy. If you're lazy, you cannot get anywhere. If David was lazy, he couldn't beat Goliath. You use what you have! Don't plan to use what you don't have. Even if I go to those countries which have milk and honey, when you don't have brains, you can't thrive. But you can achieve even if you're here.

I personally, I can have a boyfriend and we can pray together, go to church together and get married. For me, what I preach most is love. Even if you are heterosexual and there is no love between you, nothing can work out. You can keep having kids but the kids won't feel that love, because you got married because of peer and family pressure rather than love. But for me, we get people here because they find love, they find comfort, because we pray here, when we start our meetings here, we pray, because we know that God loves us so much. Even if we don't go to those churches, we can pray from our premises. And God does wonders.

I am praying The Nature Network will be okay when I leave for resettlement. I believe it won't stop here with me. There is something that our aunt said that if you are not there for someone, no one will be there for you. Even if you are a pastor, even if you are a Muslim, even if you are a big person, if you don't have people who believe in you, and you're not social, then the world isn't a better place for you. If you not only think of you and start thinking of others, good things will follow you.

Everything will come automatically when you're doing good things. Even sexuality! The Lord sees the thing that is in you, the pure you, transparent. For me, my prayer is, if I get resettled, to bring people who are like me, those in my circle, my blood. As queer people, LGBTI people, we started staying together, and now it's all about blood, like how I felt when I found those people in my community way back. You know, when people get to know the good work you're doing and they're of the same community, something will drive them: that's what they call blood. It will drive you, you come and find your friends because we do not call people to join us, they just come. But when they come here in The Nature Network, they feel so comfortable, they feel at home.

When they come here, they find home: there's mum, there's dad, and they can bring their boyfriends home, and they can go out with them; they can dress up the way they want at our premises, which makes them uncomfortable at other places. That's why sometimes they ran away. I didn't want to leave my parents, because I love them so much. My brothers, sometimes I wish I could talk to them. I wish I could call and they would pick up. But I do have that fear. And then I'm like, 'God: you know why you did this and you know how you made me to be. Just use me. Time will come, we shall be together again.'

We shall be one. Sexuality will not be a problem always. Through our sensitising, in our work we're doing, we are seeing a change in the community. Many people are not accepting – but at least the message is getting out. If you're a woman, or a dad out there, and you are seeing your child behaving in some way, don't chase him away. Chasing him away is not the solution. Listen, make time. This is what I tell people, even in my show, 'The Couch': I tell people to listen. There's a day you will say, 'Oh my God! I wish I listened. I wish I shared!'

Let's not take people for granted. We have gay people in churches. They are everywhere. It's okay not to know *but it's not okay not to know.* Get information. And let people live their life. For me, my message is love and acceptance; and even if you don't accept: understand. It's about love.

It's not like heaven here

Based on a life story interview with Tigan
(15 September 2019)

I am a simple person and I love simplicity. I care about people so much; sometimes my friends complain, asking, 'Why do you care about other people so much? You need to care about yourself too.' It's my weakness. I'm also a happy person, and I'm very sarcastic, overly sarcastic but I'm serious on some issues. I always speak my mind. It has been so hard for me to admit, but right now I can admit that I'm a gay person; I identify as gay. I'm a man attracted to fellow men, emotionally and sexually.

I am from Uganda. I'm a refugee here in Nairobi, Kenya. It's a journey I didn't choose, as I always thought I would stay in my country and be happy, like, forever. But then something happened, and I had to make the journey. I was not ready for it; I had never been out of my country at all; I always used to have my family with me, because I was one of those persons that didn't have that many friends. I was always with family. So when I got issues with my family, when they found out about my sexuality, they disowned me and it really shocked me. I didn't have anyone else. I learned my lesson, that I have to open up to friends outside, try to open up to other people and not only depend on family, because family can leave you and you are left with nothing.

When my family found out about my sexuality, they were like, 'Are you gay? We can't live with that.' I was disowned by my family; I was blackmailed by the boss I was working for then. That's why I had to run for my life. It was a horrible experience but thank God I can talk about it right now. At first it was very hard for me to talk about it, even at UNHCR. When I went to register and had my first interview, they asked, 'Tell us why you left your country?' It was really hard. But in fact, the officials there were very okay, because of course they have heard a lot of stories. I was surprised that they were so easy on the subject. What I learned is that the more I got to share my story of what happened, the more I felt healed, the more I felt comfortable. Also, because sharing my story can help others and inspire them. Every time I share it, I feel some kind of relief, like a weight is being lifted off me.

So, what happened? I had just completed school and I stayed home for five months. It's very hard to get a job in Uganda, even if you've studied. I'd been promised a job at a bank but then they called saying that they couldn't hire me. I was really shocked like, what the hell: all my friends have gotten jobs and I have nothing. So my father had a friend who had started a graphics and printing company. He was around twenty-nine by that time but he had his own company. His family was rich so they actually helped him with capital to start the business. My father said I could go and work in that start-up company. I was tired of sitting at home, so I accepted the offer thinking that maybe something good will come out of it, or I will get better opportunities in the long run. So I went and worked there. It was a struggle because I was the first employee he got, and I was literally doing everything: I was in the marketing department, looking for clients, and doing the printing. We used to print billboards, banners, receipt books, business cards, and so on. I used to do the marketing, go outside there and look for clients, moving from shop to shop, asking them whether they needed receipt books and things like that.

It worked out actually; we were doing well, and I had a good relationship with my boss. We used to share quite a lot. He always used to ask me like, 'how come you don't talk about girls at all?' Then I'm like 'No, I'm not doing girls now, they will eat my money.' He was like, 'But you should try.' But I said, 'There's no way I will.' By then I actually had a boyfriend. My family didn't know he was my boyfriend, they just knew he was my friend, they met him like once. I was that kind of person who never brought anyone home.

So, I'd been working at this job for like four months and the business was doing well. But I hadn't been paid, because my boss was promising like, 'You know what? Let's wait for the money to accumulate: we started this thing together, I want us to get a lot of money, so let's wait and do more work for clients, we shall make more profits.' He was like, 'The profit will be very big and we shall share. It's 50/50, because you've done good work for my business.' So I was like, 'Okay.' My parents used to give me money for transport to work and for lunch every day. I was patient, I was like, 'I can wait, I'll get something big out of this.'

So on a fateful day, I went to the field and found a really good client. We used to have some sort of a formula to calculate a price for, say, a banner. We would measure the width and length, and then we did the calculations to get the price. So I came back excited, telling my boss that we got this client. He said, 'Great, let's see how much you're going to charge him.' We were using my phone to do the calculations. He sent me down – we were working on the fourth floor – to get some airtime. I left him with my phone because he was busy doing the calculations. But while I was away, he went through my phone. When I came back, he looked at me, asking, 'How long have you been doing this?' I was like, 'What do you mean?' Then he showed me a picture. The previous day I had slept at my boy-friend's place and we took pictures while we were kissing and half naked. We used to take pictures like that, in bed and him lying on my chest, the way any couple does, be it heterosexual or gay. I'd forgotten to delete the pictures. I always remembered to delete the pictures, because at home my sister often used my phone. But this time I'd forgotten. He showed me the picture where I was kissing my boyfriend. He asked how long I had been doing this, and I was like, 'That's not your business.' He was like, 'It *is* my business, I can't work with someone who sleeps with men.' I told him to give my phone back; he was like, 'Even if I give you your phone, I have already sent the pic to myself.' He told me that he was not going to give me any money, but that I needed to get him a client every day. And he wanted to have sex with me. I was like, 'You're saying you are really shocked that I sleep with men; then why would you want to have sex with me?' He said he wanted to try and see what guys do. And if I wouldn't do it, he would go tell my parents, tell the police.

I had frequently seen the news when people had been embarrassed, put on the news in Uganda like: 'Two men found to be sleeping together!', 'Two men in a hotel having sex!' Then they were arrested and paraded on the streets, and everyone would be looking at them. I always thought, 'What the hell, I can't go through that.' All that passed through my mind. So I decided to do what he said. So yeah, he had sex with me, and I worked for him. That is when I started losing weight because I wasn't happy at all. I worked for like two more months. Then my mum was like, 'Why is the guy not paying you?' I was like, 'Talk to my dad, you know my dad knows the guy.' When my dad talked to my boss, he told him that I was lazy and didn't do anything. And he said he did actually give me money. So my dad was like, 'They give you money and you still ask for transport and lunch from us?' I couldn't tell my dad that he doesn't give me any money, because he has my secret and I was really afraid. I didn't want my family to know about it because my family was like, I wouldn't say they are homophobic, because I feel that homophobic is like an abuse. Okay, they might be homophobic but because they are ignorant, because of what the culture says and the churches, every religion, be it Muslim or Christian. So I was like, 'He gives me some money but it's not enough.' Then my father stopped giving me money and I was like, 'What the hell, where am I going to get money from? I'm like a slave to this guy. He wants to have sex with me, then he is not paying me, he's not even buying me lunch.'

So I used to talk to my boyfriend, I didn't tell him that this guy was using me for sex. I just told him I had some issues at work, and he said I should leave the job. And I was like, 'No I can't leave the job, I don't have anywhere to go.' I couldn't tell him the truth. So I continued to struggle. I lost a lot of weight; I was looking terrible because I was going through a lot. It reached a time that I couldn't do it anymore; it was too much on me. I felt like I was going to go into a depression and I wasn't talking to anyone. So I was like, 'I'm not going back to work.' I stayed home, it was Monday; I woke up, my mum was like, 'You're not going to work?' I was like 'Yeah, I'm not feeling okay.' And she always questioned me, 'Why are you losing weight? Why do you look like that? Aren't you eating? Your boss said you just eat the money.' And I was like, 'I have stress, I will be okay.' Because my mum was my friend, a very close friend; we were always together.

So that day he called me, he was like, 'Are you coming to work, or not?' And I was like, 'No, I'm not feeling well.' Then he was like, 'Okay, but tomorrow you come.' So the next day I told him again I wasn't feeling okay, and the next days. He was like, 'It seems like you're lying.' He came to the place where I was staying; he met me, and I was like, 'I'm sorry, I will not return to work.' And he was like, 'You don't remember that I know your secrets and I have evidence?' Then I was like, 'We've been doing the same thing together, so what secret are you talking about?' When he left, I was like, 'Thank you Jesus; I'm not going back to that job and get used.' So I started applying for other work.

After a week or so, I went to town to take my papers to different companies. I came back home around 8pm, it was already dark. When I entered the house, I saw my former boss and my father. They were sitting in the living room, and mum was seated at the dining table. I entered, and I thought that maybe he came for a normal visit. I greeted everyone, but my mum wasn't even looking at me. I went to my bedroom, but shortly after my mum came and called me. She didn't even look at my face; she asked me to go to the sitting room. When I went to the room, I was like, 'Oh my God, I think he told them.' My father stood up and slapped me really hard, so I fell down. He was like, 'I have given you everything, good education, why are you doing this to us?' I didn't say anything. I was so embarrassed. But what really hurt me so very bad was the fact that my mum said nothing to me; she didn't look at me at all. And I had a very good relationship with mum. Even when I was younger, my mum used to stand up for me every time my dad was like,

'He has to do this and that.' She was always like, 'This is my son, let him rest.' But this time, she didn't look at me or say anything. I wanted her to say something, even if it was hateful, but she didn't.

My dad was like, 'Pack your bags and leave, you're not going to stay here any longer; at least I've given you education, go hustle on your own, you're not staying in this house with those behaviours of yours.' Then my boss tried to put more fire into the situation; he was saying a lot of stuff. But I didn't say anything, I was not paying attention to him, I was really embarrassed. I left that night. Still when I was leaving, I looked at my mum: she was seated at the dining table, she was putting her head down, as if she was too embarrassed to look in my eyes. I looked at her, but she didn't look at me; then I left. I stood at the door waiting for her, and my dad was like, 'Leave! No one is going to be on your side.'

I didn't have anywhere to go. I called my boyfriend and told him, 'I have to tell you something.' I went to his place and explained everything to him. He was like, 'You should have told me; you shouldn't have kept such a big thing secret; I would have understood that even though you slept with your boss you didn't want to; we could have found a solution for this.' Now, he was still in school, so was still with his parents. So I stayed at his place for some time. But he said:

> You can't stay here, like, forever, because it's my parents' home; you can stay here for a week, but my mum can't allow you to stay here for like a month, there will be a lot of questions, she knows you have your parents, so there will be a lot of questions, and I don't want my parents to find out I'm gay too.

So I needed to find my way. I didn't have any money; I had nothing. I had just completed school with not that much experience. By then I had some friends in Nairobi; they had actually been published in the newspapers in Uganda around the time the Anti-Homosexuality Bill was passed, so they couldn't stay home, and had left for Kenya. They were not really close friends, just Facebook friends. I used to see their posts, like, 'We need food, we need help.' I'd go to their inbox and ask, 'How are you? Sorry about what is happening.' Then they would talk about the situation in Nairobi, saying like, 'It's not good, we are doing sex work to survive, but at least here we are away from danger and persecution.' Because when they were in Uganda, some of them had been beaten up, some were discriminated against, some of them used to stay in hiding and then they had to be evacuated from the plot where they were staying. So I was talking to one of them, and he was like, 'You know, Tigan, you don't have choice.'

In the meantime, my boss kept sending me messages like, 'I'm going to make your life miserable until you come back here and beg and work for me.' Then he was suggesting like, 'Okay, you come and work, I'll give you food, you can sleep in the offices.' And I was like, 'What the hell, I can't go back there.' So I texted my boss and told him I would not work for him, because I knew he just wanted sex. He said, 'That's not the end, I'll go to the police and report you.' And in Uganda, they would arrest you for being gay. So I was like, let me just get out of this drama, let me just leave, you never know something might happen. Maybe this is the journey God has put for me.

My boyfriend had been talking to his sister, who was working. She had given some money and he gave it to me. He said, 'I think you should go to Nairobi and try.' Also, the guy I had been talking to was like, 'Come, I'll help you and house you for some time, and also UNHCR will support you.' So I thought like, 'Okay, let me come and try, but if it fails, I'll just go back to Uganda.' So I got transport and came to Nairobi and met that friend of mine; he took me to the UNHCR, they registered me. Then life begins in Nairobi from 2015.

Life in Nairobi was kind of hard at first, because it's not like heaven here. By the time I came, UNHCR had experienced a lot of fraud with people pretending to be gay just to join the asylum process and also to get some money. So I came in during that time, and they were like, 'We are not giving any financial assistance to the LGBTQ community, to people who are claiming to be LGBTQ.' That friend of mine was staying with other people in a room, it was so small; we were with eight people and we had three mattresses. I was like, 'I'm not used to this at all, I can't live such a life; let me just pack my bags and at least die in Uganda.' But my friend told me not to leave, saying that at least here I'm safe, my boss can't cross the border and threaten me or do any harm to me. So I stayed, and I started coughing every night; it might have been because of the cold. It was so hard. There was a time when UNHCR refused to give us money for financial assistance, we didn't have food. Another person who was staying with us had talked to some Kenyan who had told him, 'I can give you guys some money but one of you has to come to my place then I'll give you money and you can buy some food.' We had no choice. That friend went there and had sex with him and came back with food. I remember at that time we used to sit on the mattresses, and everyone would be like, 'do you have a 50 bob, 10 bob?'[1] And most of us didn't have anything. So

---

[1] 'Bob' is a slang word for shilling.

when someone said a friend invited him over and offered like 1000 Kenya shillings,[2] we all thought, 'Wow, that's a lot of money.' It kept on happening with different people. But then I was like, 'we can't be doing this guys; we need to find a way.' Sure enough, UNHCR resumed their support, because some people had been demonstrating outside the UNHCR offices, and also some activists were pushing it so hard on social media. So they resumed giving people financial assistance again. That is when we moved house to where we are now, through a connection.

The house where we were staying was expensive; we were suffering there. And the neighbours started noticing us, because we were staying in a place that was very congested. They asked questions like, 'why is it that these people are only boys in the house, why is it they don't have any girls that come here? What kind of work do they do? How can they pay rent?' Like a lot of questions. We used to lie a lot, like, 'We are students.' And they would be like, 'But we don't see you with bags.' There was a time when our landlady called us telling us, 'People are complaining and saying that you guys are the people who the president of Uganda chased away.' So she asked, 'Are you gay?' And we were like, 'No! We are not gay!' And that was the time we were also struggling very much to pay the rent. So my friend was like, 'We can't stay here, we need a better environment.'

Through a connection we learned about this house, here in Matasia. It's very far from town, but at least it's safe. So we came here in April 2015. The guys had just moved in, and we came like in the second week. At that time it was called Ark Commune, started by a certain priest from Uganda who actually helped to secure this house and organise it into a community house. But after some time, the priest returned to Uganda and was unable to continue his support. Other people also left, as they got resettled in the US. Some other people moved in and it became The Nature Network afterwards. Raymond Brian developed it. He came in with the idea of mimicking TV personalities from Uganda, and he would pretend to be a TV personality, saying 'Welcome, this is the show!' It started as a joke, like a really jokey thing, but then he created a group, we added in more community members, and we started doing all kinds of creative things. And people started talking about it, it became a thing.

At first it was very hard to live here with all these people, like it gave me a lot of problems because these people have different characters, some are very provocative, some are not neat. But I got to learn lessons. I have

[2] Roughly GBP £7 / $9. Modern equivalents here and onwards are as at April 2021.

no choice; I can't go back to Uganda. So this is like my new family. I got to love these people as they are, I got to learn about myself and my character. I'm really happy about it. And also, people here are free, like free from being so, how can I put it? Like in Uganda, you always have to pretend, you have to pretend to your family. I remember, back home when they were passing the Anti-Homosexuality Bill, it was all over the news; so we would sit in the room with my family and we are watching news and they get people's opinions on the streets, and people are like, 'These gays should be killed, they shouldn't be in this country'; and everyone is cursing while we are watching the news, supporting the people's view on TV, and I had to say something too, because everyone is saying something. It used to kill me like so very bad inside, but again I had to say it because otherwise they would put question marks, 'Why is it that he's the only quiet one?' When I came here, everyone is LGBTQ and in the long run it felt so good, you don't have to hide even when you're holding someone's hand in the house, even when you kiss someone in the sitting room, no one will be like, 'Oh my God!' People will be like, 'Oh, normal stuff!' We were not born together but we created a family that's free, although also having our own problems, like sometimes we blame some people for doing some stuff, but at the end of the day we really do understand and we have to see those mistakes, learn from them, and get to correct ourselves.

What usually happens, every month we sit around the table, all the people staying here, and we count up all the expenses for the month ahead: this is the amount for rent, this is the budget for food and utilities. And we decide what everyone has to contribute. But sometimes it happens in the middle of the month that the food we had bought for that month is finished. Then that's a problem, and people will be like, 'Oh my God, what are we going to do? There's no food in the house!' So we try and raise funds. Sometimes we get a visitor and they help. Also the sex work continues, people used to go out to make some money, then they come back and buy some food. God!!! I had to do it myself for a while, but then I was like, 'I can't do this.' It made me feel terrible, because I come from a very Catholic family, and I used to be an altar boy and I was so much attached to religion. It felt so bad, even when I was doing it. So then I was like, 'No, I'm stopping.' It still feels terrible, but right now I look back at it and I know it was the only survival that we had. And mind you, it was not a lot of money we were given, they would give you like 300 shillings[3], so after paying transport you remain with like 150

---

[3] Roughly £2 / $3.

shillings; but again it did help at that time. Maybe you would buy some beans and then you share. I did it until we lost someone due to HIV, then I was like, 'I can't do it anymore.'

This person had just fled, he came and joined the house and started doing sex work. I won't judge the person. After a while he was diagnosed with HIV, so he got so depressed. He went to UNHCR and they were like, 'We can't give you extra help just because you have HIV, there are a lot of people with HIV and they are surviving.' So this person felt he was neglected; he didn't even come back home to pick his bag, he just left and went back to Uganda. We were looking for him, and then learned that he went back to Uganda, and we were like, 'What the hell? Why would he go back?' He had talked to someone and told him like, 'I can't be with HIV and be in this process, it's very hard, we have no food, we just live for survival.' So he went back, and after a month we got news that he had died. Then we were like, 'How can someone die just two months after being diagnosed with HIV?' But we realised that sometimes depression can kill someone, if they don't have anyone to talk to, and something bad like this is happening to them.

When he died in Uganda, it was like an eye opener for us. We had to switch our videos from the dramatic and entertaining ones to videos talking about HIV, relationships, and things like that. That's how we kept on growing, developing ourselves into this very beautiful family, The Nature Network. At The Nature Network I'm the administrator but I do quite a lot because, let me just say, because some of the people here don't have much education. When it comes to applying for grants, I do most of the writing; when there are visitors, some people struggle to express themselves because of the language. All the things to do with paperwork, mostly I do it with Raymond and someone else who's not here at the moment called Josh and another one called Jonah. I have taken them through everything that happens; we really try to involve each and every one.

As I said, I grew up in a Catholic family. My mum wanted me to become a Catholic priest. You know with Catholic priests, they don't marry at all. And also me, I wanted it. I used to feel different from other boys and I was like, maybe I should hide in this, maybe I should consider it. I almost joined. Then my father was like, 'No, you can't join, I need grand-kids. I want my son to have a woman.' And my mum was like, 'But I want him to join.' I don't know what happened but I didn't join. To be honest, I haven't gone to a Catholic church in like forever. But I have always prayed from here and I would still say I'm Catholic. Right now what I believe in is that if at all we can pray here in our own house, then God will listen. Here in

Nairobi I used to go to Cosmopolitan Affirming Church.[4] That was way back, but it was too expensive to go there all the way from here. Then we got another church just nearby where we were praying, but it was demolished. Then we were like, 'Let's organise some prayers here in the house.' So now we have our own regular prayer sessions.

To be honest, I'm not really a Bible person. But, there's a story about Daniel: he was thrown into the lions' den by the king, and he wasn't eaten by the lions; so when they came to check if the lions ate him, he was still alive and he was like having some sort of interaction with the lions. I would connect to that story in the way that the homophobic people in Uganda, our families – I don't hate my family at all, because they don't know, they are ignorant about it all – they threw us into the lions' den. But by the time they will come to check on us, we shall be prosperous, we shall still be here, we shall be alive, because God loves us. If at all God doesn't love us, God would not be creating more and more LGBTQ people, because every day LGBTQ people are being born, and it's heterosexual people who are bearing these kids, so I think God knows what he's doing. So if at all they throw us into the lions' den because of that, I believe that no, we shall not be eaten. We shall not.

Like Daniel, we have survived a lot, and we are still around, we are surviving, we didn't die when we went through persecution, blackmailing, sex work – and now we are here. There used to be a time I needed someone to talk to, but right now there are people who come to me and be like, 'Tigan, I need to talk to you, this and this is happening, I have got some issues.' And then I can advise them. I feel like we haven't been eaten yet. And I don't think we shall be eaten by any lions. Daniel was protected, you can imagine. And I feel like there's a very big ray of hope; I know we are still going through it all, but there's a very big ray of hope. Everyone here thinks about their resettlement, but I don't believe that it's milk and honey in Canada, or in the US or UK, I'm sorry to say. There, too, they have some people who are hateful. But I think it's a little better, because people there are more open-minded and also, the law protects you, so when someone does something to you, they can be charged. But the law does not protect you in Uganda, or even here in Kenya.

Say, in five years' time, I still want to do advocacy, and I still want to be there for a lot of people, mostly the young boys or the young girls who are LGBTQ and are still confused. In Uganda, but also here in Kenya,

---

[4] Cosmopolitan Affirming Church is a church community in Nairobi, LGBTQ+ founded and led.

they don't know what's going on in their bodies, they are going through puberty, it's really confusing. I don't know but you might have faced it, too? I would really want to be there for such people, and I look at myself to carry on our beautiful Network and it becomes an NGO, something big and then we support people here.

I'm in the pipeline for resettlement to the US. I hope to live in a place where I'll be safe to hold a man's hand and no one will judge; of course I might be judged, people may give me looks but they won't come and attack me, and giving looks doesn't hurt me. In Uganda you have to pretend everything, you can't even hold a guy's hand, as people will raise a lot of questions. I hate that so very much. So I'm looking for that space in the future, that space where I can hold someone, maybe can kiss someone, just like the way heterosexual people do. Like in the US and the UK they can kiss, they can hold hands on the streets and no one will be like, 'Oh my God!' But in Uganda, you can't.

Here we are free to express ourselves without fear

Based on a life story interview with Kyle
(22 September 2019)

My name is Kyle and I stay in Nairobi, in The Nature Network house, which is in Matasia, in Ngong. I'm 37 years old. I'm the Aunt of the refugees here, and I'm the welfare officer of The Nature Network. I am gay but a feminine gay. I treat myself as a woman.

I knew I was gay from a very young age. I think for me it was God who discovered me. When I was with my cousins, because we were age-mates and young, whenever we were at home alone we would just do some, let me call it, stupid stuff, like touching each other. We were all boys and I was the ring-leader who used to tell them what to do: like touch their small dicks to see if they can become big. So, after some years, my mum died in 2002 and I went to stay with my brother in Ndeeba.[1] He used to go on safaris for a very long time without coming back home. He had CDs of porn for heterosexuals. I was in Primary Five and I had a lot of friends from school that came to visit me. Some days I used to watch those porn CDs with them and they touched their penises; I enjoyed watching their penises getting hard. So, I didn't really have any person that I can say helped me find myself: it was all me.

It's certainly not white people who taught me to be homosexual. I was born in a very deep village, and I didn't see any white person in my young age coming home or near my home. It was only when we went to town for something that we used to see them. I have just started interacting and actively seeing white people these days. And I dropped out of school early, so there's no way I could talk to a white person. I disagree with that saying about white people teaching homosexuality, because I grew up differently.

---

[1] Ndeeba is a neighbourhood of Kampala, the capital of Uganda.

At home we had two beliefs: my mum was very much into cultural norms and my dad was a Catholic. I had my feet on both sides, because I couldn't decide. My dad said that when I grow up, I'll decide for myself. When mum died, things got a bit complicated, because I couldn't really practise my traditional rituals like I used to and my dad was not supportive of me doing these rituals. So when I went to Ndeeba I became Catholic, and dad celebrated it. I started going to church daily and I joined the choir. I later became the youth leader in our group. When you become a youth leader in church you must get married to set an example to all the youths in church. The church had a meeting to find a wife for me to get married, and that's where tables turned. I tried to explain to them that I'm not yet ready for marriage. The chaplain told me about an offer they had: if I introduce my fiancée they will cater for all the wedding costs and the honeymoon. But I refused it.

I'm still a Catholic. But to be honest, I'm not really good at quoting the Bible. But there was somewhere when Jesus was walking with his disciples, all the twelve men, and there was a man called Peter, and he used to sleep very close to Jesus.[2] But I'm not sure of what happened between them. Jesus decided to be with only men and not a single woman: why? He slept with Peter on his chest. Are we really sure of what happened in the night? So with the Bible we are not sure of Jesus' sexuality. So that really inspires me and teaches me not to just look at people and judge them.

In our Buganda tradition, we have a small god called Ndawula[3] and they tell us that we are all Ndawula's wives, no matter which gender you are. So that means Ndawula was gay, too. I was not sure if Ndawula was male or female. They refer to people who sleep with the same sex as 'Ndawula's followers'. So to me this means that homosexuality was in our tradition too. But they don't say much about gays, because of our African culture, which cares so much about having children and having blood heirs. I'm really sorry if anyone is disappointed about me not having children. But there are heterosexual people who are barren, too. We had some in our family. Who knows if I'm barren too.

[2] The text that Kyle appears to allude to here is John 13:23, which speaks about 'the disciple whom Jesus loved' (most likely referring to John, not Peter) 'leaning on Jesus' bosom' (in the King James Version).

[3] Ndawula was *Kabaka* of the Kingdom of Buganda in the eighteenth century. *Kabaka* is the title of the king. In Buganda tradition there is a spiritual and a material king and a *Kabaka* does not die – hence, possibly, the notion of him being 'a small god'.

I came to Nairobi on 29 January 2014. I got problems on 11 November 2013, on my birthday: that's the reason I can't forget the date. I was with my friends in the house of our friend called John in Gayaza.[4] One of our community members tried to blackmail John, and when he failed, he went and reported him to the police. They came to arrest him from his home, and when they came for John, they found us too, because we were making plans to form a certain organisation to be called Pearl Uganda. We had applied for some funding and had to sign some documents. The police came and searched the whole house; afterwards we all were arrested.

When we got to the police station the officers started separating us, putting each one of us in their own cell. We were only four. And then they started taking our statements, asking how we know John, what we know about him, and many more such questions. They had arrested us in the morning so later, when it was approaching 5pm, I requested to make a short call – and they gave me an escort, which surprised me, because they had told me I was coming just to make a statement. When I came back, they told me to remove my shoes and belt, and all my friends reappeared. They also didn't have their belts and shoes on. They handcuffed all of us and put us in one cell and we gave it a lot of drama and resistance, because we knew we hadn't committed any crime. We were only arrested because they found us in the same house as the person they had come for. We thought, 'by the next day we will be out' – but we were in there for the next five days. On the fifth day the officer in charge of Kasangati Police Station[5] came and asked us if we were gays. We said 'no', and then he asked why we are in touch with John, and everyone explained their reasons.

Because my friends had given me a lot of gifts the day they arrested us, they took my case seriously, taking the gifts as evidence. The gifts included female clothes and a framed picture of me wearing traditional female attire, you see. They took it to mean I was gay and because they had a search warrant, they thoroughly searched and found lots of evidence, such as flags, tags, and my business cards stating my sex worker status. They also found a CD that had gay porn on it; so that's when they started pin-pointing me. I tried to make up stories but it was all a waste of time. They asked us if we have families and where they were, and we each told them. Afterwards, they sent us 'doctors' to do some check-ups on us. But the 'doctors' they brought in were police officers too, so I resisted, because I knew these were not doctors. They were trying to check me because I

---

[4] John is a pseudonym. Gayaza is a town in the Wakiso District of the Buganda region of Uganda.

[5] Kasangati is another town in the Wakiso District of Uganda.

had bigger breasts and because John was a doctor. They thought he was injecting hormones into me, so that I can grow breasts, and they wanted to check if I can have an erection.

After all that, the officers called the press and gathered all the people around the station to come and see the 'evil gays in their community'. When we got outside there were a lot of cameras and unfortunately, most of them were reporting live. Even those who wanted to help us not make this public, organisations such as SMUG[6] and HRAPF,[7] came too late and could not stop it happening. I was called lots of names: 'first lady of gays', 'president of homosexuals'. While we were in the cells, lawyers came from HRAPF led by Frida.[8] Others wouldn't come, because they were intimidated by the situation: everyone who tried to check on us was called gay too. So Frida got other strong lawyers and they came to our rescue but John was taken to prison. We were tortured a lot at the station. They injected us with some medicine, poured water on us, and I lost one of my fingernails. But they released us on bond. SMUG got us a safe house where we were for two weeks, and we had to keep reporting to the police. And that was all at around the same time as the Anti-Homosexuality Bill was passed through the Ugandan parliament, late 2013.

In January 2014 we went for our regular reporting and the officer said that our case was being taken to the Attorney General for him to decide if we would be taken to court, or left alone. We were really confused and intimidated by this. As we were going back home, we visited a befriended priest, who had been supporting us, to tell him about our story.[9] He said to us that if our case goes to court, because of the Bill in the parliament, they will imprison us. We had to go back to report on 5th February and after discussion we decided not to return to the police. He told us that we were not safe. We heard about the camp in Kenya called Kakuma, and that it was a bad situation there but that we could possibly spend five to six

---

[6] Sexual Minorities Uganda, a non-profit, non-governmental umbrella organisation that aims to end discrimination and injustice towards members of the LGBTQ+ community of Uganda and to ensure all Ugandans are free to live out their sexual orientation and gender identity or expression.

[7] Human Rights Awareness and Promotion Forum.

[8] Frida Mutesi has represented HRAPF in a number of prominent cases, notably 'HRAPF vs The Attorney General of Uganda and The Secretariat of the Joint United Nations Program on HIV/AIDS' (Reference No. 6 of 2014).

[9] The priest works with youth and refugees in Kampala. He was one of the founders of Ark Commune, which became The Nature Network (see 'Introduction').

years there under UNHCR's protection, which is better than staying here where they can kill us any time. We were advised to run for our survival. We explained to our friend that we don't have money to go to Kenya and we don't know Swahili, the language they use in Kenya. He said that we'll learn it. We asked if the police won't search for us everywhere, but he said that if they don't find us, they will give up. So we all agreed to think about it.

We didn't even think about it that much! Everyone sold any possessions they had to get money: mattresses, saucepans, and other stuff. We managed to raise some little amount for transport and the border fee. Before we left, one of our friends called us to come and pick up money for food, and we were given 25,000 Ugandan shillings each.[10] When we got that money we called our friend and told him we had agreed to go to Kenya. And he helped us with transport money and some additional funds. We were three people. We chose to go on 27 February and we reached here on 28 February 2014.

We got to Mash Poa[11] offices in Nairobi. Everything was different. It was a Friday and we had no idea where to go. We decided to call the priest and ask where to go next. He told us to ask around for the directions to the offices of UNHCR in Westlands.[12] We had already exchanged our currency and a guy asked us for 6,000 Kenyan shillings to take us to UNHCR.[13] We gave him the money and he took us. At UNHCR the guards asked us where we are from, and what we had come for. We told them we had run away, because they wanted to kill us at home. They said, 'there is no war in Uganda: how come you decided to come here?' And we told them we are gays and that's a crime in Uganda. They all got defensive and told us how they don't want gays in their country either. It was a Friday on which UNHCR offices were closed. They threw our luggage to the other side of the street and there was lots of drama, because they wanted us to leave and we refused. One of us decided to ask the guards, 'When does UNHCR resume work?' And he said he doesn't know, because the offices are closed.

We decided to look for someone who can take us to any nearby guest house, so that we can rest and a man took us to Mountain View Kangemi and asked for 3,000 Kenyan shillings.[14] We didn't really know about Kenyan money, so we just paid. We paid the guest house for a full week

[10] Roughly £5 / $7.

[11] Mash Poa is the name of a Kenyan bus company.

[12] Westlands is an affluent residential neighbourhood and an administrative division of Nairobi.

[13] Roughly £40 / $60.

[14] About £20 / $30.

and we had some food and drinks. On Monday we called the priest and told him all that had happened. He told us that on Monday UNHCR is open and that we should go back. We went back to the offices and they told us that we should go and register with Refugee Affairs Secretariat (RAS). When we went to RAS, the same scenario happened because of our status. We went back and forth for a week, with them telling us that a person who is supposed to attend to us is not around – and yet they were registering others. Then one of our friends contacted a lady called Caroline[15] and told her about our situation. (Please remember: we didn't have the local SIM cards to make calls so whenever we wanted to talk to someone, we had to use a cyber café and write emails to people.) Caroline told us to go to HIAS'[16] main offices in Lavington.[17] Here the same thing happened: after we said that we are Ugandans, the guard didn't even open; he just said their workers are not around, yet we saw other people entering.

We didn't have much to say, because they spoke in Swahili and we could only use English. The most challenging thing was that we just gave out money, and we started to realise that we were running short. We decided to pay for only one room and share that one mattress, because of lack of money. We paid the lodge for more days and we were dejected. Then, one of our friends hooked up with a guy and went to Mombasa to meet him. He explained to the guy about us and asked if he would allow us to be with him until we figured out what to do next. He agreed and we all went to Mombasa. We spent some good days there, forgetting that we had emailed Caroline who in the meantime sent us several emails stating that if we didn't get help, we should tell her. But we were not aware of them. We had moved on with our lives until our friend decided one day to check his emails only to find a lot of documents sent by Caroline that we should take to HIAS to get help.

We hadn't paid attention because they had treated us badly at UNHCR and because the guy in Mombasa gave us everything we wanted, so we relaxed. When our friend came back from checking the internet, he told us about how serious Caroline is about our registration. When she asked what we are doing in Mombasa, we told her we are doing sex work. She went and called Dorris, the Director of HIAS, and told her about how we were chased from every office we went to and she threatened to report them if we get in any trouble. She asked for a phone number so that she can send

---

[15] Pseudonym.

[16] HIAS stands for the Hebrew Immigrant Aid Society.

[17] Lavington is a high-income suburb of Nairobi, northwest of the city centre, in the Westlands administrative division.

it to HIAS for them to contact us. We told the person hosting us if he could give us a number, but he told us to forget about the refugee stuff and to stay in Mombasa and work. We begged him until he got us a Safaricom[18] number and we sent it to her.

Caroline wrote to HIAS and UNHCR and sent the number to Dorris. After some time they called the number and the owner of the number asked them several tough questions, like why didn't they listen to us instead of beating us and sending us away. So HIAS and UNHCR decided to call Mombasa Police and they told them that the owner of this number kidnaps refugees. The police called the guy and warned him to report to the offices with us within hours. He went but not with us and told the police that we didn't get help from those we needed it from until he decided to help us, so how can they threaten the only person that helped refugees. The police told him that we were needed immediately, but he said they had to first make an agreement that we will be treated well, and they had to provide transport for us. They called HIAS and they sent 15,000 shillings.[19] The guy took us to the police where we signed an agreement and later he took us to the bus station where we got a bus to Nairobi.

When we got to HIAS they immediately started to interview us one by one and asked for the evidence that showed what we said was true. We told them we were on the news all over Uganda and directed them to look for NTV Akawungeezi, which was the news channel we appeared in. They said they will confirm in the morning and warned us to be sure that we appeared, because it would have consequences if we didn't. We told them we had other evidence too but we had left our luggage in the bus from Mombasa. They escorted us to the bus to pick up our bags and we showed them the police bond and the newspapers. They took us to their transit place in Kangemi[20] where we stayed for a full week.

I think they took us seriously by now, because of Caroline, and how persistent she was. After a week in transit, they came for us, took us back to their offices, gave us 6,000 shillings, and paid six months of rent. They gave us all the household things we needed. They drove us to the house in Kawangware.[21] It was a good house: one bedroom, a sitting room, a bathroom, a kitchen, and a store, which was enough for three people.

We are now registered with UNHCR in the resettlement process, which is very slow. But I have a dream of going somewhere and to continue

---

[18] Safaricom is a listed Kenyan mobile network operator.

[19] About £100 / $140.

[20] Kangemi is a slum on the outskirts of Nairobi.

[21] Kawangware is a residential area of Nairobi west of the city centre.

with my studies and later fight for those who can't fight for themselves as an activist for LGBTI people. We need to help the young generation that will face the same problems as we are having right now. We need to have a very big safe house here that can shelter those chased away from their homes. For example The Nature Network: if we can buy this house and not rent it, it becomes ours. And then I need to buy a very big piece of land to bury those who are killed because of their sexuality and those who die from within the community, so that they can have a good resting place.

I don't really miss home to be honest. You know, I left home long time ago now and I have tried to look everywhere – like Facebook, online, radios – to see if I can find somewhere that my relatives are looking for me: but not a single thing. So I only miss you if you miss me, that's my decision. At The Nature Network we have created our own family: we have a mother, aunts, and children. Here we are free to do and express ourselves without fear and we love each other no matter what. So Nature Network is more than an organisation: it's a family to all the LGBTI refugees in Kenya.

I consider this as my new family

Based on a life story interview with Cindy
(21 September 2019)

My name is Cindy. I left Uganda in October 2016. I have been living in different parts of Kenya ever since I came. I have been homeless, sometimes facing eviction from houses by landlords, because of my sexuality. Right now, I'm in the process of resettlement, and I'm at the embassy stage, which is quite a privilege. I am currently a director at Pride Umbrella Kenya, which is a community-based organisation (CBO) of refugees. We are based in Rongai[1] and I'm so happy that I am helping the community to move on, that I'm part of community work.

I define myself as a transgender but transvestite. In public, I prefer to look like a man but when I'm in a safe space like home with the community, I just love to cross-dress. Even right now, if I had cross-dressed, with my wig on, my best makeup on, I feel I would give out my best, I would feel comfortable. Yeah, I feel very comfortable when I cross-dress. Much more than when I am like this [gestures towards the casual clothes she is wearing]; I feel like I am not that person I really want to be. It's funny. But because of the public and the way people look at you in situations, you just have to be like a man, like the society expects.

When I cross-dress I feel really myself! For instance, we were at a proactive grant workshop. There was this grant that was coming, and we were called as CBO leaders to come and discuss how we are going to use this grant. So I was called and I decided that when I go like this I will not feel comfortable, so I packed my wigs and all that in my bag and I went. I was actually really confident and I gave my best. That's the day I felt that

---

[1] Ongata Rongai is a town in Kajiado County, south of Nairobi's centre and west of the Ngong hills.

when I'm cross-dressing I'm really myself, I really feel confident, and people are looking at me and they really take on what I am saying.

I came to Kenya in 2016. When I got here, I barely had anything; I was just seeking refuge with friends. And then sometimes you find yourself going into relationships that you don't want to be in, because you don't have anywhere to live and then this person is helping you and wants to be your boyfriend. It happened to me in a place called Kangemi[2]; a friend of mine was there, we met on Facebook. So when I arrived in Nairobi I didn't have anywhere to stay, because I didn't get assistance from the UN.[3] So we started living together as friends. I thought we were friends. And then he comes at night, he has only one bed, that's where we both sleep, and he forces you into sex. When I used to chat with other people, trying to get to know the community, trying to talk to other people, he was limiting me, saying, 'why are you talking to this person, why?' And when I talked to other people on Facebook, you know, gay people love gossiping, they are like, 'Simon[4] told us you are his boyfriend.' And I was in fear, I couldn't confront him about it, because he was giving me somewhere to sleep. I was completely dependent on him; he was paying rent, buying the food and all that. I was new in Nairobi. The situation went on for about two months. Then I reported this situation to Raymond and Jonathan. I told them about my situation and they actually came for me. So I had to lie to Simon. I told him I'd been given a place to stay in Matasia, at The Nature Network house. When I left, I felt like life has given me a chance because I wasn't really comfortable being forced into a relationship I didn't even know about. So that's how I was introduced to The Nature Network. My first safe house was here and I lived here for like a year. The experience was good, like the care, the love, and the safety was really fine.

I left The Nature Network when the process became a bit difficult, when the UN decided to take all new arrivals to the camp. We went to Kakuma refugee camp, in Turkana County. Life there is really terrifying; it's not as good as here. And when it comes to the LGBTIs it becomes worse. We faced a lot of homophobia from the locals and from fellow refugees as well. You know, when you hear of the camp, at first you hear that it's a community of free living, it's a community of no expenses, like you don't spend anything, you don't pay rent, you don't buy food, the UN provides everything. True, it provides, but then the camp is really not a good environment – especially for LGBTI people. Because different refugees

---

[2] Kangemi is a slum on the outskirts of Nairobi.
[3] Cindy refers to the UNHCR simply as 'the UN'.
[4] Pseudonym.

are mixed together in one camp, you find the Somalis that ran from their country because of war, you find the Sudanese that have other issues, and then these people are straight, they are not LGBTI and they have their cultural beliefs. So you find yourself coming to the camp, there's no one there, and the network coverage for phones is very low. So you find that life is difficult, and you try to find ways of coming back here.

Like I said, I have a community where I live, so when I come home from work or meetings I put my dress back on. But in the camp you can't do that because when you put it on you find people attacking you; they used to attack us when they see you with makeup, they beat you. And there's no one to report to because the UN offices are very far from the camp, and there are no vehicles and also no cash allowances to help you go to the UN offices and all that. What I would say about the camp is that the community is harsh. Also, the police is harsh there, especially on the LGBTI people; even if you try to raise issues, like maybe you put on a strike when you are not really satisfied with what UN is doing out there, the police will not listen or even give you protection, but they will beat you instead and take you into custody. They lock you up with the locals who are not friendly with LGBTI people.

So that was my experience in the camp, we were a group of around eighteen and most of us were transgenders, we used to cross-dress. We didn't want to live there but wanted to come back to Nairobi. I remember that time when we said 'enough is enough', so we decided to put on a demonstration to request to be brought back to Nairobi where we can find work, we can find a place to stay. Because some CBOs in Nairobi used to write to the UN requesting for us to be brought back. They told them that each CBO could accommodate, like, six people, but the UN failed to respond. During the strike, the police from that area came, they beat us up, they put us on trucks and we were taken into custody, into police cells, before we were taken to prison. We slept there for three days and after that we were taken to court, without knowing why. In court the judge said that we had been arrested because the camp reception had reported that we caused a disturbance at the camp premises, and the community had complained about the way we dressed, calling it improper, but then this is us who are trying to be us.

So we had been taken there, to a place that is supposed to be safe, but we could not be the way we wanted to be. It's kind of difficult. In court we were sentenced to 30 days in prison. We were taken to Lodwar prison, which is the main prison in Turkana County. Lodwar prison also wasn't very good; life was difficult there.[5] Sometimes we were made to do a lot of work, because the prison wardens would be telling us, 'Why are you like a woman? You should do work, you are a man.' So they would give us a lot of work. You know, that place is very dry so there is a lot of sand. We were given sacks. Each of us had to fill a sack with 100 kilograms of sand, and then pull it to the side, because they were putting up a fence there. And this work was given specifically to us, the LGBTI. We used to be mocked, teased, and bullied.

The wardens used to come every evening to do what they call mathematics, prison mathematics.[6] They used to pick on us every time, asking 'Where are those ladies?' and the others would laugh. So we would sleep in terror, in fear, not knowing what's going to happen at night as you sleep, because everyone has gotten to know why you are in prison. We tried to write, we tried to request, we tried to apologise, so that we could get out of the prison but it never worked until we had served the entire 30 days and then we were taken out. In the camp, right up until now such things have been going on, because there's another group including some of our friends, they were beaten and others were stabbed, you know to the extent of people almost killing them. Fortunately, the UN has now decided not to take any LGBTI refugees into the camp.

I am a person who loves living a life that's moving on, you know. Because others are moving, so you also have to find a way. When you leave here, you are going to be resettled and then what will you be going to do after you get resettled? So, I went back into my field of work, because I have been doing beauty since I was in Uganda. I said, 'This is the turning point!' Ever since I left the camp, I can't let life be the same. So I went to Rongai, a nearby town, and I looked for work. There's a friend of mine called Steven, he helped me with bringing back my beauty skills, like skills of nail technology, skills of makeup. So we worked together and, luckily, I went back to work. I was working in Rongai until my boss found out about my sexuality. Then things started becoming difficult. We started having fights here and there. She was picking on me now and then, so I decided to leave work. After leaving work, I lost my house where I was renting, and then I met this other group that also didn't have anywhere to live. Life was bad for them; they were living in others' houses. But they wanted to create something, so we came together as a group and we created Pride Umbrella Kenya. That's where I am currently.

[5] Lodwar is the largest town in north-western Kenya and the capital of Turkana County. Its prison is notoriously congested.

[6] A term referring to the process of counting the prisoners.

In Pride Umbrella I'm working as the director. So far, we are a group of fifteen, with seven being on board. Pride Umbrella started as a solidarity group with a mission. We want a society where refugees are freely accepted, a society where I can wear my dress and go out and no one picks on me. We have a safe house where we are staying in Rongai. The safe house has been able to accommodate ten members. We have been at the safe house since May 2019; we haven't yet made a year. We have hens at home; we are doing agriculture, growing tomatoes. The other project we have, we make tumblers out of empty bottles, tumblers and decoration bottles. We cut bottles and make wine glasses out of them. We also produce a magazine; it's a queer magazine sharing information about us as refugees. We are not only Ugandans, we have people from South Sudan, one member from Somalia and another member from DRC.[7] So, some of them are from countries that don't speak English, and we teach them English in preparation for their resettlement.

I was never accepted by my family but here I am; I have a family here: they accept me, support me, love me, and cherish me. These are the people I live with every day; they know how I feel, they know what I go through. Back at home they didn't want to know anything about me, because I am gay. So I can't call *them* family: yes, we share blood but I consider *this* as my family. Even when I wake up, I actually don't remember the last time I dreamed of my mum but then I dream about these people I am with, like sometimes you dream that Raymond is calling you for something. I feel like I am a parent to my community, for instance. When I am away from home, I miss them and when they don't have some stuff, I try to help. We had parents in Uganda like my mother: I thought she would never let me go, come what may, but when I came out as gay, she didn't want to even look into my eyes, not even want anything to do with me; I don't want to be that kind of parent.

I am a Catholic. I was raised Catholic. But I'm really embarrassed; I have gone so long without going to church, because of the things that are taught in church. I used to go to a church in Nairobi town, at Ebony Chambers.[8] I used to go there but because of transport issues and all that, you find yourself not able to go. But sometimes The Nature Network organises church sessions, so I attend as it's nearby. It's really important for me to go to church, because I need to be connected to God, and everyone needs to be connected to God. Church can even be in your bedroom:

---

[7] The Democratic Republic of the Congo.

[8] She refers here to Cosmopolitan Affirming Church, which is an LGBTQ+ affirming church in Nairobi.

you wake up, kneel down, and start to pray. I myself believe that no matter how people look at us as a disgrace, we are still God's children.

In the society the way they understand God, they think God doesn't like gay people. But then I look at this straight person who doesn't have anywhere to stay with a bunch of kids and then I look at myself, I have family I am living with; well, life is difficult on my side but not the way it is on the other person's side, so I am like, 'Maybe God knows why he created me.' Some days I am like, 'Today I should hit on a girl.' But then I can't, which means that it's me. And sometimes you find yourself praying to God about your asylum process to move to another level and then something good happens; then you are like, 'God really cares for me. And I think he understands us.'

In the Bible, it says that no human should judge the other. There was a situation where people sent away a prostitute but Jesus welcomed the prostitute. This was also a person, who can change. I think that really reflects on our lives, because the society sends us away; they don't want us; they don't want anything to do with us. But again, we find ourselves more blessed: God really cares for us; God doesn't see us as bad; as long as you don't hurt anyone, live a faithful life, faithful to God, you are not hurting anyone, you have not killed anyone, just living as normal as others. Then the other story is about Zakayo:[9] he was short, like me! So he had to climb a tree trying to see Jesus. People wouldn't let him but Jesus saw him, got him out of this tree, and helped him. So let me give an example: in the community, when I had nowhere to live, when I was living in that unknown relationship, I talked to Raymond and Jonathan, and they came as friends who pulled me out and gave me somewhere to stay. That story helps me to know that however much there may be obstacles, difficulties that come your way, there's always someone who will pull you and help you to follow your road to success. These stories really encourage me. Like the story of the prostitute: whenever I get to meet these people who say gay people are bad, I am like, 'You believe in Jesus, you go to church and then this is your Jesus who called upon a prostitute, you know: he welcomed a prostitute, he welcomes me as well and he will always welcome me.'

As for my resettlement, you know you can't plan it yourself; it's the UN that plans everything for you. But I'm so happy that the UNHCR put up this process so that at least you can go somewhere where you can find a future, where you can find a life. It may take long, actually it does take long, but at least some day you reach your goals. Sometimes here you find

---

[9] The Luganda name of Zacchaeus.

employment for like two months and after they find out that you are queer, they fire you. I'm at the American embassy, which takes a bit longer but I have future plans of helping my friends that I will leave here at Pride Umbrella. I will work and help them out. In five years I will look at my life as a parent, not a parent of children of my own but a parent of the others. I will look at myself as a successful beautician, because that's what I do, and I will look at myself as a person who will change people's lives here. When I look at my shelter where I am living, in five years I will look at this shelter as a community that helps very many people achieve what they want to achieve in life.

Personally, I think God is gay

Based on a life story interview with Henry
(21 September 2019)

My name is Henry. I'm gay, and I'm a refugee here in Kenya. The problem I got is that they chased me away from Uganda because of my sexuality; that's why I'm here in Kenya. I've been here since December 2014. I decided to leave because people wanted to kill me, even my family chased me away. I didn't have any plan where to go because, you know, Uganda is like a small country. I just ran away from my family to a friend's place, then they found me there; after that they put my name out on a radio station and said that if anyone sees me, they should just kill me. So that's why I decided to come to Kenya, because of my life. I want my life.

My family got to know about my sexuality sometime back when I was at school. I had a friend and we tried to play sex, so we fucked when we were in school. So that boy then went to the teachers and told them about what we did. They called my family, and then they chased me away from school. My father thought that young kids would not do that. So he said, 'You won't be going to school again, you are going to stay home and help your step-mum', because my mom had died. While I was home, sometimes I went on Facebook, I posted my picture on Facebook and I got another boyfriend. One day he had a birthday party. So I told my step-mother I wanted to go to my friend's birthday, and she told me to first finish work and then I could go. So, I reached there, I met many gays; I was so surprised and happy to see them; it was my first time seeing so many gays. I was so excited and started visiting them on weekends at their place. I got a phone, and we used to send each other messages, saying 'love you' and also send a lot of porn. One day, I had gone to buy something, and I left my phone home, because my brother used to play games on my phone. My step-mother started checking my phone and went through my chats. She told my dad. That's how they got to know about me.

When my father came home, he called all my sisters and brothers older than me. They all came and started beating me. I was badly beaten; I still have some scars. They told me that they were going to burn me. They threatened that they would take me to the police station. So when I got a chance I ran away and I went to my friend's place. I stayed there, crying. I had left my phone behind when I ran away so they started talking with my friend on my phone, asking him where I was. They tried to call my friend asking where I was, and he brought them. So, I ran away again. I called my boyfriend; he was on his job and I told him what had happened; he told me to find him at his job. When I reached there, I told him the full story. He said he had nowhere to take me, so he advised me to call Frank Mugisha,[1] he is an activist in Uganda. But Mugisha told my boyfriend, 'No, we are in the Christmas season and all the offices are closed, we don't know how we can help you guys. Maybe you could go to Kenya.' My boyfriend gave me transport money. He said I could not stay with him. I think I was burdening him. Then I came here to Nairobi and I didn't know anything about Nairobi. I came by bus. When I reached here, I didn't know where UNHCR is; I didn't understand Kenyan money; I didn't speak the language. I struggled so much. I asked people directions to UNHCR, but when I reached there, they had closed for Christmas time. After that I was seated there, crying. One security officer saw me crying, so he went inside and told someone in the UN, so they came and asked me about my problems. I told him everything, that I didn't have money to buy food, didn't have anywhere to sleep, and didn't know Swahili. After that he took me inside the office, and I was taken to the transit centre where I was registered after being asked many questions. Then I was given money for rent.

I have to say that overall, the experience in Kenya has been so bad. First of all, there's the language barrier. And people here are so homophobic. That's why we have to change places all the time, because they keep chasing us away from houses. I think even some UN officials, they don't care about us. If you have an appointment with someone at the UN, they ask you rude questions. And even the interviewers are homophobic; sometimes they ask stupid questions like, 'Why are you like that? Why don't you change? You guys, I don't believe that you are normal.' These are some of the challenges we get here.

The situation got so bad that one time I decided to go to Kakuma camp. I thought, 'at least I will have shelter there, and food'. But Kakuma was

---

[1] Dr Frank Mugisha is one of Uganda's most prominent LGBTQ+ advocates and the Executive Director of Sexual Minorities Uganda.

worse, people were beating us. They have communities of Sudanese and Somalis, and these people have their cultures, so they used to beat us all the time. I spent like three months there, after which I came back to Nairobi. I decided to come back to Nairobi even though I didn't know what I was going to do, because in Kakuma it was so bad. We got a lot of injuries. I came back here and couldn't even walk, because my leg had been badly beaten. So I struggled, I struggled. In the end I found one of the CBOs and they tried to help.

We started doing some beads and handcrafts, and we'd sell them in order to get some money and pay for our house. But you can spend a day without eating. We are just struggling. It's far from easy to survive, but maybe, I think, it's God, because every time God is there. Sometimes I know God helped me. You know, sometimes I used to hate God. I thought God hated me, he had given me the wrong feelings and therefore people would see me as a bad person who isn't normal. But I reached the time when I came to realise that God didn't make a mistake; I think God wanted me to be like this. So that's why sometimes I believe in God. Sometimes, you know, I tried to kill myself; I tried to take medicines to die, but it failed. There was a time I took an overdose. I thought I was going to die. I went sleeping, thinking that by tomorrow I would be dead; but the next morning I woke up, not dead.

I tried it several times because the situation here is so bad. I don't have a brother; the situation is that you have to struggle alone. Like the situation of getting something to eat. We cannot be employed because we are gays and also refugees; they don't give us jobs. We need to work but they don't give us work permits, those are some of the problems we face. I just used to feel like I was the only one, and no one was going to help me. You know, that feeling of being alone in the country and that no one is caring about you, you are just struggling hard. You just decide to kill yourself because you can't do anything and no one can give you a job. They only take you for granted. They just know that if you are gay, you have to be a whore. They just want to beat you. So sometimes you just feel like committing suicide.

It is hard to survive. Sometimes I do sex work. The other time I was doing sex work there used to be a lot of blackmailing. They call you to come, then when you reach there, they just fuck you, and after that they chase you out of the house without giving you money. Another thing is that when you reach there, they just use you – like four of them like that; you just say 'ok', because you need money. You can find like three guys and they want to fuck you for 1,000 shillings.[2] They want to fuck you, the three of them, and you can't deny it because you need that little money. It makes me feel bad, because if you need sex of course you can get it, but with sex work you do it for the money, because you need money to survive and pay rent. That's why we end up doing sex work. But it doesn't even pay rent for a month, it just helps you to buy food for eating, just for surviving. Sometimes they just give you 500 shillings. It makes you feel bad. Someone can use you, fuck you like for one hour, and you feel bad because he told you, 'I will give you my money' but then they take advantage of you. Because they know that you are not Kenyan and you are a refugee. Sometimes you meet someone who doesn't pay you, and they say that they are going to call the police because you are a refugee. And then there's the risk of HIV, because you don't know his status; also other kinds of diseases, such as gonorrhoea and syphilis. They may say like, 'I'll give you a thousand shillings if we can do it without a condom; I don't want to use a condom.' And because you want something to eat you just do it like that.

I stay in one of the community houses. We keep ourselves busy, we have a timetable and a rota. If you are the one to cook, you have to cook; and if it's your turn to mop the house, you have to. We also have small projects that we started doing, like beads, they keep us busy at least. We have a lot of talents but the problem is that it's difficult to sell our products. Like for making beads: Kenyans do the same and the competition is high and sometimes you don't sell anything on a day. Or sometimes, you get a client and you sell like only two items today but nothing the next day. We started like seven of us, after they had chased us from our houses. That's when we decided to do something as a group, get our own place with privacy and keep ourselves busy. We used to sleep outside the UN and in the streets. But then we decided to come together to get our own house. I've been here for like three months. The house is called Pride Umbrella Kenya. Before that time, when I stayed alone, I used to be panicking, for rent, food, and so on. I couldn't survive alone because you must pay a house, you must pay all the bills and we are not working. But then at least we came together, and we helped each other, shared our problems; there's always someone to comfort you, like you ain't alone; so at least you feel good. As I said, when I stayed alone I almost committed suicide. But here we are like brothers, like a family; so at least I have another second family

2 Roughly £7 / $10.

here. Different from my family in Uganda, here they look after me, when I get sick, they take care of me.

I grew up in a Catholic family. But whenever you go to church, they talk only bad things about gays. So you go there but you can't be comfortable, because everyone will be speaking badly about you. Thus, on Sundays I'd rather sit and pray on my own, or I'd sit with friends and pray. Me personally, I think God is gay. Because at least God can't chase us away, as I think God created us. He thought like, 'Let me create this: let me create people who are straights and let me create gays.' So he decided to create straights, and then people like me. So, God created us like that, yeah. You know me, sometimes as I see it, God is my best friend, my mum and my father. Sometimes like if I have stress I just sit there and talk to God that I have stress, I ask him to come and fight for me please.

Sometimes when you walk, people abuse you, they shout 'Gay! Gay! Gay!' Someone can beat you, so in that situation I just call for God, that God at least helps me, helps me to survive, because people don't want us, they just want to kill us, they just see us like an animal. I pray that at least they change their hearts and they get to know about us.

Angels don't have a gender

Based on a life story interview with Dhalie
(21 September 2019)

I'm Dhalie and I'm gender-fluid. In Uganda they call us *basiyazi*.[1] It's just the harassment we go through. I feel like I identify as a man and when the time comes, I will go through transition, like hormone therapy. Seriously, me, I don't like my boobs.

I wish I could have come here, to Kenya, like for a vacation or something. That would have made a difference. But I came to Kenya, because I thought it was the nearest place where I would be safe from what happened back home and where I could afford the transport. So that's why I came. I boarded *matatu* buses and I was like, 'Let me just go where no one knows me: maybe there I can be myself.' At least, if someone doesn't

---

[1] *Basiyazi* (sg: *musiyazi*) is a derogatory Luganda word for gay people. Our participants came up with various meanings and backgrounds. One, it comes from the word for margarine, *siyaaji*, and became the word for homosexuals, because of the idea that they use margarine as lubricant. Second, it comes from the word *kusiyaga*, which refers to non-penetrative sex where partners (either same-sex or different sex) would rub thighs (intercrural sex). People involved in this are called *omusiyazi* (sg.) or *abasiyazi* (pl.). Participants came with some anecdotal evidence of such sexual acts happening between boys at school and between men in the army. Third, it comes from the word *siya*, which refers to sighing and moaning during love-making. Fourth, it comes from the verb *okulya ebisiyaga*, which means 'eating rubbish', with *basiyazi* meaning 'people who eat rubbish' (which might be a metaphor for anal sex). For an academic discussion of its etymology, see Sylvia A. Nannyonga-Tamusuza, *Baakisimba: Gender in the Music and Dance of the Baganda People of Uganda* (New York and London: Routledge, 2005), 215. Whatever its origins exactly are, participants agreed that nowadays *basiyazi* has a negative connotation ('a hate tone') and is used in Uganda to refer to LGBTQ+ people in general.

know me, they won't talk about me, or pre-think about me in their mind. I thought, maybe I will be safe and they will just see me as me, as Dhalie, who identifies as a man; not like those guys who saw me as a young girl. I left my country because I didn't want to be tied up. My sexuality had never stopped me from going to school, or from doing what I am supposed to do.

When I was growing up, I was a girl. When I was in secondary school, around when I was 13 years, that's when I would like to play outdoor games: volleyball, soccer, and I love volleyball! When I was around 16, I met this girl at school, and we became friends. We would write each other letters. We would share our lunch and eat from the same plate. Then, we would share our beds, you know. At school they wouldn't let us share our beds; it was prohibited. But we would find ourselves sharing the bed. I didn't know anything yet about sexuality. It wasn't even in my vocabulary at all! The time they expelled us, we were actually sleeping in the same bed, but doing nothing. At least at that time we had never kissed. There was nothing like any sexual contact. But by then the student leaders were watching us. Imagine waking up by someone hitting you with a stick! The next day, we went to the disciplinary committee and they were asking, 'What were you guys doing?' Yet it was nothing: we were sleeping! And they asked, 'How many times have you fed her? How many times have you people shared a plate together?' That kind of stuff. And then they made us cut our hair, a shabby cut. We had to walk barefooted to class the next day. That's when they called our parents. I was being expelled but still I didn't know my sexuality.

So, I was forced from school, expelled from school. And when I was expelled, my mum didn't even take me home: she took me to some old lady who used to stay around near the school, because it wasn't yet the end of term and she didn't know how to explain to my father why I'm home before end of term. My mum kept me there. It was because they can't just accept me. At first, I thought, 'Maybe my mum would accept me.' But no. And then, my father had an impact on her, when I had to change schools and the questions came.

I reached a time when I was an adult, around 18, and they started taking me through what they call conversion therapies. The rumours were there, because they never saw me hang out with a boy, or have a boyfriend. They said, 'She's starting to dress this way, and she has gotten spoilt. She is having this homosexual behaviour.' When I finished school, I had the liberty not to be in my parents' eyes 24/7 and that's when I started dress-ing the way I want. But then relatives would come and be like, 'How could you let a girl do this. Those are homosexuals! They are paid to be homosexuals!' Yeah, they thought I was being paid – even though I was working and supporting myself.

At home they were expecting me to get married. Those conversion therapies had an impact on me. It even reached an extent that they would affect me at my work place. I would dress like the way I want but then, reaching the dressing room where I work, I would put on a dress. It was really, like, draining. And I wasn't really feeling attraction for guys. No, not at all! There was this particular time: a guy was vibing on me and saying one day, when we were wearing the same clothes, like jeans, 'You could put on a dress or something.' And I was feeling so uncomfortable. Then I started to explore. I tried to study myself. I couldn't put on a skirt, not even when my father said I could wrap a *leesu*[2] around myself. I chose to discover myself, rather than caring about what others felt.

I am Muslim. My father was actually a deputy mufti of Uganda.[3] My parents took me to a sheikh to pray for me.[4] It was tormenting: they take you to a sheikh, this guy you've never known, and he reads you the Qur'an. And it's like he's abusing your body: you know, touching your body, trying to convert you from being a homosexual. They even forced me to fast! They don't understand that you feel in a wrong body, a wrong body!

It had reached a time – my sexuality, my gender identity – where it affected my family. My dad tried to actually blame my mum for what I was becoming. Dad had to leave home, he was like, 'I can't live in this house'. And he would fight with my mother, saying that it was coming from her side. And, oh my god, my other sisters thought I was bringing trouble home; they thought I had taken away their father! My dad left home; but I think he was using me as an excuse: maybe he wanted to have another wife. So, I was like, 'I'm causing all this. I have no choice but to leave.'

When I applied for asylum, I identified as a Muslim and as LGBT, and they were like, 'What?!' Meaning, 'You can't be a Muslim *and* be LGBT.' I don't get it. They think these things, faith and sexuality, have to be exclusive. But I read the Qur'an and I grew up in a Muslim family. I went to Muslim schools. I fast for Ramadan. I pray. And I know that angels in Islam are genderless. Angels, they don't have a gender. I never heard anyone referring to my guardian angels as 'she' or 'he'! If God created those angels genderless, I needn't be tied to a certain gender either.

---

[2] A piece of fabric that women in Uganda commonly wrap around their bodies.

[3] The Uganda Muslim Supreme Council is chaired by the mufti, who is assisted by two deputy muftis. Together they present the highest level of religious authority in matters of Islamic law in the country.

[4] 'Sheikh' is a term used for Islamic religious leaders and Qur'anic teachers.

I know there are five pillars of Islam, and if I'm a homosexual, or a trans, that doesn't mean I don't believe in Islam. The first pillar is to believe in the oneness of God. The second is to pray five times a day. Then there's pay charity, fast, and the fifth one, to go to Mecca for pilgrimage if you can. Maybe, there are six pillars? The sixth one is to believe in the day of judgement.[5] Whatever happens, whether good or bad, it's coming from God. In any case, I'm not breaking any pillar. So, no one can use my faith against me. And even when they used it against me, I went away to learn more about my religion, and I loved it more. I need to stop beating myself about this thing of, 'Am I sinning against God?'

I am not breaking any pillars and when I learned all that, I came out and proud. I am not scared *and* I am a Muslim – even if people sometimes force me out of a mosque here in Kenya. I had to make a report about it, because we were in Ramadan. We had this *duwa*,[6] more like a charity event, where you prepare something for people fasting, when you break the fast with them. I attended this particular one and I had put on a *kanzu*[7] not a *hijab*.[8] So, this person recognised me and said, 'She is not supposed to be here, 'cause she's a homosexual.' It was very embarrassing. They picked me up out of the room. They had to embarrass me by saying, 'That woman was making herself a man!' But I had put on a *kanzu* for prayers. I was not sinning against God.

When I first came to Kenya, I hadn't really reached a point of needing resettlement. I was just looking for safety, away from home, and having this feeling that I will go out, prepare my CV, write applications, and get a job to start my life. Starting a new life: as simple as that. But the thing is, we do want to work but the working environments do not cater for us. You get me? They tell you to be who you're not – wear a skirt. And for me, I don't want to be referred to as 'she' or 'that woman'. Call me either by my name, or say 'they' or 'them'. But people don't get this.

When I first got here, I didn't register with the RAS, the Refugee Affairs Secretariat; it's a government entity, under the Ministry of Interior Affairs

---

[5] This is not a pillar of Islam (of which there are only five) but one of the six articles of faith in Islam.

[6] In Islam, *du'a'* refers to an appeal, or invocation. It counts as a profound act of worship.

[7] A *kanzu* is a white or other pale-coloured robe worn by African men in the Great Lakes region, including in Uganda.

[8] A *hijab* is a covering traditionally worn by some Muslim women in the presence of any male outside of their immediate family. It covers the head and chest and conforms to Islamic standards of modesty.

of Kenya, where you're supposed to register as a refugee. Instead, I went to a friend who was here, from my former school. She's a Kenyan. She did not really know about my sexuality, not really. But she would let me be, with my dreads, because here in Kenya you find guys that have adopted Rastafarian style and that makes it a bit easier. It's okay to go around here with dreads. They just think, 'She's a Rastafarian.' But back in Uganda, they relate dreads with homosexuality. I looked for jobs, went to hospitals, till I was told, 'You know what: you don't have a work permit. You're not a Kenyan? You're what?' That's when I registered.

So I went to a place called Shauri Moyo[9] where the RAS offices are. That's the place where you have to be at 5am. For a full week, I went every day to Shauri Moyo – and they couldn't register me. They'd say, 'You're Ugandan. What's wrong in Uganda? There's no war in Uganda!' Refugees are supposed to be running from wars. Wars are the thing that threatens one's life. And then, when I'm telling them I am from Uganda and I am queer, they ask what that means. Even if they know, they make you explain. And then it's like, 'So you're one of those people that love girls? Why do you love girls? Why don't you want to get married? Why don't you want to have kids?'

There is so much injustice in that place. You answer and then they give you a paper telling you that you have to go to Kakuma. Kakuma is in Turkana County! You're seeking security and protection, and then someone takes you there! You have to tell them why you are who you are, and explain why. And they say, 'If it's sending you away from people you love, why don't you let it go?' Oh, my God! So this woman at the reception gives me a paper to go to another room, and that's where I had to go through the entire story of the conversion therapies. And then someone tells you that if you saw your own father beating up your mum because of what you are and it hurts you, and if you saw your father walking away from your other siblings and it hurts you, then why don't you stop? They ask, 'Why don't you just stop?'

Eventually they registered me. Trust me, at Shauri Moyo they don't have time for you. They gave me this paper and I was like, 'What's next for me now? UNHCR? Where do I go?' I'm not going to stay at this person's place, because I was supposed to be getting a job. And now they are not giving me a work permit, just an asylum seeker pass. I cried. I cried, because, first of all, I was having a hard time, because I was living with someone and it was beyond what we expected, because I also came with

---

[9] Shauri Moyo is an eastern part of the city of Nairobi, Kenya's capital.

my own expectations, you know: 'I am just going to get a job and start life!' And then, coming here, it's not like that.

I went to a place called GALCK, it's the Gay and Lesbian Coalition of Kenya. I got details from Google. I reached there and I told them my issue: I told them I just want somewhere safe so I can resume my career, and a normal life. And they said, 'We can't do that: you have to go to UNHCR.' 'UNHCR, where is it? I don't know.' So I got to UNHCR and they told me, 'Are you going to the camp, or do you wait for an exemption? We don't have anywhere to put you. We don't have anywhere. The transit centre is full and we don't want queer people in the urban area. Oh, you have to go to HIAS.' I didn't even know where or what HIAS is!

I saw some people outside, speaking Luganda. I talked to them and there was this one guy called Memory and he took me to HIAS. He told me, 'since they haven't worked on you at HIAS, we shall go back the next day.' I told him I have my stuff on the other side and so I have to go back there. And he says, 'Okay: you will pick up your stuff there and then you can start staying with us.' Memory took me to his home, on that side of Mwiki.[10] They were four boys, three girls, and me, in one bed sitter. It was such a relief to meet up with fellow Ugandans – trust me, I was crying.

Memory is gay. I was crying when I met him but he and the guys they told me 'Don't worry.' He told me I will have to do an assessment at HIAS. It became tough but these guys gave me a home. There wasn't much room and they told me that you're not supposed to move about, you don't go anywhere till you get an urban paper. They told me that if the police find you, and you only have an asylum seeker pass, which has an expiry date, then there's trouble. HIAS gave me a stipend, and I paid part of the rent, because we were sharing the rent. I told them I don't want hand-outs, I want to sustain myself. They told me, 'We can't help you with that, 'cause now you have to be having an alien card to get a work permit'. So hard!

But then, eventually, I got to interact with the community. When I met these guys, they showed me other people, where I could go to parties and then, that's when I met people from CBOs, those community-based organisations: people like me. And most of them were Ugandans and some of them were, like me, asylum seekers, in different stages of the process. The process has assessments and there's what they call RSD (Refugee Status Determination), RAS interviews and then resettlement assessments, and then you go ahead to the embassy so you can eventually be resettled. It's a long process. It used to be that people took a short period of time but

[10] Mwiki is a ward of the Kasarani residential area of Nairobi.

these days you can spend five years waiting for it. I think it's taking longer because the government wants to make people think we are safe. It affects the LGBT community especially, because we are not safe. Trust me, no one is trying to kill a pregnant Somali woman here in Kenya but a trans woman is not going to be safe to just move freely. Other refugees are also escaping trouble back home but when they are here, no one is trying to kill them. But, for us, as LGBT refugees, even the Kenyans themselves don't want us; they don't love us; they don't want us to be here.

It's hard to navigate through public spaces, to go your way, even if you're hard-working, or if you have your papers: the fact that you're a refugee and then you're LGBT makes it very hard. Sexuality, then your gender identity too. For a transgender person it's hard. You don't want to live your entire life pretending. We settle, we create jobs, but then we are competing in an environment where first of all, we don't speak the same language. So, even if you're, like 'I am going to make my own beads!' and you go to sell them, you sell them just to your own community. You're selling them within your circle. This is why we have trouble with working. You know, everyone is just trying to survive, within the same environment. It's really hard. I am a medic and counsellor. I now embrace myself; I've come to understand there's nothing wrong with me. There's nothing wrong with me and with the way I dress, the way I walk; and who I sleep with, has nothing to do with intellect. I can still perform; I can still do good in the community; I can still be there for my friends. You get me? Instead of being tied up, I now embrace myself.

I was like, let me stick to my community, the queer community. Let me be with people who understand me, people who let me explore what I want, my dreams. You know, I eventually got to accept myself, and when the world is closing in on me, I go to be with the queer community. I found the people very embracing in the community and they had formed groups, like those community-based organisations. I would go to Nature's,[11] Team No Sleep[12], getting to know those community-based organisations. Like whenever I visit here, at Nature's, I feel good; I feel in a safe space; it feels like coming home; it's the place I go to see friends. I go to people in the community, thinking 'I can do something!' Before that I used not to tell people that I'm a doctor. Why? Because some would be like, 'she wasted all that', and others would ask me, 'how could you leave your job?' I now find freedom in being me and being queer. I got a family

[11] The Nature Network.
[12] Team No Sleep is an LGBTQ+ refugee organisation in Nairobi.

here; I really feel comfortable. I have everyone here, I have people who already call me 'mum', people who call me 'daddy', people who call me 'love', people who call me 'bro'. I belong to the Foundation for Lesbian, Bisexual, and Queer Women Refugees. We formed that because in most cases women even in our small community tend to be drawn away, they draw themselves away, they don't want to be actively involved, because women are very vulnerable.

For my future, I would love to go through the transitions of my body. For me, I know I'm a man but the hormone therapies are not accessible here and expensive. I don't want to reach that time when my body can't handle such anymore. That's what I really want and am planning on when I get resettled. That's what I want: to go through the transition and then I will feel it's me. I can't put a limit to myself. So I will just spread my wings for whatever comes my way. I just want to get resettled and go through the transition and be who I am. And then, trust me, no limit!

As I said, I'm a practising Muslim. I love this *surah*;[13] it's called Ad-Duhaa.[14] Allah is talking to the Prophet (peace be upon him). He was telling him, 'Don't despair: I haven't forgotten about you.' Because this was a period where the Qur'an was revealed in stages, like seasons, and then there was a time the Prophet (peace be upon him) wasn't receiving revelations from God, so he thought maybe God had forgotten about him. He was even like, 'Maybe I sinned, I'm no longer anointed; I'm no longer getting revelations from God. God is not showing me any signs!' You understand? So, he was berating himself. Even people who used to come to him, he would send them away, like, 'I'm no longer getting revelations: just go, and live your life.' So, God came and told him, 'Don't despair: I have not forgotten you. Do you remember when you were an orphan and I raised you? Do you remember when your uncle sent you away and I raised you?' It's called Surah Ad-Duhaa. It talks about how God never forgets about you. You don't have to despair: He's *always* around. So, I think:

> How did I cross the border to Kenya and now I'm here? How come when I lost my job, I still had food? How come I left my family, I was born with, but now I have family here, who call me 'bro' and call me 'love'!?

It's God. The other one is in Surah Al-Baqarah, that's like the second surah in the Qur'an where God promises us that he never gives a man a challenge he can't handle. He never tests you beyond your limits. So those

---

[13] A surah is a chapter of the Qur'an. There are 114 surahs in the Qur'an, each of which is divided into *ayahs*, or verses.

[14] Ad-Duhaa is the ninety-third surah of the Qur'an.

surahs keep me strong. I'm inspired and I am like, 'Wow! This means God knows I can do it.'

To conclude, let me say, guys, I'm Dhalie and I would love to really give this special message to all the Muslim queers: 'You're not breaking any *sharia* law. Like, Allah is love; the Prophet (peace be upon him) spread love; the Qur'an talks about love. There's nothing like condemnation, yeah. And be you. Be who you are.'

God loves me more than they love me

Based on a life story interview with Drake
(12 October 2019)

My name is Drake. I came to Kenya because of the insecurities I faced back home in Uganda. Not only insecurities, but also the stigma, the difficult life. Because of my sexual orientation I was stigmatised, I got insults, both verbal and physical; I got some scars but I managed to escape and came to Nairobi. It was because of my sexual orientation, because they discovered that I was queer. Or let me use the word that everyone uses, that I was homosexual. I myself am okay being homosexual but I don't think the community thought that it was okay for me to be homosexual. First it began verbally, when I would pass by. I tried to keep ignoring them, as I want to live my life in a very simple, humble way. Then it turned out to be physical, and yeah.

I came to know my sexuality in class three at primary school. I used to have friends, let me just mention one of them. He was called Tom.[1] He used to be my friend. I went to a Catholic boarding school; it was a mixed school. Actually, the first time we met, we became friends, we clicked so well. At that school, every night after showering, they told us to go to the dormitory. When we reached the dormitory, we started playing until 8:30pm; then they switched off the lights. That was the time where we had to go to sleep, because we had to wake up early the next morning. One night, I went to his bed and we did something, something dirty. We never had any idea about what to do. What we knew was kissing and if you kiss, you have to lick someone's tongue, the whole lips. Not like in the professional way. We continued that act again and again. So, in primary seven we still had the same thing going on. Still with him. But I also had other partners whereby we mingled, not him alone. So he developed jealousy

---

[1] Pseudonym.

somewhere somehow. Because I had some other friend of mine, it was also lights off and then we found ourselves doing certain things. So, if I'm honest, it's in my primary school when I enjoyed myself, more than at my secondary school. Stigma, you understand, because in secondary school we can't just do something; because we're already older, you are afraid to be embarrassed; but when you're young, it's like normal; you just think that when you grow up, it will disappear.

I didn't know that it would keep on growing and growing and growing from now, you know. We used to shower together as boys, but in secondary I stopped showering with boys, because I used to get a hard-on. And when it's hard-on, my friends could suspect something; and you know, my dad has this reputation of his name, because he was on the board of the school. So, I would either go first in the bathroom or last. It was in my form one, at the beginning of the third term, I had something with some boy, he was Kenyan I remember; he used to leave school during the day, I still remember his name and I curse him, I'm sorry. So, he was called David;[2] I still remember David's face. David and I, we did something and he enjoyed it. He really did, because we sucked dicks and he was the first person to teach me how to kiss. He told me like, 'if you want to kiss someone, get the upper lip and I will get the lower lip. Or, you either choose to get the downer lip I get the upper lip.' So, I enjoyed it. Before that, I had it with some small boy called Peter, so cute with round eyes, you know someone with these big round eyes; and Peter and I used to do stuff and he never said anything to anyone. But David is the one who blackmailed me. He wanted something from me and he had never gotten it from me. Then he told me, 'I am going to tell the deputy.' The deputy's name was Madam Ochieng,[3] and she was very tough. So, when David told me that he would take me to Madam Ochieng, I was like, 'Okay, but I'm gonna deny everything.' To be honest, I thought he was literally kidding, but he went. Boy, he went! So, five boys came to call me. It was like at seven, we were about to go for dinner. They came and they were like, 'You boy *olya ekuyu*!', meaning, 'you boy, you eat ass!' Because Madam Ochieng had already told them. They said, '*Olya ekuyu* blah blah and Madam is calling you.' And I knew that you couldn't disobey Madam Ochieng. So, I was like, 'I'm not going to embarrass myself.' So, behind our rooms, behind the boys' dormitory was our bathrooms, and in the bathrooms there were these small windows through which you could squeeze yourself and drop onto the street outside the school. I said, 'I'm not embarrassing

[2] Pseudonym.
[3] Pseudonym.

myself.' Because I knew that either, they would call my dad, or I would be taken to the evening prayer – remember, it's a Catholic school, so we used to have evening prayers – and I'd get embarrassed there. So, I escaped out of the school.

I ran and went back home. I found my dad home; they welcomed me, but they were like, 'Tomorrow morning you're going back to school, and we'll find out what's wrong.' Because the school principal had set a rule, saying *bwotoloka kusaomero, todda* ('if you escape from school, never come back'). So, my dad talked to the principal. They knew each other from church, the Rubaga cathedral.[4] Before we went, I told my dad like, 'Whatever they're going to tell you at school, it is a lie. I can do anything but I can't reach that extent of embarrassing you.' My dad was like, 'I know my son is not lying.' That was the first time my dad believed in me. So, we go to school and they called David; he described me from head to toe. And I was like, 'We shower together at this school, we share the same bathrooms. Of course he can describe me.' But the principal was like, 'If you want to come back to this school, you have to apologise to the school.' I told my dad, 'I'd rather you beat me up than me embarrassing myself in public.' I had pride, even when I was young. I was like, 'You beat me up, rather than me reading that apology letter they want me to read at the assembly.' But they took me to the assembly. They said, 'Let's call all those children with bad manners in school, they have learned bad manners from outside the school.' Then they pointed at me and said, 'Now this one was trying to sodomise his friend.' Can you imagine them saying that about you in public?! At my age, calling me a sodomite! It was something very bad. I was young, I was in form one; I was like fourteen, fifteen around that age.

So, after they introduced me, I just walked away from the assembly and went out of the gate. And they were like, 'Huh, this boy has guts!' I then spent something like a week sleeping outside, in some unfinished houses. Then my dad sent some people to look for me. They found me and caught me at midnight, when I was sleeping. When they brought me home, my dad was like, 'My son has become too stubborn.' So, he took me to rehab on Entebbe Road. I stayed there for six months, but I refused everything. You know, I refused to talk when it came to my sexuality. At that time I used to say, 'I'm not gay, you understand?' They used to tell me that it was part of my adolescence, that these things would stop when I'd grow up.

---

[4] Officially known as Saint Mary's Cathedral Rubaga, in Kampala.

But now I know that being homosexual is not an addiction but a feeling inside you. It's not something you can stop.

By the time I ran away from the rehab, my dad told me to look for a new school and go to school. People had told him, 'This boy just needs attention and love.' He even went to church, and they advised him, 'Just give the boy attention and love, he's going to change.' So, my dad said, 'You go to a school, and I will pay for it. I will be happy as long as you won't disturb me; please go to school and study.' My dad didn't believe I was gay. But my step-mum kept saying, 'Me, I know that this boy can do that.' Not because of hate but because my step-mum knew the kind of person I was. She was like, 'That boy needs prayers. Take him to church.' But me, I cared about convincing my dad, because I believed that my step-mum had not any say in the house, apart from crying out loud!

So, when my dad told me to look for a school, I remembered I had cousins who were studying at Kabojja International.[5] I went there with my step-mum to look for a position; you know, my step-mum loved me so much at that age. So we go to Kabojja, I got a place, and they are like, 'You have come in the middle of the term; you have to pay for this and that'. So we bought a uniform and I started. My step-mum was like, 'You just need to concentrate', and she left me there. So, there I was in Kabojja secondary. You know, when you're paying your tuition, it's like you're paying for an apartment. They built apartments for the children to rent. They're like flats, and the girls were in a different block. My dad had put me in my own cottage – because there was a cottage for one, a cottage for two, and then a cottage for four; it depends on the money your parents can afford. But for me, because I was big-headed, I told my dad that if you don't give me this single cottage, I won't study, I won't go to school. So, there I was at school. Oh my God, I used to change boys like clothes in my cottage! I would call them to my room, the schoolmates in the same block. It was like a demon in my head, you understand? I'd bring you into my cottage, we'd talk about stuff, we'd talk about sex, and then I'd pretend like, I am teaching you sex. Because these were boys, they didn't know anything about sex; they had never slept with anyone, but I was so crazy, so stubborn.

I was good at manipulating guys. As a kid I used to go to my cousin brothers' place when they were watching porn, so I knew how to manipulate someone.[6] I used to see heterosexual porn. So the moment I bring you

[5] Kabojja International School is a private co-educational school in Kampala.
[6] A cousin brother is the son of a father's brother, and is culturally regarded as a brother.

to my room, I would pretend teaching you sex and then ahu! I put your dick in my mouth. One thing I can tell you, even if he's heterosexual, once you put his dick in your mouth, it will harden. But we never had anal sex; no one knew anal sex; no one knew lubricants. The only thing we would do was sucking dicks and kissing. But thank God, I left school without them finding out.

I actually tried dating girls; I had a girlfriend in school. But it was always hard for us to meet girls at school; they kept us apart. So we used to meet during the holidays; but it wasn't something that I wanted. I kept doing what I knew was in my head. I thought I was the only one sleeping with the boys and no one else. One day, during the holidays, I was home. That's when I found a boyfriend; I won't say the name. I met this man, short, smelling nice, dark, he was with a friend who had dreadlocks. It was at the Barbeque Lounge in Centenary Park.[7] I was there with friends. We used to hold a bottle of Smirnoff for the whole night because we couldn't handle more. One Smirnoff can take you off. That's how young I was. But me, because I was big-headed, I used to show them I can manage. To show the boys that I'm bigger than them, I had to take two bottles. And then this nice man got us shots of tequila, which we had never even tried. I'd only seen tequila in movies! So, I took shots of tequila and I got drunk. I never made it home; I slept at his place. So, in the morning he dropped me at home. And my dad was like, 'Where did you sleep last night?' I said that I slept at my cousin's place. He said, 'You smell like alcohol.' I denied it. But I was beaten up thoroughly.

My boyfriend gave me money to buy a phone. It was a lot of money. My father always refused to get me a phone. He was like, 'You will get a phone when you leave my house to join university, but as long as you're under my roof, no phone.' But my boyfriend and I, we didn't do anything, he respected me. When I went back to school in form six, that's when he started coming to school visiting me, doing anything to please me. So my character started changing, you understand!?

I used to be a church boy. I come from a very Catholic family. I used to sing in the church; I used to pray in church. I was an altar boy. When I was seated on the altar and the pastor would start condemning homosexuality, I would tell myself that it's just a stage. I was like, 'I will get over it.' But somewhere, somehow, I started discovering myself. When I left my father's house, I entered the LGBTQ+ community. I came to know myself,

[7] Centenary Barbeque Lounge was a fast-food place and bar in Centenary Park, Kampala.

that it was not a stage. When I entered the community in Uganda, I got to know many people. I was the happiest ever. Because they used to say that we are going to burn in hell, so I said, 'At least I'm not going to be burnt alone.' I felt amazing. I felt like I'd been having something on my chest and finally let go of it. Because I thought that I was the only person, I have bad manners and am going to burn in hell if I don't stop with this stage; I thought it was a sin. I was like, 'Maybe one day I will go and apologise to my father and say, "Father I have sinned, I've been sleeping with men, but I have stopped, please forgive me."'[8]

My parents got to know about it. One day my father asked me, 'Are you gay?' and I said, 'Yeah I'm gay, get over it.' I remember we were having dinner. He told me, 'Go and pack everything that you want and get out.' That's when I picked up my phone. Remember, he didn't know about it, so he was shocked and he's like, 'Really, this kid can stay under my roof and no one gets to know about it? He can just disrespect my house and no one gets know about it?' So, I was chased away from home. And I was like, 'Drake, it's time for you to die. I'm not gonna suffer and hustle forever.' So, I hit the streets of Kampala. I slept there for four months; we used to sleep in boxes that we got from retailers. But you had to keep the shoes inside your trousers, because if you didn't, you would find them gone the next morning. The first thing I lost was my phone, because they steal everything.

I knew some Ugandans who stayed in Nairobi. Social media is very great, Facebook, oh my God! I respect Facebook. So, they suggested I should move to Nairobi and be safe. But Nairobi hasn't been a very easy place to stay, because we all know it is a very expensive place to live in, in terms of accommodation, in terms of feeding, in terms of transportation, in terms of, let me say, in terms of the life style. It's very expensive.

I have been in Nairobi for four years and some weeks now. I stay at The Nature Network. I knew some of them from back in Uganda. So when they began this movement, let me call it a movement, I wanted to join. I learned a lot. It has given me skills, you understand! It educates you on how to do everything. For instance, I had some problems with my drinking habits, because I had my own stress. I had become a drunkard, every time in the bar. But they welcomed me, because they knew me, and they gave me some time to sort myself out. Since I started staying with them, my life has changed. How people portray me, my character, my drinking habits – I

---

[8] The words with which Drake narrates this part of the story echo almost word-for-word the biblical parable of the prodigal son (Luke 15: 11–32).

cannot say that I quit but it reduced, also the way I use drugs. So, they literally helped me and put me in line; they have taught me how to be me, Drake, and how to handle my stress and problems.

The situation here has been so bad. We never get enough support from the UNHCR. So we had to do sex work to survive, and then when you start doing something that you haven't been used to, it traumatises you; so you have to take drugs, so you find yourself getting addicted to drugs, alcohol, walking at night and not caring. Since I stay at The Nature Network, things are getting better. It has taught me skills: how to take care of myself, to stop doing what I was doing. You understand? And when I stopped doing it – although sometimes I still do it because I need money – but when I stopped doing it, I reduced my drinking. I said to myself, 'I'm not meeting anyone for sex work, so why should I drink myself out?' The reason I was drinking was because you can't sleep with someone when your mind is switched on – drinking helps to distract your mind.

I'm not going to blame myself for being gay. Because if God never mentioned it in the Ten Commandments, that means he never cared about it! Tell me, where it is written that man shall not sleep with fellow man? Where is it written in the Bible? In the New Testament, I remember that when Jesus came, he used one word: 'Come the way you are.' You under-stand?! Like, 'Cast your burden, come to me, because I do care about you. Come the way you are.'[9] We once had a pastor who visited The Nature Network; he said something interesting, 'If Jesus had to keep himself around a prostitute, what about homosexuality? Like Zakayo[10] was a tax collector and a thief, but Jesus even visited his house.' Homosexuality did not begin right now, it began a long time ago. In the time of Alexander the Great there were homosexuals, the whole of Rome.

In the Bible what I can quote is, 'Come the way you are; I will love you the way you are, whether a prostitute, a thief, whether a murderer, whether a what?' So why do they just remove the word homosexuality? Yes, it's not in the Bible, it's not written anywhere. But at the end of the day I think we are also humans, we sin. When God was punishing Sodom and Gomorrah, do you know why he punished them? It's not because of homosexuality, it's because when the angels visited, there were people outside the doors knocking saying, 'Let them out, we rape them; let them out, we kill them.' So God wasn't mad about homosexuality, he was mad about the too many sins that were happening in Sodom and Gomorrah. Homosexuality ain't a

[9] The biblical verses paraphrased here might be Matthew 11:28; John 6:37; I Peter 5:7; Psalm 55:22.
[10] The Luganda name for Zacchaeus.

sin. Where is it written clearly in the Bible that it condemns homosexuality? Where in the Bible is it written that kings were killing homosexuals? In the Old Testament they tried to talk about homosexuality, because men were too much sleeping with men; they were afraid that the population was going down and then the king was like, 'men should sleep with women', because the king wanted an army, you understand! He's like, 'Men will no longer sleep with men, men should sleep with women to reproduce.' The king wanted men to sleep with women, for them to get pregnant and give birth. Because they never had an army.

I love reading the Bible when it comes to homosexuality, partly because we get attacked by the Christians. So I can explain to you, because I know myself, I discovered myself and I accepted myself. Whoever is homosexual – let me call it homosexual because that's how they call us – it's an ugly word but it's the reality – they have to accept who they are; it's a feeling, not an addiction, and they won't be punished for it.

You find that those church leaders talking about homosexuality all the time actually sometimes are the ones practising it. The person will come out and say, 'Don't practise homosexuality!' Yet he's sleeping with a boy behind closed doors. In my experience, I've been in relationships with pastors, fathers,[11] and everything so, at the end of the day, if I'm sleeping with a father or a bishop and then I'm in church and hear other fathers speaking this nonsense about homosexuality, I'm like, 'I wish you knew father!'

I'm not ready to go back to society, asking them to accept and love me. God loves me more than they love me. My mum loved me as her kid; my father loved me, too, although we had misunderstandings. But God loves me most.

[11] Meaning priests.

I just wanted an opportunity to express myself

Based on a life story interview with Doreen
(21 September 2019)

I go by the name Doreen Andrews. My government name is a dead name, my before-name. I am now living my life as Doreen Andrews. Doreen is many things but to put it in a few words: I am a non-binary person, a calm person, a community person. I am recently a mother. I didn't biologically give birth to these kids, but they look up to me and they like some of the attributes I have that motivate them to live their lives, to be happy with who they are. They look up to me for that. So, now they are like my daughters. It's so hard, and it's so fun; it's a responsibility but it's a loving responsibility: you get an opportunity to have someone who relies on you, and also, you rely on them. I worry about them and they tell me, 'Oh, mummy, I need money to go somewhere! Mummy, I want to buy something!' But it gives you that kind of acceptance of yourself, that I am no longer just living my own life, but having someone else who is looking up to me.

Right now, we are at The Nature Network: a resource centre, offices, a home, a safe house to so many refugees, the place where refugees are free to express themselves. Nature Network is a home, it's a mother to me, I cannot ever repay Nature Network. But I wasn't always so safe. You know, there are those events that happen in your life that you wish never happened, you wish didn't exist in your life. You know? Sometimes I want to forget them. Some of this brings back traumatic moments. But I want to share; I want to tell the world; I want to show people that what happens now doesn't determine tomorrow; what happened in the past doesn't determine today. So, when I came to Kenya, for me it was a way to escape the life that I was living in Uganda, the life I was living when my family was putting up all these rules and barriers for me so I could not express who I really am.

I grew up in a really strong Christian family. It was so strict that we couldn't even talk about sexual topics. Anything regarding LGBT life was seen as an abomination to their beliefs, to their standards, their principles. So, I grew up as a loner mostly, because I fell out of the family that I was raised in. And then the Bill passed in 2013 in Uganda. I think it was early December 2013.[1] Then the commotion got more and my family said more, too. Pictures from the gay community started being put in the tabloids. You'd find coverage in the newspapers, online, on TV stations. All the time, everything and everyone was talking about that and it became the atmosphere we were in. So you'd find yourself in one day, having three or four members of your family telling you, 'Uh, you're so weird, you behave the same way as those people behave.' You know? And for me, I had lived my whole life trying to escape that kind of attention. I don't know how God created it that way. However much I tried to escape it, that attention was still on me somehow. I felt like they were blaming me for something I am not doing, you know? I'm thinking, 'Why are you blaming me so much, yet I am trying so much not to live that life; I just want to be normal like everyone else.'

I am a beauty therapist: a hair stylist, a makeup artist, and a nail technician. In 2014 I was supposed to go back to college to finish my diploma in beauty therapy. So, beginning school in January 2014, people were back from the Christmas holiday, and they came back thinking about this topic, 'the Gay Bill' that had been passed. Everyone came back with a story to tell: 'In my village two were beaten'; 'In our church, two were beaten'; 'In our home, this happened'; 'When we were going to our Christmas function, this happened to some gay person'. I felt that guilt all the time, every time I would hear that: I felt that they were talking about me, because you relate to the situation, you feel like it's you. It was tormenting me. So, I failed to continue with school. And I found an excuse to give people at home, because I couldn't tell them that I left school because I am gay, or because they're talking about gay people! With Christian people you can't tell them that, and they already had a bias against me. This is because they had said, 'Since you're a man, there are some jobs that you can do to get some money. Go study electrical engineering.' But when I went to college to do electrical engineering, I went and asked the principal if there are other courses, any other careers that I could join. He gave me a list and I

[1] The Anti-Homosexuality Bill.

chose beauty therapy, because that is what I wanted. It would fit right with me; I like my art. There's no better way to express art with humans, with people. Art is not supposed to be stagnant; art is a story; art is an experience, you know? To let someone be different, with makeup on their face, different nails, to *be art*.

Makeup is an amazing thing. Ok, I grew up with girls. I have a big sister, then there are two sisters, and the one right after me. So, these are the people I grew up with and they *loved* makeup. They loved it so much, even at a young age. Me, I didn't do it, because I was hiding a lot. But I would tell them, 'That lipstick doesn't match: put on this.' Deep in my heart I would say, 'If I was the one putting on that dress, I would put on *this* makeup. I would put on *that* lipstick and *that* shoe would match with *that* colour.' Now I know that there's a way to make money out of my passion. You know, for me, I didn't think of a career to have cars, or a house: I just wanted to have an opportunity to express myself.

Now, when I chose beauty therapy, most of my family members were against it. But my mother was doing it, so she supported me. She told me to go ahead, and she even paid for my tuition for the first year, because the family refused to pay for me. I knew my mother knew I was queer and she was also against it as well. But because she's a mother, when all were against me, she always protected me, even though she had problems because of me. I finished the first year, going up to the second year. But when I came back in 2015, because of the commotion I felt at school, I felt like the whole world was against me. I was feeling like everyone is judging me, pointing the finger. Now, I had a friend on Facebook and he had already started the process in Kenya. After the Bill passed in Uganda, UNHCR offices in Kenya had opened slots for asylum seeking. If someone was running away from such stuff, they were free to seek asylum and get help with the process for resettlement. We used to chat, what, what, what; chatting like, you know, like courting. So, we were chatting, and he told me, 'Why don't you come to Kenya? No one will judge you; no one is going to care.' And I wanted to hear only that. I wanted just to explode everything away. To just be me.

There's this organisation in Uganda called 'Ice Breakers'.[2] Ice Breakers was in Luwafu and I was staying in Salaama[3] but we used to buy things

[2] Ice Breakers Uganda is an organisation that runs a clinic and advocates for the health and human rights of LGBTQ+ people, based in Kampala; it also serves as a community centre.

[3] Luwafu and Salaama are both in the Makindye Division of the Kampala District in Uganda.

in Luwafu, because that's where the market is. Every Monday morning when I was going to school, because my school was near Ice Breakers, you would find them coming or swaying-walking around freely. And when you're passing them, there's this look they give you. Like something is pulling you, you know! Have you ever met someone and you're like, 'I think I have met this person before! He looks familiar.' I found out that they're called the Ice Breakers and people around said things like, 'That house is for gay people, they do homosexuality. Don't even talk to them!' Blah blah, such things.

I even met two, and when they saw me they started asking, 'Hey you look familiar! Have we seen you somewhere?' I was like, 'Oh my God!' At that time, I couldn't even talk to them. I just couldn't say, 'Hey!' All I could do is just pass by them and when I saw someone looking at me, I'd hide that feeling that you have. This was the time that leaves me with black spaces, that time of whenever I met someone, there'd be that desire to know more. I wanted to know them, because how come they had friends? How come they lived happily? How come they lived freely? Yet me, I can't even walk out of my room and have the same joy that these people have. They were happy. It's both so sad and also really good that whenever I saw them, I knew I wasn't alone. Every Monday morning, I saw people that showed me that I'm not alone. I found out later on, when I came to Kenya, that they were always coming from a gay night club. So, they were coming from that club on Sunday and now, on Monday morning, when they were going back to their places, they would pass by my school. I was so surprised! I wish I'd known that there was a gay night club!

I think I'm still fresh in this discovery of myself. Because this discovery is still happening, because it started just two years back, and I've had so many drastic changes. Remember when I came to the process in Kenya? I was first of all escaping a particular part of my life and now moving into the community. But I had to first learn about the spectrum.[4] Where do I really fit into all this? I found different kinds of people: I had a little bit of that, there's also something that person has that I can't do at all. So, you have to first know yourself. You've grown up living this image that you've been creating to fit into a particular society – and now, you have to leave that image and go into the image that you are. The one that you've been hiding forever, the person you've been hiding so much. It's like even parts that were so easy to express have been hidden for such a long time they've been getting erased.

[4] Meaning the spectrum of gender and sexual identities.

So how do I identify? Let me say I am 80 per cent a woman, 20 per cent a man: in between but on a scale of balance, one side is heavier than the other. I am more woman, but I still accept the other parts of me that are masculine-male. I don't believe that there will be a time that I will say, 'Let me go cut my genitals'. I might transition but not fully. Let me say, I'll have boobs you know! For like, two or three years – and then take them off.

I'm a Muganda and my mother's name means that she's the daughter of a princess. My father was not a Muganda; he was from a different culture. So, when I was born, my father was pushed out of the family picture, because he was not from our culture. Our family is of a lineage of royalties, so they expected to keep the blood pure, the tradition pure. My mother raised me with my family and all that, but she had this problem with the rest of the family, who were asking her, 'Why did you give birth to a child from such a man?' She protected me since childhood, because of my origin, even when the time came that my sexuality, my orientation, was coming out. She was so used to protecting me, so she still protected me.

My journey to Kenya was not easy at all. I came here knowing only one person in Nairobi. Reaching Nairobi, I called this guy and he tells me he's in the Kakuma camp but that he was expecting to come in about two weeks. He gave me directions to the place where we could meet. So, I went to the place and met his friends. They were gay people, and they helped me; they took me to UNHCR. I went to transit for a week and then, coming back, I found out that they had been resettled and then I had to fit in with these new people I didn't even know. Let me say, I had to survive; I had to do what I had to do to survive.

It's better now. I am working with two organisations. Next year – because I have not yet started with my status in the resettlement process, and because I am going to stay for a long time, I won't sit back and let things go, when I can do something – when next year begins I will have a new project, so I will be having three projects. So, first of all, I'm the assistant director and programme director of the Refugee Trans Initiative, a transgender-focused organisation that works with transgender refugees regardless of their country of origin. We know that other organisations may fail to focus on transgender people but this is an organisation that makes it easy for us transgender-identifying people to relate. It's dangerous, because we're living in a situation where we're limited. The truth is, we can't work unless we're working in a place that is LGBT-affirming, or LGBT-tolerant. In most cases the places we work are LGBT-focused groups, and most of the work is voluntary. That's the truth, you don't get paid, yet you have bills to pay, you have rent to pay.

Let me use my example, I have a feminine outlook. I have feminine characteristics; I have a feminine way of walking; when I am doing my hair, I rely more on my feminine side. When I'm doing someone's makeup, the way I talk when seeing my work is coming out, it reflects me. The things I do are inspired by my femininity. But when other people see that, I get attention, and then I am targeted, you know. It's easy for you to lose your job; it's easy to lose a client. And so, you find yourself working in an LGBT-focused organisation. I say, 'Yeah, if that's what is available, let's do that.'

In terms of challenges in Kenya, let me separate it into three sections: there's the political section; there's the social section; and then the economic section. The economic section is about employment and it's tough because, as I just explained, we're not allowed to work here. The social section involves society, religion, beliefs, and all that, and I will explain that when I talk about religion, shortly. Let me first talk about the political: I have been arrested by the government of Kenya three times. The first time was because the landlady found out that I am a trans person; she didn't want 'such a tenant in her house'. It was the neighbours who, when they found out, called the caretaker. They embarrassed me when my boyfriend was there; they embarrassed us both; and we were kicked out, you know.

The second time was when there were two community-based organisations sharing the same house in Nkoroi.[5] Again, this landlady wanted us out of the house. When she was renting the house initially, she didn't know she was giving it to LGBT people. After three months, when she did, even though we had paid, like, five months' rent, with still two months remaining, she found a way of kicking us out of the house. She was making excuses: she called the police, saying that we are loud, we move around at any time, we don't have work, we are idle, you know! She used excuses and then the police came and took us to prison. By the time we reached prison, the charge changed: so now it was about we'd been caught practising homosexuality in the house.

Still on the political: recently the Kenyan government criminalised the bill on homosexuality, the 162 law.[6] So, if anyone is caught in homosexual

[5] Nkoroi is in the Ngong region on the south-western outskirts of Nairobi.

[6] In 2016 three Kenyan human rights organisations presented a petition arguing that the Kenyan Penal Code violates the rights of LGBTQ+ persons. The petition pertained particularly to articles 162 (criminalising 'carnal knowledge against the order of nature') and 165 (criminalising 'indecent practices between males'). Disappointingly, on 24 May 2019 the petition was rejected by the High Court in Nairobi. An appeal against this decision is currently pending in the Supreme Court.

activity, the government can target us. If you're found dressing in any kind of way that is seen to suggest homosexuality, or you are caught in any way practising homosexuality, you're arrested. I was caught by the police again at UNHCR, where we were having a demonstration about how UNHCR is limiting its services for the LGBT community. When I first arrived, services were available, things were easier. But after a while, some funders pulled out and things became harder. The numbers of refugees became more and exceeded available services. UNHCR was not communicating about this, so we went and demonstrated – and they arrested us.

Right now, UNHCR provides no financial support. How do I get my money?

I do beauty therapy; I have clients based in the community, and there are some others who are accepting. I call clients on my phone and I go to their place or they come to my place. I created a salon in my house. I offer nail services, hair services, and makeup services. In the future, I believe it's going to turn into an academy. I may be able to teach things that I know to the rest of the community.

The world looks at us and says that the only thing that we think about is sex. I can't blame them; that's their perspective. When they talk about 'homosexuality', even the term they're using has the word 'sex' in there! So, for them, when they talk about a homosexual person, the only thing that stutters in their mind is sex, different kinds of sexual activity. But it's not like that: we don't eat sex; we don't pay our bills with sex, you know! Although there *are* some bills that we *do* pay from sex, from sexual activities! But after sex, what's next? After sex, how are you going to make an impact? How are you going to live your life? What about tomorrow? We have dreams and ambitions.

Ok, now about religion: I grew up where everything I was reading in the Bible and everything I was taught in the church – or, let's say, 70 per cent – was against my flow of life, against my nature, against my being, against my experience. It was telling me what is expected of me to be a man: to marry and have children, leave a legacy, create a lineage, and all that. And when a man takes up his life and decides to live it as a woman, that is abusive to God, it's blasphemous, it's like you're telling God, 'You don't know what you are doing.'

I identify as non-binary; it's a third sex. But the Bible says God created a man and a woman; he did not create any other sex after that. And then here *I* am, saying I am a non-binary; I am neither male nor female. I am bringing confusion. And the preacher, the readers of the Bible, scholars, they use the Bible to tell you that you are doing the wrong thing. But it's not what *I'm* saying. It's the life I'm living since I was a child, ever since

I've known myself. I believe that if I had grown up in a way that is more accepting, or more tolerant, I would actually not be a non-binary: I would be a trans woman, completely. But because I was raised up like this, raised to be a man, a part of masculinity, of being a man, stayed attached to me: the 20 per cent I mentioned. I have lived so long trying to cover up the woman in me, that the guy got cemented into my life.

In the Bible there is the story of Job. Job was a person who believed so much in God; everyone around him knew him for that. And then the Devil decided to tempt him, and told God, 'Give me Job, so that I can tempt him for some time and we will see if he will still believe in you.' And then God did it. God said, 'Job believes in me so much and I also believe in him.' So, for me, I believe that you can believe so much in God that even God reaches a point and starts believing in *you,* a mere human being.

The story of Job inspires me a lot, you know. All the things that happened to him: the Devil took away all his property, all his richness, all his money, gave him all diseases; he made him a street beggar, like a person who once lived in mansions and now he's living on the streets. But Job still had faith in God and believed that God was still there. However much the world turns away from you, if your family turns away from you, if all your riches go away – everything belongs to God. Now, I relate to that, to your family leaving you, being left all alone. As for my family: when I couldn't hold it inside anymore, before I started living my life, I told two of my sisters, the ones I grew up with, my big sister and my small sister, because they were the closest people in my life, I told them I'm gay, because for me at that time I didn't know that I was trans. I believed that they would support me: not necessarily tell me to continue doing what I feel, but at least give me their backing. We've been through everything together. My young sister said, 'I knew', but my big sister abused me. She said, 'You can never say that, never! Do not ever let anyone hear you say that!' Then she reported me to our mother, and she reported me also to the rest of the family and they wanted to imprison me. They believed that if they take me to prison and I serve maybe 10 to 20 years, I will come back a straight person. I didn't want to go to prison. Who wants to go to prison?! I didn't do anything to anyone; it's just me, it's my life. When I found out that even the closest part of my family had left me, then the Job story inspired me. I left for Kenya.

After I'd left for Kenya, my mother came looking for me, because she was always the one fighting my battles. She was the first one to even come and she told me, 'We go together!' Let me share a little bit of it, because it's part of my life and I know I am not the only refugee that is going through this. So many LGBT refugees are going through so much but because we don't want that part to exist, we hide away from it. But it's the life that we're living. Like I was saying, when I left Uganda, I hadn't had that conversation with my mother. We hadn't sat down and I hadn't said, 'Now this is what is happening. So I am going to move on.' I didn't get a chance to do that. Everything happened so fast and I just left. She stayed and worried, scared actually, 'Where is he? What has happened to him now?' I would always be her baby, she was like, 'That's my baby.' My father said that he doesn't want to hear about me again. He said, 'That one is spoilt!' When I came to Kenya there were still some people, close friends, who I was talking to back home in Uganda. They told my mother, 'He's living in Kenya.' My young sister said she wanted to visit me, the one who was tolerant. She said, 'We cannot just leave you! You are still my Andrew! You cannot just go away! I am used to having you around, we're used to you and you cannot just leave! I want to talk to you about my boyfriends' – like a sister talks! So, by then I was living in Kasarani[7] and I let her come. She came, spent a week, and then she went back. I don't know if she was sent to spy; I can't tell you that. I don't know whether she went back and they forced her to tell about me. I don't know. She told them, 'He's not doing bad, he's saving and he will survive.'

A month passed and then my mother came with my little sister. I just cried! I'd missed her so much and I didn't know what she was going to say, whether she was going to abuse and beat me. So, I cried, and she also cried. And she told me she had problems after I left, because whenever anyone was arguing, she was always the one to fight my battles even now when I wasn't in the picture. Some were saying to her, 'See you're the one who's been spoiling that child!' And then I felt guilty, because when she told me about it, I felt, 'It's me who brought all this on her.'

So, my future plans, long term and short term. For the short term, the time I am going to be spending here in Kenya, I want to help build the Refugee Trans Initiative into an organisation where every transgender is able to get services that can help them exist in such a difficult place. Even if the world doesn't want to receive transgender people, they cannot live on the streets. But when they're in a house, they may be able to do so many activities that can help them to make some money. I have dreams for my academy. I call it Silent Screams, because the activities that we're doing, the talents and passions that we have, is how we scream into the world. But we are forced to not express our feelings in the community, so we have to scream silently.

---

[7] Kasarani is a residential area of Nairobi.

I call it the Silent Screams Academy and the academy is not only for beauty therapy: we want to teach people how to handle money, manage financially, turn your savings into something else that can bring you money. I want to teach people in the academy: I want to teach people how to turn their passion into generating capital. Right now, we have two people who are painting, Julie and Emily, my daughters. The long-term project is for when I will be resettled from this continent. I want to study for a degree in advocacy and start practising advocacy in our community. As for my children, my daughters: the reason why I want this academy is to know that I'm leaving something behind for them. I am sure I've left them a way to sort themselves out. And they can always call me and talk to me.

I was chased away from the garden of heaven

Based on a life story interview with Shamuran
(22 September 2019)

I'm Shamuran. I'm a fun person and I'm gay. I'm a Ugandan refugee, LGBTIQ, and I'm in Kenya, Nairobi. I grew up having girly behaviour. I didn't make many friends. I only had my sister who didn't care how someone behaves – not like my brothers and my step-mum. And my dad was always busy.

Back in 2016, I decided to go for a Pride march. We were arrested and that's when my family found out that I'm gay and so they chased me from home. It was like this: we were at a club called Venom, during Pride month, and the police came in and arrested all of us at a Pride event. We were taken to the police station and given the right to make a phone call. I called my step-mum, because I was staying with my dad and my step-mum. She came and asked why I was arrested. After knowing the reason why, she said that she can't take me back, because I'm gay. She didn't bail me but left me at the police station. Now, there was an organisation called Trans Equality Uganda and they came and bailed us out, and then I had to go home. When I went home, my step-mum, my dad and my brothers started asking me questions like, 'Why are you gay? What do you get out of being gay?' Everyone was unhappy when they realised who I was. No one was on my side. They were so mad, and they started beating me. They said they can't be with a person who's gay and one of my brothers said, 'We should kill him instead of him shaming our family.' I had to run from home, because it had reached the extent of them wanting to kill me. And so, I was forced to run for my life. At first, I thought they will just beat me and that will be it, and I was not ready to leave home. But when they talked about killing me, I got afraid and had to run.

I was in school at that time. When I left home, I went to a friend who hosted me for some months. After that, I decided to go start a new life. I got a job and started renting with a certain friend to survive. But my family kept on following me; my step-mum went to my boss and asked him why he's hosting me. She said to my boss, 'Who are you to be with my son? I'm looking for my son and I'm going to report you to the police and say that my son is lost and you have him.' So, my boss had to let me go. The good thing had been that my boss was also a member of the LGBTIQ. So, he had understood my situation. But when it came to the police, he couldn't help me anymore. I left the job and got another one after, and the same thing happened. My first job was working in a restaurant, as a waiter. My other job was as a shop attendant. I had even changed areas. But one day I was at work and my mum came with my brothers and started shouting from outside the shop, yelling that I ran from home and I'm gay, blah blah blah. The second boss didn't know I was gay, and she wasn't around when my step-mum and brothers came, but the neighbours told her. But I was young and hard-working, and she had been happy with me doing the job. But now my boss got scared. She was like, 'I would like to help you but I might lose my business.' So, she had to let me go too.

I changed area again and found another friend to stay with. I also left social media and I changed my SIM cards. But I couldn't get over the fear of my family interrupting my life. And then that friend started using me for sex so I could get what I needed, because I wasn't working. I wasn't ok with that but that's the only thing that I could do to give back for me staying with him and get all the services, food, clothes, and all that. I did try to find work but, you know, I had that fear, of my mum ruining everything for me. And again, my family got to know where I was. Again, my mum came with my brothers and caused chaos at my friend's place. They shouted things, like that I ran away from home because I'm gay and that she's my mum looking for me, and all that. And they made it look like *I'm* the bad person – because people didn't know that they wanted to kill me. The landlord threw us out, saying that he can't have gay people in his houses. My friend couldn't help either. He got another house and lived alone. I couldn't go to the police to report my family for harassment and stalking, because they would have told the police that I'm gay and the police can't protect a gay person in Uganda, because being gay in Uganda is not allowed.

In 2014 there was a Bill that says homosexuality is not allowed and I always had fear. So, I had to go back to the organisation which had bailed me out and explain the situation. They said, 'This won't stop happening if you still live around your family.' They said they can help me and connect me to an organisation in Kenya: 'Maybe you can seek asylum or just keep yourself safe there?' So, they connected me to an organisation called HOYMAS[1] in Nairobi, and Trans Equality Uganda gave me the transport fare.

I travelled and entered Kenya in January 2017 but I didn't know anyone there apart from the guy the organisation connected me to, and I was talking to him while travelling. So that guy was Kenyan and from HOYMAS and he came for me at the bus stop and took me to his home. At the border they gave me only 30 days for the visa, and the guy told me I have to make sure I get proper documents that very month. Because I had to rest for the day, he told me, 'Maybe tomorrow you'll go to UNHCR and see if they can help you, because I can't help for long.' So, I had to get proper documentation. The guy said, 'You'll have to go to UNHCR and they will help you, and then we can add you on, because we are partnered with UNHCR.' When I went to UNHCR, they took me to RAS and I registered; then they brought me back to their offices. They asked me what happened, and I explained. They offered to connect me to one of the CBOs they work with, The Nature Network. I was only with the guy from HOYMAS for one night, so I don't have that much experience of his organisation. I wanted to go back but they told me about a CBO that helps fellow Ugandans. So, I found a safe house at Nature Network and they still had a grant, so we were not paying rent. They took me to HIAS to do assessment interviews. HIAS also works with UNHCR and it's an organisation that gives financial assistance to refugees. I did the assessment interviews but the bad thing was, they were no longer giving out financial help. They told me they will give me feedback after a panel meeting. So, they got my story and then they had a panel to see if I'm eligible for help. So, I had to be where UNHCR recommended me to stay, at The Nature Network.

It was safe and a very big house, so we stayed there with many people. But after some months, The Nature Network funds stopped. So, I had to contribute to the rent, 4,000 Kenyan shillings every month.[2] Not only that, but we needed to eat, and pay other bills too. I stayed but I started doing sex working, because I didn't have any other way to survive. I didn't know anyone at all. I had lost contact with my only family, so I started sex work, to pay rent and other bills, and also to survive. I still do it. But now I have some other skills, too, because the organisation did some training, like

[1] Health Options for Young Men with HIV/AIDS/STIs, a Kenyan community-based organisation formed in 2009 by male sex workers and persons living with HIV.

[2] About GBP £27 / $38.

videography, which kind of helps. We went to the Nikon store and we had photography training there. Sometimes we get gigs to go and shoot but, because we are LGBTIQ, it's very rare. Occasionally, I leave sex work and go shoot and get some money. I don't feel good, because I'm not proud that I do sex work. But it's my only means of survival.

The Kenyan community is also homophobic. A while ago we were arrested, just because we are gay. We spent one week in police cells and UNHCR had to get us out. UNHCR bailed us out. Prison was not good. Cellmates and police officers used to call us names, like 'girl-boy', *shoga*,[3] and they used a lot of bad language. I have a belief that me being LGBTIQ is not the end of me. I tried fighting it but I failed – so instead, I embraced it. At first, I was a Muslim, but with all that when I came to Kenya, I was like, let me become a born-again Christian. I converted. In the past, I hated myself so much and I tried going to churches and to pray for myself, so that one day I would change how I feel and go back home. Because my mum used to tell me I have a demon in me, so I wanted to pray to get rid of it. But later, I realised that I can be gay and Christian. I still pray.

In the Bible there's a story I feel connected to, about Adam and Eve. Like them, I was living in the garden of heaven, that's my home, and after my parents found out that I'm gay, which they believe to be evil, I was chased away. The story helps me in a way, because after they were chased away, Adam and Eve, God gave them a chance to have kids and start a family. So in the future, I would like to go back to my family, because I grew up with them and I share a lot of memories with them. I pray that they can understand me one day. In the future, I see myself as a professional photographer and videographer. I think, after some time, I will be resettled in another country, which God will give me.

I believe homophobia will come to an end in Uganda and Kenya but only after sensitisation, which needs to be done by us, the LGBTIQ community. We need to stand for ourselves, but it will take some years.

---

[3] A derogatory Swahili word for gay people.

First and foremost, I want to be a free person

Based on a life story interview with Julius
(22 September 2019)

My name is Julius and I am a pop artist and a song writer as well. I do pop-style music, rock, gospel, as well as country. I am a free-hearted person, social, and I love making new friends. I love people, and most of all I love LGBTIQ persons, because every time I see them, it's like I meet my brothers. They feel the same way I do; we understand one another; we go through similar difficulties: it really touches my heart.

I identify as LGBTIQ. I am the 'G' – that is, gay. Actually, I am trans versatile: transgender and versatile. But I am gay. I am a refugee and fled from my country, because I didn't have the freedom I deserve to have as a gay person and as a human as well. My country of origin is Uganda. I got into this 'gayism' situation. I found that my freedom was taken away from me. I wasn't free. I was hiding my sexual orientation for a long time. For many years I did not want anyone to know who I am. I actually pretended like I am not gay but this put my life in a closet and it became so hard, very hard. So, my life reached a point of 'enough is enough'. There were other problems I got through, but my orientation was the main issue that made me flee to Kenya. The people in my community were not okay with my sexual orientation. I won't go so deep into it, because I'm not feeling comfortable sharing my testimony in detail, but it related to my sexual orientation.

I have been in Kenya three years and nine months now. I reached Kenya on the 28th of January 2016. I have found it very difficult. Kenyan citizens are so homophobic; they don't want to be near us or give any assistance once they realise someone is gay, someone is a lesbian, LGBTIQ. We are finding this a difficult situation here in Kenya. It has made me relocate from one place to another; it makes me not even want to engage in love relationships. I would – but I fear being killed by citizens of Kenya and I fear being caught by the police and to get imprisoned. Kenya doesn't accept gays. The law doesn't protect LGBTIQ people in Kenya, just like in Uganda. In 2014, back in Uganda, when the anti-gay law was passed, many gay friends of mine got scattered. It was unexpected to all of us.

It is crucial to understand that gay people are not safe in Uganda and it is the same way in Kenya. There is no difference. We are in a very hard, difficult situation. We live by faith and we live with great risk. Yeah, I can say that. I came to Kenya, because, first of all, it's a neighbouring country, an easy country for me to access. And I thought, 'Maybe I will get the assistance I want. Maybe, I will be welcomed and be a free person.' If I had known! I have come to the point of saying that I wish I would have gone to somewhere else. I have come to realise that here I am like a prisoner. And there are many other Ugandan LGBTIQ people who fled from Uganda to Kenya, facing the same problems I am facing. It's a big challenge, a big problem.

Kenya also has refugees who fled from other nations, who are not LGBTIQ. But I think, according to the experience I have gone through here, that LGBTIQ refugees are facing the most challenges and are the most at risk here in Kenya, even more than refugees who are not gay. I don't feel the government, or the police are protecting us. I registered first with the Kenyan government, with RAS. After I got recognition by the government that I am legally in their country, I realised that this did not make me safe. That's what led me, searching for my protection, to the UNHCR. I am registered with UNHCR now. UNHCR listened and they started working on my case. It goes step by step and it is a long process. But they did help me to where I am right now, though it has been a very long, difficult journey and process, you know. I survive through the financial assistance through HIAS. HIAS is partnered with UNHCR. It was UNHCR who forwarded me to HIAS. But HIAS cannot give assistance unless you are registered with UNHCR. I have been living and surviving from the assistance of HIAS. They help me with paying my rent and food. The little I get has been helping me to start my life here.

In Kenya it is not easy for a gay person to get a job. It's not easy to be accepted by Kenyans. When you show your alien card, employers will not give you work and also, LGBTIQ refugees get kicked out of their houses, because of failing to pay their rent or because they are gay. Many of us refugees engage in sex work to survive. It's a heavy question. Personally, I have never been involved in the sex work business myself. I think I cannot do that. But it can be a way of surviving. I'm a love-relationship person. I would rather be in a love relationship than being a sex worker, because gayism doesn't mean I have to sell my body. But I can tell you that sex workers do sex work to face their big challenges. Many are not getting any assistance, like the assistance I am getting. They go through great risk as a way of surviving. I wouldn't recommend it to an LGBTIQ person, to go into sex work. Some are raped, some are caught by the police and it can cause their death.

I am an Anglican Christian. As an LGBTIQ person here in Kenya I connect my life to that of a man called Daniel, in the Bible. Daniel, too, went through a lot of problems; he got thrown into a lion cage or something. It was a terrible moment for him; he had to look at how to get out of that lions' cage but he couldn't manage. It was because of God's strength that Daniel survived that very difficult situation. That is like the kind of situation that a gay refugee is facing: you look that way, and the other way, and you don't see *where* the help may come from for you. Living today, you don't know what tomorrow may bring. You don't know if you will have something to eat, whether you can stay alive or if you will be killed.

I want, first and foremost, to be a free person. I want safety. Because, now, I see myself as a prisoner in my condition. So being free and safe, that's my great prayer. And I want to be able to express my sexual orientation. You know, it matters a lot to me. As an artist, I want to be able to do my singing work freely, not fearing when being on stage that something may happen. There's always a ray of light at the end of the tunnel. I keep my faith in God.

God has a purpose for us all

Based on a life story interview with Kennedy (21 September 2019)

My name is Kennedy. I discovered that I was gay when, after primary school, I joined a single-sex secondary school. I got a friend who was a very brilliant guy. He was a fellow student, called Richard;[1] he was a brilliant student, one of the best at the school. One day when we were in form two, secondary school, I interacted with him. So, the more we interacted, we became friends. There's something I discovered that was unique, each time that we were together: the sense of humour. Like there was a good form of communication; we had chemistry. What was so funny is that when we joined form three, we became dorm mates. He was following me and I was following him. I remember one day when I fell sick, he came and looked after me back in the sick bay. So, in a school of a thousand boys, this one individual is taking care of you. I was very close to him and I started feeling emotional attachment towards him. Even if I would go back home for the holidays, we kept communicating. And I remember we first made out in form five. Actually, we were in different schools by then; I think that's when we missed each other more and when we developed such a strong emotional attachment together. That's where I discovered that this is who I am, that God has planned this for me. I can't fight the emotion of being who I am.

Most of the time I would avoid negative spaces, where people talk badly about homosexuality and go against who you are. I would either keep quiet or move away from people who talk like that. You know, there's this negative perception about homosexuality, they look at it as a sin, and gay people are seen as worse than murderers. But we are talking about people who breathe the same air, people who are human beings. You can choose what you want as long as it doesn't affect the space of others. To

[1] Pseudonym.

me, when people look at homosexuality, when they look at people who are gay, they judge you for who you are, but they are not looking at how you can improve society; they will not look at your education, they will not look at your professionalism, how you will contribute to society, but they will judge you for your sexuality. These people seem to think that we have partners just for sex, or engage in sexual relationships without consent. Yet whatever action we engage in with our male counterparts, we propose, we are happy, we go for dates and seek consent. They look at it like it is bad, it's a sin; they regard us as inhuman, which is so hurting. It's that kind of perception that has always made me so active to fight against such abuse in society, such bad vices.

I came to Kenya at the end of 2015, because of the persecution that I went through in Uganda. Sometime in 2015, I finished my degree in law, and I went into activism, supporting some of the marginalised groups in society, because I myself am part of the LGBTQ community. I had a friend who was queer; he told me about how different students were being expelled from school, and about situations where children were going homeless. So then the question was, how do we help them? Back then my friends and I managed to put together a small fund; we used to do projects so that we could raise money to help those that were homeless. We also started getting some money from where we work, from our law firms; we saved from that money to help our queer friends who were marginalised in different parts of Uganda. We did not establish an official organisation, because of the policies and the law in Uganda. The laws in Uganda about homosexuality do not even allow us to start an organisation that supports LGBTQ people.

In the year 2015, in August, one of our friends borrowed some money and yes, he was LGBTQ but he defrauded us; when he borrowed this money, he didn't pay back. So, when we tried to follow up why he was not paying the money, we discovered he had used the money for partying. When we tried to push him to pay us back, he went to the police. He tried to expose the kind of activities that we were doing. So that Friday, we were invaded by the police at our place; they took everything that was in the house and they arrested us. I think that's the first time I went into police custody. They found some lubricants in the house and some flags of the LGBTQ and other items that made the police concerned. Usually in Uganda there's that weird perception that people go into LGBTQ business for the money and have access to resources. So the police asked for money from us. We paid around 800,000 Ugandan shillings,[2] after which we were released. But after a week the same guys who arrested us, invaded us again. They wanted more money. I think they knew we had some funds.

I can tell you, I have never gone through a worse situation in my life than being in police custody. The first time we were there, we were beaten on our way there, and while in the cells we were seriously tortured, and we were not provided with any warm clothing. It was a disgusting place. We were starving for two days, and the beatings were really bad. But we managed to get someone, one of my colleagues I was working with in the law firm; he helped us to secure a bond and we were released. We were supposed to report to the police station after every two weeks. But then after a week, they came again. We were beaten; we were tortured; I remember having wounds on my ankle, because we were told to put our hands down and our knees. The second time we were invaded, we spent a week in the police cells. But we managed again to pay some money so we bribed. It was like 500,000 Uganda shillings.[3] It may seem little money, but imagine we had saved that money to help, to support our brothers and the queer society. That was the last time I was in Uganda, because when we left the police station, I told my friend, 'we can't stay around.' So that's when we left the country. I managed to get some of my academic documents from the house. I jumped on to the next bus to Kenya. And that's how I found myself in Kenya, because I had a few friends who had studied in Kenya.

When I arrived here in Nairobi, the situation for refugees was really horrible. Unlike today, where at least life has kind of improved with the community houses, back then housing was very expensive and unaffordable; unlike today where you can have at least one meal a day, back in the day you would have one meal in two to three days, and a cup of hot water with some little sugar. Life was very horrible, also because of the persecution by the police and the general homophobia in society. When I arrived, I didn't immediately register with UNHCR as a refugee, because I had the benefit of having a friend who connected me to a sponsor who supported me to go back to law school. So I didn't register immediately, but then my sponsor died late in 2017, and life became so hard for me. After life becoming so hard, I had no choice, if I wanted to survive in a foreign country. So I registered myself as an asylum seeker, and I'm looking forward to the day that God will bless me with a safe space where I can be resettled.

[2] £160 / $220.
[3] About £100 / $140.

Being an asylum seeker feels like being an alien in this world, like you're seeking permission to be in this world; you're seeking doors to be opened for you, opportunities to be opened for you, but because you don't have a legal status nothing opens. An asylum seeker is like a new-born baby and the decision about who's going to push the child lies between the medical doctors and the mother. So it is a tight situation, because there may be laws to protect you but you're still treated like shit. Anything bad can happen to you. You don't know your neighbours; they can report you. Now that we stay in safe houses we can still be invaded anytime. When the police ask you for your legal documents and you show a document stating that you're an asylum seeker, the police has the right to put you into a prison cell;[4] from there, you can be taken to prison, the local prison in your jurisdiction, or you can be taken to the camp and thrown in there. So you can imagine, being an asylum seeker is one of the toughest situations. The UNHCR has not dealt with such situations adequately; and there's this organisation called RAS, which is the Refugee Affairs Secretariat, which is also not doing its job in terms of helping asylum seekers and refugees to cope with life both in and outside of the camp.

Being what I am professionally, a lawyer, is a blessing, especially in this community where there's a lot of discrimination. I have managed to study human rights for the past four years, and I'm currently completing my course at law school here in Nairobi. Human rights, the way I understand them, is about the right of people to do what they wish with conscience, with a free will but without affecting the will of other people through their actions. Here in Kenya, I would say the penal code is subsidiary to the constitution, and the constitution provides the Bill of Rights, which is very clear: there are fundamental rights to every human being. And if you're saying fundamental human rights, that means we are talking about *every* human being – every-one who breathes, who lives in this world. So the LGBTQ community is part of that. So I believe that the Bill of Rights, which is in the constitution, recognises the free will to do anything you wish in a safe space, in your own space. Then why should the penal code on the other hand come and follow you to your bed, to take *away* your rights? Why does it follow you to see what you're doing under your blanket?

I volunteer as an activist in a community-based organisation. I can't say we are 100 per cent living the dream life; we are supported by the world out there through donations and funding, and by visitors coming to check

---

[4] Because of the encampment policy requiring urban refugees to relocate to official refugee camps.

on us as LGBTQ refugees in the country. I can say our livelihood and our health is not very good, it's not pleasing at all. I don't remember the last time I had a balanced diet, because you find that food that is rich in proteins is expensive and food that is rich in carbohydrates is very cheap, so you find that we have more carbohydrates and not enough proteins.

I work for The Nature Network, which is a community-based organisation, and also for the Refugee Coalition of East Africa which is an umbrella body for all LGBTQ refugee community-based organisations in Nairobi. That is where I do my voluntary work. I found out about The Nature Network two years ago, when I got an invitation to attend a psychosocial event. That event was about HIV and things like that, and we talked about our stories. Those counselling sessions piqued my interest to join the organisation, and it has been a nice privilege, it has been a nice opportunity. I had to learn about other people's problems, share my own challenges, and be supportive to the community. Among the refugees, back in the day, sometimes you found people making suicide attempts. So at least I feel life has become better thanks to these community-based organisations. In the long run, if we can get more funding, these organisations can support more people. Being at The Nature Network, it feels like home for me, because it's a safe space, unlike when you go back to the community where you are being looked down upon as someone who is an offender of the law, as someone who's committing sin. There's a way they look at you. But for me when I'm here in the community house, I feel at home. I feel a great connection as we bond as fellow queers, and I'm very happy. In the future, I believe we shall become a bigger organisation that can support many. Right now we have limited resources so we can't support each and every LGBTQ. But in the next few years, with connection, with the networking and with the kind of testimonies from each and every one who has stayed with The Nature Network and has now been resettled, I believe it will become a bigger brand, and that we can support many LGBTQ asylum seekers and new arrivals in the country.

Personally, I see myself continuing to advocate for the LGBTQ community and refugees as a whole; I see myself standing in the courts of law, defending those who have been prosecuted and persecuted falsely, even those that are undergoing different challenges. I hope to get resettled in another country, but I see myself coming back one day to start up a big international organisation that takes care of refugees across the world. I look at Elton John as my inspiration, I hope to meet him one day; when I meet him my dream will come true.

I'm Christian but the time I spent going to church I often found people talking ill about the LGBTQ community. They regard our actions as sinful, they look at us as being sinners, which is weird because God says that the first commandment is 'love your neighbour like you love yourself', and the same Bible tells us to never judge someone. If you look at the story of that woman who's a prostitute, they wanted to throw stones at her, but then Jesus says: 'Why are you throwing stones, yet you are also sinners?' So to me the definition of sin is that everyone is a sinner. Whether you steal a small pen or commit murder, it all comes down to sin. So the magnitude of you, as a human being, measuring other people's sin and judging another person, it is unfair. I believe that the way the church perceives the LGBTQ community is very ill and bad.

The church needs to change. The theological schools where those pastors go for studies, they need to teach about issues of gender and sexual orientation. Then after that, let them go to each and every story in the Bible. When you look in the Bible, in the Old Testament, God sometimes seems very harsh, sending fire and diseases, and other ill things to punish people. But then, when you look at the New Testament, Jesus seems to be the new brand, the one who comes and washes away the sin of the world. That means if God still gives us breath, if we are still breathing as human beings, apparently God still needs us in this world. And the same Bible talks about us making the world a better place. In Genesis God says, 'humans: go and make this world a better place'. So that means that, irrespective of your sexuality, it is about making this world a better place. The people who preach the gospel should focus on love as the key word in their preaching. They should look at people's value: there's a queer doctor out there, there's a lesbian soldier who's protecting the country, there's a police officer who's gay. The church is supposed to be a safe space for each and every human being, because in religion you can find peace, but sometimes instead of a safe space where you can talk to God, in the church you find people using the words of the Bible as a sword to attack other human beings, which is very unfortunate.

I'm inspired by two stories from the Bible. First, the one I have just shared, about that woman – I don't remember whether she was a prostitute or I think she was adulterous – that story where they were going to throw stones, because according to the law back then if you're caught in adultery they will throw stones at you and they will kill you. That's one of the stories that inspires me, because Jesus comes in and says, 'whoever has never done a sin, kindly throw a stone'. All the people present felt shy when God talked about sin, and they disappeared. Then the other story would be the story of Joseph, who was sold by his own brothers, and he was sold to another territory. Joseph's story is so amazing, because he was sold as a slave, but it was through his slavery that God blessed him with a second chance. He ended up serving the king and the queen; and imagine, the queen fell in love with Joseph and she wanted to sleep with him; he tried to resist. Joseph was a brilliant guy, he won favours from the king, and he became a big prominent person in the palace. So later his brothers were experiencing some challenges in the province, they came back and found that Joseph had grown, he had become a big person in the palace, and he was the one in charge of the treasury. That story shows me that irrespective of the persecution, and all the challenges we go through as LGBTQ, we may be prosecuted for who we are, but at the end of the day we find God's favour. As long as we breathe, believe and walk in faith, as long as we happily coexist among each other, then I believe this world can be a better place. And Christians out there should know that the biggest commandment is to love your neighbour as you love yourself.

The biggest message I always want to give is, know the law. Wherever you are in the whole world, if you do not know the law then you'll be prosecuted. And my message to the religious leaders is simple: if we are still breathing, and if God is still blessing us in this world, and we share the same resources as other human beings, that means God has a purpose for us all and there is a reason why we are still living to make this world a better place, with or without the queerness, with or without being straight. Sexual orientation should not be a basis for discrimination, for breaching human rights. This brings me to the commandment to love your neighbour as you love yourself. Let's have peace and let's live in harmony and the world will be a better place for us all.

God doesn't make mistakes

Based on a life story interview with Keeya
(16 September 2019)

My name is Keeya. I came to Kenya due to the situation I was facing back home. I am from Uganda but the situation wasn't good. However much I want to be still in Uganda, because that's where I was born, the situation didn't favour me to stay. Instead, it pushed me to leave the country I love so much. I came to Nairobi in 2015. I have seen a lot, which made me leave Uganda – a lot! I was ministering in church, I was a singer, a preacher, and a pastor; I preached the gospel and encouraged people to come to the Lord, and I strengthened them in different ways so that they could stand and believe in God. Because being gay doesn't make you leave God. It means you were created that way.

I personally understood later that maybe I was created that way. I now believe that's how I was created, but at the time it was hard. Because we used to be in church where they would speak out against homosexuality – and you are gay and you hear them abusing you, talking bad against homosexuality; if that's what you are, you don't feel good and you have to encourage yourself. But the fact is that it wasn't me who created myself, and no one taught it to me; rather it just came. I started realising that I have feelings for my fellow man, and it used to stress me so much.

I used to pray a lot. I was raised Muslim, and Muslims used to say that homosexuality is bad, so it made me think that I'm a sinner. Muslims also used to say that the cities of Sodom and Gomorrah were burnt because of homosexuality, but they also failed to explain clearly that there were a lot of sins going on there. The sheikhs would just say it happened because of homosexuality. But if God destroyed them due to homosexuality, then God would also have killed me – but I'm still alive; I don't have any curse. Later I got saved, I became a born-again Christian. But it didn't change the struggle with my sexuality. When I started to feel that I'm gay, I had that feeling inside me, and I couldn't remove it, not even through prayer or fasting. Because in church they used to say that when you pray and fast, those feelings will go. So I used to go to the prayer mountain along Entebbe Road, in Seguku.[1] I prayed and prayed. At that time, I'd become a strong minister in church: prayerful, worshipping, and preaching the gospel, chasing each and every devil – but the spirit of homosexuality didn't go. In the end I understood that God himself is the one who knows why I'm gay and I became free. Of course, my family was still Muslim. They were already angry about me having changed from being a Muslim to becoming Christian. And then, in Islam they say it's a curse if a person is a homosexual. They say that if they find out that you are a homosexual, you just have to be killed, because you were cursed. You have to be killed because you don't deserve to be in the family; if you stay in that family you will infect others, because they think it's a disease – but it's not.

I felt the feelings when I still was a child. Then I thought it was only me alone in the world and I used to fight it. But even if I was with a girl, I couldn't have any feelings and when I saw a boy I could be with feelings. Of course, I couldn't tell anyone else. Only later, at an older age, I was introduced to the society for homosexuals and I understood that there are others like me. It happened through a friend. He used to sing and was a dancer. He had come to perform in our church, we hosted him. When I looked at him, I got attracted, and so did he. Within two weeks we hooked up. He was the one who introduced me to the community. It was so interesting! And it was fun! I got to know that I wasn't alone. From there, things kept on coming. I used to visit and hang out with them. Then I'd go back to church and it was like I had something pulling me. Whenever I had free time, I would call someone from the community so that I could meet them; being in their company helped me to feel fine.

What pushed me to leave for Nairobi was torture. I had my boyfriend but it was secretive. We connected through church and I was leading him, teaching him. I saw that he was doing things I liked and I used to bring him home. He would come to my place; he used to come and go. But one day we got some misunderstandings. It was about money issues. It ended up in an argument. He reported me to the police. That's when it became so bad. They also found out about me in church. And I used to sing and preach there! So, I got tortured. It reached an extent of them wanting to kill me just because I'm a homosexual. The problem was that I had told one of the

---

[1] The Africa Prayer Mountain For All Nations is a hill along Entebbe Road on an 80 acre plot of land at Seguku, just outside Kampala. It was established in 1999 by Apostle John Mulinde of the World Trumpet Mission, and Christians from across the region visit the place for prayer and fasting.

pastors about the feelings I had. He said that homosexuality is bad and that whenever those feelings would play up and disturb me, I should come and he would pray for me. So one day I went to the office and I shared with him. I thought he would keep it secret, between me and him. But then, next time he came to the pulpit he called me, like he was going to pray for me. He called to pray for me and said, 'this child, let everyone pray for him because he has a spirit disturbing him'. He told the whole congregation that I had the spirit of homosexuality! I felt like they had poured water on me! I became so silent, sweating, and drying up as they were all praying and rebuking the spirit of homosexuality.[2] Then the service ended and everyone was looking at me funny and shocked. And those who were my friends, they didn't even greet me because they did not want demons to enter them. You know, they call homosexuality a demon; they don't know that it's natural; it's really hard to explain that to people. I feel it's natural, because I prayed for it but all in vain. After this happened, I never went back to my church. I prayed to God to help me find another church. I attended a few other churches, in Kabalagala and in Kasubi.[3] But the news about me started circulating almost everywhere. I didn't have anywhere to go, because when they get to know that you are gay, no church would allow you in. In Uganda it's rare to find a church that would welcome you. Actually I have never heard of one.

I came to Nairobi without knowing where I was going. No one gave me a hand, I just came on my own. On my arrival in the city, I asked myself where I was going, because I had nowhere to go. I was so confused, because those who were my friends had disowned me. So I went to the UN, because I used to hear it's an organisation which helps those people who have no one to help. When I told them my story, they welcomed me and they said, 'You are not alone; so many of your colleagues come here. Do not worry, you will live.' They helped me. I still appreciate that they helped me. It's now four years and some months here in Nairobi. In Nairobi, there are some Kenyans who love you. Even if they find out that you're gay, they don't care. But there are also those who torture you. They look bad at you, don't even greet you, due to their culture, just because you're gay. Africans have their ways or beliefs. One of them is that you need to have children. Especially me as a pastor, I need a child. So I hope that there's a possibility of God doing a miracle in the near future; you never know, I may have a child. Otherwise there would be many questions from people.

---

[2] Most likely the storyteller means 'getting a dry throat' or even perhaps 'becoming dehydrated' as a result of the anxiety and panic.

[3] Kabalagala and Kasubi are neighbourhoods of Kampala, Uganda's capital.

I became part of The Nature Network, because my nephew stays here. He inspired me to come to The Nature Network and I requested to stay with them. It's been like two years now, and they have been so helpful. I have a place to sleep, eat, and live; at times that I wasn't able to support myself, they have helped out.

My family is here, we have different people we stay with at The Nature Network; it's a big beautiful house, it caters for quite a number of people. I'd rather stay here with this family than with my family in Uganda. I don't miss them. How would you miss them if they wanted to kill you? Would you even feel like going back, if it's your own family that is torturing you? My family back home started torturing me, the reason being that I had changed from being a Muslim to becoming born again. And also, they heard that I'm a homosexual, so that made it worse to the extent of me no longer being able to stay with them. In Islam if you change from being Muslim to another religion, they call you *kafir*[4] meaning that you deserve to be killed, because you have no value.

I'm still a pastor, even here in Nairobi I'm still a pastor. One day I sat down, and I said that I'm a minister of God and I respect myself; I have to minister among these people. They are in the same process: many people fled Uganda to Nairobi. I realised that I have to mobilise them for God, so that they don't judge themselves. They judge themselves believing that when they die they will automatically go to hell, because that's what they've been told in church. I mobilise them, we meet, and we preach the gospel to them, and we pray for those in our community. There are some things we'd like the world to know, that the person was created like that, that's how you were created when God created you with two hands; it's a mistake to try to remove that from someone. Because it's God who created you, he created you with your two hands and your eyes. And everyone he created, he loves them. God doesn't make mistakes, so everything you see on this earth under the sun was created by God and he loves it.

People say the Bible is against homosexuality. But God says a different thing. The Bible says it somewhere:

Come to me, all you who are weary and burdened, and I will give you rest. Take my yoke upon you and learn from me, for I am gentle and humble in heart, and you will find rest for your souls, for my yoke is easy and my burden is light.[5]

---

[4] *Kafir* is an Arabic term, which means 'infidel', 'apostate', 'disbeliever' or 'nonbeliever'. It is applied to one who rejects Islam.

[5] Matthew 11:28–30 (New International Version).

Human beings disappoint and may dump you but the Lord doesn't disappoint you, because he's the one who created you and we are all God's children. I know he created me this way; you can't take me away from God, I love him so much. There was a time I reached to God when praying and I told him: 'Lord please could you take away this burden torturing me?' And he listened, but he didn't change me as he wanted me to be like this. So now I'm free and very okay to be who I am. As a gay pastor, I believe that God has called me. But not everyone would believe in you; not all will like what you do and not all will love you. But there are those who love you. Me, I feel so free and okay if I find that there's someone who likes me and I can help them. Not everyone will hate you. And even if they are against you, you can still help. There's a reason why God got me from Uganda and he brought me to Nairobi. He knows that reason and even me, I'm just getting to know that he had his reasons.

The story in the Bible which I like to relate to is from the New Testament, about how Jesus Christ used to walk around, preaching the gospel, but always with his disciples. He selected twelve disciples and there were no women among them. Jesus never married. Jesus never gave birth. There's a certain verse in the Bible which states that Peter used to sleep on Jesus' chest.[6] On Jesus' chest! I don't want to be vulgar, but there's a certain revolution in it. He used to sleep on Jesus' chest. Not once but time and again. So now I have no way to explain that. Even pastors don't go so deep, they just stop there. If Jesus would allow his male friend to sleep on his chest, why can't I sleep on my fellow man's chest?

Pastors say that homosexuality was brought by whites, but yet way back, we used to see those kings such as Kabaka Mwanga who was well known in the history of Buganda and he slept with fellow men.[7] Even in my village, as a kid, you could see a woman who was like a man. And there could also be a man growing up like a woman. There's nothing new about being trans. Only, we didn't have the language for it back then. And today, those in our community who are trans, they are so interesting and also very free, the reason being that they feel themselves and you can't change them. Even here in Kenya, in previous generations they had gay men. They introduced those laws against homosexuality which indicates that it happened, because you can't put laws on something that's not existing or unknown. And it's not like this law was just introduced, it was there

---

[6] The verse that Keeya references here appears to be John 13:23, which speaks about 'the disciple whom Jesus loved' (most likely referring to John, not Peter) 'leaning on Jesus' bosom' (in the King James Version).

[7] See note 2 in Story 1, Raymond Brian.

even before we were born, which means those things used to happen. It's not me or you that introduced it. God knows where it comes from. So, whenever I'm preaching the gospel in our community, I tell them to look up to the Lord; he knows why you were created that way; when you get to know yourself, you will get peace.

Kenya isn't okay for the reason that most Kenyans don't like our community. The LGBTQ+ community, they don't like it. That's the reason why we are not going to stay here for a long time but are going to be resettled to a third country. In fact, I'm leaving for Canada very soon! What I'm proud of and what I thank God for is that my future is going to be so nice. I'm going to a place where I'll be accepted and able to be who I am, and I will really feel so much peace. I can dress the way I like. I will continue to preach so that people get saved and born again. Because even in those countries, there are many who still condemn themselves because they think they are sinning, and they have pastors who keep on telling them that they are sinners and cursed. But those pastors should realise that whenever they point a finger at someone else, the other four are pointing at themselves. If *they* want to be at peace, why can't they leave *others* alone in peace?

Let no one judge themselves because of their sexual orientation. It's not you who created yourself. I would like you to identify yourself, by looking in your heart, there's that inner person; for us, we see the physical, but there's that inner person in you who bears the image of God. The Bible says that even when the tree is cut, there is still hope that it can grow again thanks to the water underground. You may have been tortured, struggling to survive. But the tree can still come to life and start growing again.

Shall we end with a prayer?

Oh Lord, I thank you, for your mercy and power, for your glory because you're a wonderful Lord. God, you know our sexuality. It's not us who pours the rain on ourselves, but it is you. You have created us for a purpose. We thank you, Lord, for your mercy. Lord, we thank you for this organisation, we thank you for The Nature Network, we thank you for the leaders and even for this research to continue and reach everywhere in Jesus' name. Let the hand of God heal those who have been heartbroken, in Jesus' name. For everyone who will listen to these testimonies, we pray that they will understand God; that they will understand that it's you, God, who created us, and that you know us. You are the great Lord, you're trustworthy. I pray for the mercy of God to bless. That through this research people will know the truth. The Bible says that if you know the truth, the truth will set you free. Lord, I thank you for this ministry. I thank you for your people; they are going through a lot. Lord, please help them, those who judge themselves, those who feel like giving up. Some feel like committing suicide because of their sexuality. Lord help them, set them free, understand them and give that they also understand you. May your name be glorified in Jesus' name, Amen!

Inter-reading Ugandan LGBTQ+ Life Stories and Bible Stories

1

Inter-reading Life Stories and Bible Stories

The first part of this book has presented the narratives of twelve gay and trans refugees from Uganda who at the time of sharing their stories lived in Nairobi, Kenya. As stated in the Introduction, these stories are part of, and contribute to, a recently emerging body of African LGBTQ+ life narratives, and they add to the building of queer African archives. Having shared these life stories, Part II of this book engages in what we call an inter-reading of the life stories with select biblical stories. The present chapter offers an account of the rationale for, and methodology underlying the research presented in this book. First, it discusses the significance of LGBTQ+ autobiographical storytelling, relating this to traditions of feminist, postcolonial, and queer activism and scholarship, specifically in African contexts. Second, it examines the status of the Bible as an authoritative religious text and a popular cultural archive in contemporary Africa, explores biblical hermeneutics of liberation, and discusses some examples of using biblical texts for purposes of community empowerment and social transformation. Third, it introduces the specific approach of community-based participatory research that was followed in this project and outlines the process by which community members creatively engaged the selected Bible stories, transforming them into plays that set the stories in their own present-day context.

The significance of life storytelling

The use of autobiographical storytelling has a long tradition in feminist, postcolonial, and queer activism and scholarship. This has to do with the ability of storytelling to render visible the lives, and to make heard the voices, of those who hitherto remained marginal, if not invisible and unheard, in academia and in society at large. For marginalised people and communities, as the feminist philosopher Shari Stone-Mediatore puts it, life storytelling has great political and epistemological significance as it produces 'knowledges of resistance':

> Narration that serves a feminist and democratic politics ... must reclaim the agencies of people who have been excluded from cultural and political centers and for whom epistemic and political agency remains a struggle. ... The act of telling one's own story is empowering for the storyteller, especially for people who have been excluded from official knowledge-production institutions. Telling their own stories enables them to claim epistemic authority as well as to counter the objectified, dehumanized representations of them circulated by others.[1]

Thus, feminist scholarship has sought to provide space for women's stories to be told and shared, and to treat such personal stories as legitimate forms of knowledge in society and academia. Scholarship in queer studies has followed a similar strategy by foregrounding the stories of people who are marginalised on the basis of their 'deviant' sexual and gender identities and performances. Similarly, postcolonial and decolonial scholarship has engaged with storytelling by indigenous people, people of colour, and other groups representing what liberation theologian Gustavo Gutiérrez has called 'the underside of history'.[2] For instance, African life writing has been adopted as a method that 'authenticates African lived experiences' and as a 'medium of self-expression' through which Africans can 'construct their own subjectivity and agency'.[3]

Stone-Mediatore makes several important points in the above quotation that are relevant to the research presented in this book. First, storytelling by marginalised people is empowering to them as it acknowledges their agency. As the anthropologist Michael Jackson puts this, '[w]e tell stories as a way of transforming our sense of who we are, recovering a sense of ourselves as actors and agents in the face of experiences that make us feel insignificant, unrecognized or powerless'.[4] As such, autobiographical storytelling is a universal human phenomenon, but it is particularly crucial

---

[1] Shari Stone-Mediatore, *Reading across Borders: Storytelling and Knowledges of Resistance* (New York: Palgrave Macmillan, 2003), 150.

[2] Gustavo Gutiérrez, *The Power of the Poor in History* (Eugene: Wipf and Stock, 2004), chapter 7.

[3] Delphine Fongang, 'Autobiography's *Other*: The Untold Life Narratives from Sub-Saharan Africa', *a/b Auto/Biography Studies*, 32:2 (2017), 393.

[4] Michael Jackson, *The Politics of Storytelling: Variations on a Theme by Hannah Arendt*, 2nd edn (Copenhagen: Museum Musculanum Press, 2013), 17.

for groups who are systematically marginalised or excluded by structures of economic, social, and political power. Storytelling is a critical means through which the subaltern can and does speak – to adapt postcolonial feminist theorist Gayatri Spivak's famous phrase.[5] It transforms them from objects into subjects, and from victims into agents, and allows them to put themselves in the centre of their own life story. This empowering effect is true at an individual, but also at a collective level. The title of a recent collection of Kenyan LGBTQ+ life stories captures this fittingly: *Stories of Our Lives*.[6] Storytelling enables community building on the basis of shared life experiences, struggles, and dreams for the future.

Second, such storytelling produces counter-narratives to popular representations in society and helps to debunk these. Where popular narratives tend to objectify and dehumanise people of marginalised groups, telling their own stories allows them to present themselves and depict their own lives in ways that affirm and reclaim their human dignity. This is relevant, for instance, in African contexts where LGBTQ+ people are too often depicted in the media and by political and religious leaders as 'un-African', 'morally corrupt', 'godless sinners', and so on. In such a context, life stories provide critical insight into the multi-layered identities and experiences of LGBTQ+ people. As the South African queer studies scholar Zethu Matebeni puts it, personal life narratives complicate the 'ridiculous notion that same-sex desire and sexuality is un-African … by fusing religion, family and sexual desires with everyday practices of being African'.[7]

Third, life stories have epistemic significance; that is, they insert new, critical, and alternative forms of knowledge into academic and other formal processes of knowledge production. The South African scholar of religion, Sarojini Nadar, argues as follows, with reference to black and African feminist scholarship in which stories are seen as 'data with soul':

Feminists boldly declare that story is a legitimate and scientific part of research – the telling of stories, the listening to stories, the construction of stories in a narrative in order to represent research findings – all of these

---

[5] Gayatry C. Spivak, 'Can the Subaltern Speak?' in Rosalind Morris (ed.), *Can the Subaltern Speak? Reflections on the History of an Idea* (New York: Columbia University Press, 2010), 21–78.

[6] *Stories of Our Lives* (Nairobi: The Nest Collective, 2015).

[7] Zethu Matebeni, 'Introduction', in Unoma Azuah (ed.), *Blessed Body: The Secret Lives of Nigerian Lesbian, Gay, Bisexual and Transgender* (Jackson: CookingPot, 2016), 1.

processes are counted as legitimate components of the research process and an essential part of feminist epistemology. And nowhere does this notion of narrative research cohere more than in Africa.[8]

Nadar's key point is that stories result in forms of 'narrative knowing' that call into question oft-valued norms of 'objective' and 'detached' scholarship. She instead argues that stories not only give a human face to abstract theoretical concepts but can also interrogate and critique such concepts and allow for alternative, narrative ways of theorising. Such theorising, she suggests, is not an end in itself, because the stories of members of marginalised groups express and engender 'a yearning for change that can be translated into a working for social transformation'.[9] In the context of the research for this book, the life experiences of Ugandan LGBTQ+ refugees are utilised as the key to the interpretation of biblical texts. Not only does this make biblical interpretation more democratic and inclusive, but it also generates liberatory readings that indeed reflect a 'yearning for change'.

We will return below to the comment in the above quotation that the notion of narrative research particularly resonates in African contexts. First, let us address a terminological issue. This book adopts the term 'autobiographical storytelling', or, in a shorter version, 'life storytelling'. The term 'autobiography' may have the connotation of referring to a complete, factual, and historically correct account of one's life. The stories presented in the first section do not pretend to be anything like that. These stories are fragmented, selective, and subjective, as they only focus on certain experiences and narrate these in particular ways and for particular purposes. For people who identify as LGBTQ+, the telling of life stories is likely to follow certain patterns of categorising sexual and gender identity and of narrating sexual self-realisation, such as in the genre of coming-out stories.

Specifically in relation to LGBTQ+ refugees, they often have learned to tell their life stories through the asylum application process, which requires emphasising particular aspects, such as discovery of the sexual self, the event of (voluntary or forced) coming out, negative responses (verbal and physical) from family and the community, persecution by state officials, life-threatening experiences, and so on. This is not to say that such stories are 'not true', but that the truth of autobiographical storytelling is not necessarily located in the historical correctness, completeness,

---

[8] Sarojini Nadar, '"Stories are Data with Soul" – Lessons from Black Feminist Epistemology', *Agenda*, 28:1 (2014), 20–21. She derives the notion of stories as data with a soul from Brene Brown.

[9] Ibid., 23.

and coherence of the account but in the momentary and performative articulation and actualisation of the self through self-narration.[10] As the Kenyan queer studies scholar Ombagi puts it, LGBTQ+ life stories are

> narrative constructions that position queer bodies within a structure of negotiated exchanges and processes, telling how these bodies build and rebuild conceptions of the self. Narrating the self, therefore, becomes a way to understand the narrator through language and personal experience to build an (in)coherent subject.[11]

In order to acknowledge this processual and dynamic nature, in this book we avoid the noun 'autobiography' and prefer instead the verbs and gerunds 'autobiographical storytelling' and 'life storytelling', highlighting that the stories capture and reflect a specific moment within a life-long process of self-narration.

Storytelling in Africa

It is perhaps a bit of a cliché to say that African cultures are oral cultures. Yet, as many studies have demonstrated, oral literatures are indeed at the heart of African traditions of cultural production and transmission of indigenous knowledge.[12] Traditionally, this takes forms such as poetry, songs, folktales, myths, proverbs, and riddles. These forms remain important and constantly renew themselves through contemporary styles, such as theatre, cinema, music, and dance (and also preaching as one of the most popular oral literary forms practised in Africa today). The boundaries between these various genres are fluid, and so are their different purposes, which include marking and celebrating life events, narrating historical events, transmitting cultural and religious knowledge, providing socio-political commentary, and entertainment. Not only the style, but also the content of oral cultural forms is renewed over time. It is inherent to the process of oral transmission that each time a poem, folktale or proverb is performed, the text may change, or the performance

---

[10] Thomas C. Spear, 'Introduction: Autobiographical Que(e)ries', *a/b Auto/ Biography Studies*, 15:1 (2000), 1–4; Thomas C. Spear, 'Autobiographical, Queer We's', *a/b Auto/Biography Studies*, 15:2 (2000), 167–170.

[11] Eddie Ombagi, '"Stories We Tell": Queer Narratives in Kenya', *Social Dynamics*, 45:3 (2019), 412.

[12] Some key texts are Ruth Finnegan, *Oral Literature in Africa*, rev. edn (Cambridge: Open Book, 2012); Isidore Okpewho, *African Oral Literature: Backgrounds, Character, and Continuity* (Bloomington: Indiana University Press, 1992).

may place a different emphasis, or the context of the performance may affect how its meaning is perceived in the present.

Issues of power and marginality are critical in relation to African oral literature both in the past and today. In their book about this topic, the literary scholars Graham Furniss and Liz Gunner identify a range of questions to be asked: for instance, how oral forms function to articulate, represent, and possibly transform existing relations of power in society, how those in positions of power appropriate certain oral forms for particular political purposes, and how members of marginalised groups can use oral forms to redefine their position and signification as construed in broader social discourses.[13] As they put it, 'it is then in the field of oral genres that the relations between the powerful and the dominated in a variety of spheres are seen to be acted out, ideological assertion being met by a variety of forms of "resistance".'[14] An obvious illustration of this point is the current controversy about issues of sexual and gender diversity in Africa. Those in power, such as politicians and clergy, use oral forms, such as political speech and religious sermons, to denounce divergent sexual and gender identities. But members of LGBTQ+ communities also appropriate oral genres, such as poetry, drama, and in some cases preaching, as part of queer arts of resistance.[15]

Although, traditionally, oral narrative forms tend to emphasise collective experiences, that is not to say that they do not have (auto)biographical elements. For instance, tales may narrate the lives of people, some of them ordinary, others legendary heroes or mythical ancestors. Songs at initiation ceremonies often are 'songs of self-proclamation', articulating the young man's or woman's feelings at the passing into adulthood.[16] In the late nineteenth and throughout the twentieth century, this has developed into forms that can be recognised as autobiographical storytelling as understood in this book. For instance, in the context of colonial and apartheid states, life narratives were adopted as an 'important mode of counter-asserting

---

[13] Graham Furniss and Liz Gunner, 'Introduction: Power, Marginality and Oral Literature', in Graham Furniss and Liz Gunner (eds), *Power, Marginality and African Oral Literature* (Cambridge: Cambridge University Press, 1995), 4–5.

[14] Ibid., 12.

[15] For the notion of queer arts of resistance in contemporary Africa, and a discussion of various examples, see Adriaan van Klinken, *Kenyan, Christian, Queer: Religion, LGBT Activism, and Arts of Resistance in Africa* (University Park: Penn State University Press, 2019).

[16] Okpewho, *African Oral Literature*, 120.

the existence and value of the cultures and individual lives' that the state 'attempted to occlude and even to obliterate'.[17] Likewise, women have engaged in life storytelling, alongside other oral cultural practices, as a way to resist patriarchal traditions in African cultures and societies, and as a basis for building an African women's sisterhood.[18] Most recently, as discussed earlier, African LGBTQ+ storytelling has emerged as the latest trend in this genre.

In contemporary African societies, oral cultures continue to play a prominent role, not only as methods of cultural transmission but also to address issues of social and political concern, and to achieve community empowerment and social transformation. As the literary scholar Russell Kaschula puts it: 'Oral literary performances are used as acts of communication, and sometimes even defiance, between individuals and communities ... in situations that are politically complex and delicate.'[19] One particular form of the contemporary use of oral literature is the method of community-based theatre – also known as theatre for development. It has been used for purposes such as promoting HIV awareness and prevention, addressing gender-based and sexual violence, enhancing youth and women's empowerment, and engaging boys on issues of masculinity.[20] One example (among many) is the work of the community-based organisation Girl4ce in Lesotho, where drama and music are used to educate and mobilise communities around issues of the protection and empowerment of girls and women. The drama performances developed as part of this book project, and discussed in detail in the next two chapters, build on this tradition, but expand it in innovative ways by using biblical stories to narrate contemporary African life experiences, in particular those of Ugandan

---

[17] M. J. Daymond, 'Self-Translation, Untranslatability: The Autobiographies of Mpho Nthunya and Agnes Lottering', in Michael Chapman (ed.), *Postcolonialism: South/African Perspectives* (Newcastle: Cambridge Scholars Publishing, 2008), 84.

[18] Mercy A. Oduyoye, *Daughters of Anowa: African Women and Patriarchy* (Maryknoll: Orbis, 1995).

[19] Russell H. Kaschula, 'Introduction: Oral Literature in Contemporary Contexts', in Russell H. Kaschula (ed.), *African Oral Literature: Functions in Contemporary Contexts* (Claremont: New Africa Books, 2001), xiii.

[20] See Kamal Salhi (ed.), *African Theatre for Development: Art for self-determination* (Bristol: Intellect Books, 1998). For recent work in this area, see Zindaba Chisiwa, 'Using Theatre for Development to Engage Boys in Examining Masculinity and HIV in Two Malawi Schools', *Journal of Applied Arts & Health*, 10:1 (2019), 87–98.

LGBTQ+ refugees. Likewise, the two poems presented in between these chapters exemplify the use of poetry, weaving together biblical stories with contemporary African queer experience. Both the poems and the drama performances address social and political concerns, such as discrimination, exclusion, and marginalisation, but they are also empowering and transformative as a canonical sacred text is appropriated in an affirming and liberating way.

Narrative methods in African religion and theology

It is for the above reasons, relating to the importance of storytelling in African cultures and knowledge production, and to the political and epistemic significance of life storytelling by marginalised groups, that narrative methods, including autobiographical methods, have been embraced in African theological and religious studies scholarship. For instance, the Ugandan theologian Emmanuel Katongole has advocated a 'narrative theology' that takes as its starting point the life histories, the struggles, and aspirations of 'ordinary Africans'.[21] Traditions of African oral literature and storytelling have been adopted as a method for the inculturation of Christian theology.[22] African feminist theologians, such as Mercy Oduyoye, Musa Dube, and many others, have embraced stories as a 'source of theology', in particular as a method to foreground the experiences and voices of women.[23] Oduyoye, in her book *Daughters of Anowa*, performs a creative act of re-storying by telling the story of the mythical figure of Anowa in order to create a narrative space to reclaim women's contribution to African religious, cultural, and political life, both in the past and the present.[24] Dube has similarly re-storied biblical narratives about women,

---

[21] Emmanuel M. Katongole, '"African Renaissance" and the Challenge of Narrative Theology in Africa', *Journal of Theology for Southern Africa* 102 (1998), 29–39.

[22] Joseph Healey and Donald Sybertz, *Towards an African Narrative Theology* (Maryknoll: Orbis, 1996).

[23] Mercy A. Oduyoye, *Introducing African Women's Theology* (Cleveland: The Pilgrim Press, 2001), 10. See also Sarojini Nadar, 'Her-Stories and Her-Theologies: Charting Feminist Theologies in Africa', *Studia Historiae Ecclesiasticae* 35 (2009), 135–150; Isabel A. Phiri, Devarakshanam Betty Govinden, and Sarojini Nadar (eds), *Her-Stories: Hidden Histories of Women of Faith in Africa* (Pietermaritzburg: Cluster, 2002).

[24] Mercy A. Oduyoye, *Daughters of Anowa*.

using these as points of identification for African women today in order to challenge patriarchal structures in society, including in the church.[25]

The use of storytelling as part of African feminist biblical hermeneutics is particularly relevant vis-à-vis the work presented in this book, and we will return to it later in this chapter. At this point, it is worth mentioning that African feminist scholars of religion and theology have not only used the archives of cultural myths and biblical stories but have also engaged in autobiographical storytelling themselves. As Nadar captures this: 'While telling their stories places them in a position of vulnerability, the stories also become authoritative dialogical texts.'[26] The dialogue alluded to here is one between women's stories and other canons of knowledge, such as cultural, theological, and biblical traditions. It is through such dialogue that critical insights emerge, and new knowledge is produced. Patriarchal structures and practices are subjected to critique, and pathways for gender justice are narratively imagined and constructed.

In the same way as African feminist scholarship in religion and theology has adopted narrative methods to generate knowledge from women's perspectives, in this book we propose that methods of storytelling are also of crucial importance for the insertion of LGBTQ+ perspectives and the development of African queer religious scholarship.[27] Building on the narrative methodologies developed by Dube, Nadar, Oduyoye, and others, and contributing to recent scholarship on LGBTQ+ issues in African theology and biblical studies, we therefore engage in a dialogical reading of LGBTQ+ life stories and biblical stories.[28] This is motivated by the

---

[25] Musa W. Dube, *Postcolonial Feminist Interpretation of the Bible* (Nashville: Chalice Press, 2000).

[26] Nadar, 'Her-Stories and Her-Theologies', 143.

[27] Adriaan van Klinken, 'Autobiographical Storytelling and African Narrative Queer Theology', *Exchange: Journal of Contemporary Christianities in Context*, 47:3 (2018), 211–229. About life storytelling as a method in queer theology, see Chris Greenough, *Undoing Theology: Life Stories from Non-Normative Christians* (London: SCM Press, 2018).

[28] For recent work on LGBTQ+ issues in African theological and biblical studies scholarship, see for instance Ezra Chitando and Tapiwa P. Mapuranga, 'Unlikely Allies? Lesbian, Gay, Bisexual, Transgender and Intersex (LGBTI) Activists and Church Leaders in Africa', in Ezra Chitando and Adriaan van Klinken (eds), *Christianity and Controversies over Homosexuality in Contemporary Africa* (London and New York: Routledge, 2016), 171–183; Masiiwa Ragies Gunda, 'African Christian Theology and Sexuality: Some Considerations', in Elias K. Bongmba (ed.), *The Routledge Handbook of African Theology* (London and New York: Routledge, 2020), 367–380;

awareness of the status of the Bible as a highly influential religious text and as a well-known cultural archive in contemporary African societies that are predominantly Christian.

Engaging the Bible in Africa

There is a popular anecdote, sometimes attributed to Kenyan independence leader and first Kenyan president Jomo Kenyatta (1897–1978), or to South African Archbishop Desmond Tutu (1931), but in fact orally transmitted across sub-Saharan Africa. It exists in slightly different versions but basically goes as follows:

> When the white man came to our country he had the Bible and we had the land. The white man said to us, 'let us pray'. After the prayer, the white man had the land and we had the Bible.[29]

This anecdote captures how the history of the Bible in most parts of Africa is intricately connected to the history of European imperialism.[30] This history started with the first wave of European exploration and (slave) trade (15th–18th centuries), followed by the second wave of conquest, colonialism, and commerce (late 18th–20th centuries).[31] Each of these waves had mission at their core, as part of a broader project of 'civilising the natives'. The South African biblical scholar Gerald West identifies a third wave

---

Melanie Judge, 'Navigating Paradox: Towards a Conceptual Framework for Activism at the Intersection of Religion and Sexuality', *HTS Theological Studies*, 73:3 (2020), 1–10; Lilly Phiri and Sarojini Nadar, 'To Move or Not to Move! Queering Borders and Faith in the Context of Diverse Sexualities in Southern Africa', in Daisy L. Machado, Bryan S. Turner, and Trygve Eiliv Wyller (eds), *Borderland Religion: Ambiguous Practices of Difference, Hope and Beyond* (London and New York: Routledge, 2016), 74–86; Megan Robertson, 'Queerying Scholarship on Christianity and Queer Sexuality: Reviewing Nuances and New Directions', *African Journal of Gender and Religion*, 23:2 (2017), 125–144; Gerald West, Charlene van der Walt, and Kapya Kaoma, 'When Faith Does Violence: Reimagining Engagement between Churches and LGBTI Groups on Homophobia in Africa', *HTS Theological Studies*, 17:1 (2016), 1–8.

[29] Quoted from Dube, *Postcolonial Feminist Interpretation*, 3.

[30] The exception being North Africa (in particular Egypt) and the Horn of Africa (Ethiopia and Sudan), where the Bible and Christianity were introduced much earlier.

[31] For a historical overview, see Gerald O. West, 'Reception of the Bible: The Bible in Africa', in J. Riches (ed.), *The New Cambridge History of the Bible* (Cambridge: Cambridge University Press, 2015), 347–390.

(1920–1959), when the mission churches were gradually indigenised, when some converts established their own (African independent) churches, and when liberation movements began to resist colonialism, with the Bible being appropriated to 'talk back to power'.[32] He concludes that, through-out these three 'waves of imperialism and mission the Bible was present, playing a variety of roles, from iconic object of power, to aural authority, to vernacular textbook, to the medicine of God's Word, to political weapon of struggle.'[33] What is noteworthy here is that the history of reception of the Bible, despite being embedded in imperialism, is characterised by a remarkable level of African agency and local appropriation.

It is worth reminding that in postcolonial studies, appropriation is a sub-versive political process through which 'post-colonial societies take over those aspects of the imperial culture – language, forms of writing, film, theatre, even modes of thought and argument such as rationalism, logic, and analysis – that may be of use to them in articulating their own social and cul-tural identities.'[34] This is what happened to the Bible in postcolonial Africa, too. From a 'tool of imperialism', it has become an 'African icon' and even a 'people's Bible'.[35] As a result of the translation of the Bible into many African indigenous languages – which itself is a complex process of power imbued with colonial ideology[36] – ordinary people could hear, read, and understand the Bible in their mother's tongue, and it came to resonate with their religious, cultural, social, and political concerns. The strong narrative elements of biblical scripture also chimed with the traditions of storytelling in African cultures: the poems, songs, proverbs, parables, and rhetoric that make up much of the Bible suggest an extensive oral (pre)history, and an ongoing oral afterlife after being written down. The Bible, particularly so in Africa, is much more than either fixed or just written text.[37]

One might think that when African countries became independent, they would shake off the colonial legacies, including Christianity, given that its teachings and its sacred text had, after all, been used to justify the

---

[32] Ibid., 355.

[33] Ibid.

[34] Bill Ashcroft, Gareth Griffiths and Helen Tiffin, *Post-Colonial Studies: The Key Concepts* (London and New York: Routledge, 2000), 15.

[35] Gerald O. West, *The Stolen Bible: From Tool of Imperialism to African Icon* (Leiden: Brill, 2016).

[36] Musa W. Dube and R. S. Wafula (eds), *Postcoloniality, Translation, and the Bible in Africa* (Eugene: Pickwick Publications, 2017).

[37] See Elizabeth Mburu, *African Hermeneutics* (Carlisle: HippoBooks, 2019), in particular chapter 6.

colonial project. However, probably because the Bible had already been widely embraced as a sacred text, and perhaps also because it had been appropriated by social and political liberation movements, the opposite happened. In the postcolonial period, Christianity has gained tremendous ground and increased its following across sub-Saharan Africa. The Bible is enormously popular, not least in the Pentecostal-Charismatic movements that emerged from the 1980s and that have transformed the African Christian landscape.[38] On Sundays, but also during the week (for instance, for the popular Pentecostal overnight prayers), one can see many people carrying their Bible to church with great care, or see people reading it with concentration on buses. Young people have e-versions of the Bible on their smartphones. The Bible is widely read, plays a prominent role in people's daily lives, and affects cultural, social, and political practice.[39] In addition to the role of the Bible as a sacred text to be read and for its meanings to be applied, there is also a common ritual use of the Bible as a symbol of God's presence and a protection against evil spirits. See, for instance, the following examples given by the Ghanaian theologian Mercy Oduyoye: 'Christian lawyers who keep a Bible on every shelf of their library; houses built with Bibles buried in their foundations and individuals buried with Bibles in their coffins; Bibles in cars that may never be read but whose presence proves comforting, a sort of Immanuel, or God-with-us.'[40]

Not only is the Bible popular in the religious domain strictly defined but, because of the fluid boundaries between that domain and others, biblical language and imagery is also widespread in the public sphere, from political speech to popular culture.[41] The boundary between political and cultural expressions can, in fact, be rather fluid. For instance,

---

[38] Paul Gifford, 'The Ritual Use of the Bible in African Pentecostalism', in Martin Lindhardt (ed.), *Practicing the Faith: The Ritual Life of Pentecostal-Charismatic Christians* (New York: Berghahn Books, 2011), 179–197.

[39] Joachim Kügler and Masiiwa R. Gunda (eds), *From Text to Practice: The Role of the Bible in Daily Living of African People Today*, 2nd edn (Bamberg: University of Bamberg Press, 2013).

[40] Mercy A. Oduyoye, 'Biblical Interpretation and the Social Location of the Interpreter: African Women's Reading of the Bible', in Fernando F. Segovia and Mary Ann Tolbert (eds), *Reading from this Place: Social Location and Biblical Interpretation in Global Perspectives* (Minneapolis: Fortress Press, 1995), 34.

[41] Harri Englund (ed.), *Christianity and Public Culture in Africa* (Athens: Ohio University Press, 2012); Masiiwa R. Gunda and Joachim Kügler (eds), *The Bible and Politics in Africa* (Bamberg: Bamberg University Press, 2012).

performances of popular culture, such as songs and dance, were used in Malawi both to support and to oppose the dictatorial regime of the first post-independence president, Dr Hastings Banda (from 1964–1994), and they often invoked biblical tropes, such as of Moses and the Messiah.[42] The same could be witnessed more recently in Zimbabwe, where biblical language and imagery were used by the regime of former leader Robert Mugabe (1980–2017), but also by those protesting against him.[43] In many African cities today, one can encounter biblical allusions and quotations in advertising, the media, Nollywood movies, and the popular music industry, both 'secular' hip hop and gospel music – and, of course, on the minibuses that serve as the main means of public transport. This very brief discussion is far from complete, but it suffices to support the following conclusion: 'That the Bible is sacred and significant in sub-Saharan Africa there is no doubt.'[44] Given this status, the Bible is not only an important religious text – sacred scripture for Christians – but is also a well-known cultural archive. People may not necessarily read the Bible on a daily or weekly basis for themselves, but they will often be familiar with biblical stories which they may remember from growing up in church and from school. Also, even when they are not fervent, church-going Christians, they will often interpret these stories, and the Bible as a whole, as sacred. That is, they will take its divine status as self-evident, and are not likely to question its authority. As we will discuss later, this was certainly the case with our community of Ugandan LGBTQ+ refugees.

African readings of the Bible

Obviously, people in Africa read and interpret the Bible in many different ways. This reflects the diversity of the continent, its cultures and peoples, as well as the diversity of African Christianities, and of other traditions in which the Bible holds a primary or secondary sacred status, such as African Jewish, Muslim, and Rastafari communities. Biblical interpretation is further influenced by the reader's positionality in terms of age, class, gender, and so on. In this section, we discuss a number of readings of the Bible

---

[42] Wiseman C. Chirwa, 'Dancing towards Dictatorship: Political Songs and Popular Culture in Malawi', *Nordic Journal of African Studies*, 10:1 (2001), 1–27.

[43] Eliot Tofa, 'The Bible and the Quest for Democracy and Democratization in Africa: The Zimbabwe Experience', in Masiiwa R. Gunda and Joachim Kügler (eds), *The Bible and Politics in Africa* (Bamberg: Bamberg University Press, 2012), 42–60.

[44] West, 'Reception of the Bible', 378.

that have been developed by African biblical scholars and theologians in collaboration with local communities, and that have been described with terms such as 'liberatory', 'emancipatory' and 'empowering'. This review of what is often called by an academic term, 'African biblical hermeneutics', will identify stepping stones towards the particular ways of reading select biblical texts in the next two chapters. Here, we focus specifically on hermeneutics concerned with gender and with HIV/AIDS, and we ask what these bring to bear on African readings of the Bible concerned with sexuality. The basic insight provided by these hermeneutics is that as much as the Bible is used to reinforce and justify situations of oppression, it can also be appropriated to critique such situations and to imagine pathways of affirmation, liberation, and empowerment both at individual and communal levels.

Hermeneutics concerned with gender are particularly developed thanks to the trail-blazing work of African women theologians and biblical scholars. As South African theologian Tinyiko Maluleke states in his afterword to the volume *Other Ways of Reading: African Women and the Bible*, 'no dimension of Christian theology in Africa has grown in enthusiam, creativity, and quality like women's theology'.[45] This unquestionable vitality and creativity derive from deploying both analysis and retelling of biblical stories through feminist, womanist, and postcolonial strategies with a strong sense of purpose and urgency that incorporate also distinctively African sources of knowledge and experience.

We will discuss three brief examples.[46] First, the South African scholar Madipoane Masenya (ngwan'a Mphahlele) practises an interpretive strategy that is emphatic in its bifocal reading of biblical texts alongside proverbs and traditions of her own Sotho heritage. In her reading of the poem in Proverbs 31:10–31, for example, which praises a woman of valour (or worth, or strength), Masenya also celebrates women of fortitude from her own context, thereby making them a part and sharing in the honours of the sacred text. This is an explicitly womanist (Masenya specifies it as Bosadi, or 'Womanhood') and liberatory endeavour.[47] Second, the South

---

[45] Tinyiko S. Maluleke, 'African "Ruths", Ruthless Africas: Reflections of an African Mordecai', in Musa W. Dube (ed.), *Other Ways of Reading: African Women and the Bible* (Atlanta: Society of Biblical Literature, 2001), 237.

[46] These examples are all from southern Africa, where feminist biblical hermeneutics seem to be more strongly developed than in East Africa.

[47] Madipoane Masenya, 'Proverbs 31:10–31 in a South African Context: A Reading for the Liberation of African (Northern Sotho) Women', *Semeia* 78 (1997), 55–68.

African scholar Makhosazana Nzimande offers another, also carefully delineated approach, which she calls the *Imbokodo* method of reading.[48] *Imbokodo* is an isiZulu word, which recalls the rallying cry of the 1956 women's protests against the racist pass laws of the South African apartheid regime. The complete cry, which translates as 'you strike a woman, you strike a rock, you will be crushed!' has come to signify African women's resistance and resilience. Its application by Nzimande to biblical hermeneutics makes clear her political and liberatory intentionality. One way Nzimande achieves this is by not only focusing on women in biblical texts but also on excavating them in texts where they have been completely elided. Hence, in her examination of 1 Kings 21, describing the corrupt trial and subsequent execution of Naboth, Nzimande goes beyond the surface of the story to imagine and retrieve also Naboth's unmentioned wife, who would also have suffered from loss of land, loss of income, and widowhood. Such retrieving of women's stories is a popular feminist practice but it is brought here into view within a distinctively South African setting.[49] Other commentators have taken Nzimande's analysis further to devise models based in the Bible for improving the lives of marginalised South Africans, including dispossessed women, again demonstrating the 'tooling' of biblical hermeneutics for concrete liberatory action.[50]

Third, and in some ways closest to the repurposing of biblical narratives to be explored next in this book, is, among African women's biblical hermeneutics, Musa Dube's interpretive retelling of John 4, the story of Jesus's encounter with the Samaritan woman at the well.[51] In this story, Jesus requests water from a Samaritan woman he meets at a well. She

---

[48] Makhosazana K. Nzimande, 'Reconfiguring Jezebel: A Postcolonial Imbokodo Reading of the Story of Naboth's Vineyard (1 Kings 21:1–16)', in Hans de Wit and Gerald O. West (eds), *African and European Readers of the Bible in Dialogue: In Quest of a Shared Meaning* (Leiden: Brill, 2008), 223–258.

[49] One well-known example is the feminist novel *The Red Tent* by Anita Diamant (New York: Wyatt Books, 1997), which retells the story of Dinah (in the Bible confined almost entirely to Genesis 34) from Dinah's perspective, in the course giving her a full life story and rich inner life.

[50] See Ndikho Mtshiselwa, 'Re-Reading of 1 Kings 21:1–29 and Jehu's Revolution in Dialogue with Farisani and Nzimande: Negotiating Socio-Economic Redress in South Africa', *Old Testament Essays*, 27:1 (2014), 205–230.

[51] Musa W. Dube, 'Five Husbands at the Well of Living Waters', in Musimbi Kanyoro and Nyambura Njoroge (eds), *A Decade in Solidarity with the Bible* (Geneva: WCC Publications, 1998), 6–26.

responds that Jesus's request is unusual, given that he is Jewish and she Samaritan – because the two peoples do not associate. Jesus then reveals that he can provide living water and asks if the woman desires some. In the conversation that follows, the odd detail emerges that she has had five husbands and lives with a sixth man who is not her husband. Dube's purpose is to offer a postcolonial and feminist retelling of the story. She includes details, such as references to ancestors, a sacred mountain, and to divisions between different peoples, that speak to African settings. The five husbands are reimagined as five historical stages of southern African history, in particular, waves of ideological and colonial influence and oppression. More radically, the salvific figure of Jesus is revealed at the end of Dube's retelling to be feminine: her name is Justine. Thus, Dube, a biblical scholar from Botswana, brings in African experiences and traditions of storytelling to make the biblical story meaningful and powerfully poignant, especially for women in her own context. In that sense, her work, and African women's hermeneutics more generally, especially in terms of the creative and empowering liberties taken with the biblical text, has affinities with and is influential for our sacred queer storytelling in the chapters to follow.

In the context of the HIV pandemic, too, African theologians and biblical scholars have sought to develop hermeneutics of HIV and AIDS, re-reading biblical texts in the light of experiences of disease and stigmatisation, and the quest for inclusion, justice, and healing. Feminist scholars have been leading this theological response to the challenges posed by HIV and AIDS in Africa, out of the awareness that women are disproportionately affected by the epidemic, both in terms of infection rates and the burden of caregiving for those infected. In the early 2000s, the Circle of Concerned African Women Theologians made combating the HIV epidemic, and addressing HIV-related stigma, and the cultural, religious, and social factors informing them, its long-term focus and goal.[52] This has resulted in a significant number of publications, some of which are explicitly concerned with re-reading the Bible through lenses of gender, sexuality, and HIV.[53] For instance, Dorothy Akoto, a theologian from

---

[52] E.g. see Isabel A. Phiri, Beverley Haddad, and Madipoane Masenya (eds), *African Women, HIV/AIDS, and Faith Communities* (Maryknoll: Orbis, 2003); Isabel A. Phiri, and Sarojini Nadar (eds), *African Women, Religion, and Health: Essays in Honour of Mercy Amba Ewudziwa Oduyoye* (Pietermaritzburg: Cluster, 2006).

[53] Musa W. Dube and Musimbi R. A. Kanyoro (eds), *Grant Me Justice! HIV/ AIDS & Gender Readings of the Bible* (Maryknoll: Orbis, 2004); Musa W. Dube, *The HIV & AIDS Bible: Selected Essays* (Scranton: University of

Ghana, reads the text of Ezekiel 37 – where the prophet receives a vision of a valley of dry bones that come to life – in the context of the social, spiritual, and physical death as a result of HIV, reflecting on what hope this prophetic vision speaks into the present situation.[54]

Out of the awareness of the gendered aspects of the epidemic, the question of men and masculinities has also become an emerging interest in scholarly work, resulting in re-readings of the Bible and other faith resources with a view to the transformation of masculinities.[55] The Ugandan Anglican priest Gideon Byamugisha was one of the first African faith leaders speaking openly about their personal experiences of living with HIV; he and others have engaged in autobiographical storytelling as a way of reflecting theologically on issues related to the HIV epidemic.[56] Although there is now a wealth of scholarship on the Bible and theology in relation to HIV and AIDS in Africa, much of this reflects the assumption that HIV in Africa is a mostly heterosexually transmitted disease, with little attention being paid to sexual minorities and their particular risks and vulnerabilities.

In recent years, there has been an emerging interest in issues of same-sex sexuality in African theological circles from progressive angles.[57] This has resulted in a renewed engagement with biblical texts and with

---

Scranton Press, 2008); Ezra Chitando and Masiiwa R. Gunda, 'HIV and AIDS, Stigma and Liberation in the Old Testament', *Exchange: Journal of Contemporary Christianities in Context*, 36:2 (2007), 184–197.

[54] Dorothy Akoto, 'Can These Bones Live? Re-reading Ezekiel 37:1–14 in the HIV/AIDS Context', in Musa W. Dube and Musimbi R. A. Kanyoro (eds), *Grant Me Justice! HIV/AIDS & Gender Readings of the Bible* (Maryknoll: Orbis, 2004), 97–111.

[55] E.g. see Ezra Chitando and Sophie Chirongoma (eds), *Redemptive Masculinities: Men, HIV, and Religion* (Geneva: WCC Publications, 2012); Adriaan van Klinken, *Transforming Masculinities in African Christianity: Gender Controversies in Times of AIDS* (Farnham: Ashgate, 2013).

[56] Gideon Byamugisha and Glen Williams (eds), *Positive Voices: Religious Leaders Living with or Personally Affected by HIV and AIDS* (Oxford: Strategies for Hope Trust, 2005).

[57] E.g. see the special issue of *Journal of Theology for Southern Africa*, 155 (2016) entitled 'Sexuality in Africa', with contributions on sexual diversity, sexual ambiguity and sexual minorities. For a broader overview, see Adriaan van Klinken and Masiiwa R. Gunda, 'Taking Up the Cudgels Against Gay Rights? Trends and Trajectories in African Christian Theologies on Homosexuality', *Journal of Homosexuality*, 59:1 (2012), 114–138.

questions of biblical hermeneutics in the light of LGBTQ+ issues.[58] Nevertheless, a queer African biblical hermeneutics is yet in its infancy.[59] Very many interpretations of biblical texts from African contexts are not queer-affirming, and some are overtly queer-condemning. A good example of the dominant tenor is the *Africa Bible Commentary*, which is a landmark volume with contributions from over seventy African scholars, mostly from evangelical Christian backgrounds.[60] Interestingly, a text box on 'Taboos', accompanying Leviticus 18, does not single out the clobber verse (v.22), which is standardly translated along the lines of, 'You shall not lie with a male as with a woman; it is an abomination', and is often weaponised against LGBTQ+ persons. Instead, the commentator points out that 'African taboos are similar to prohibitions found in the Bible' and that 'taboos are not necessarily wrong in themselves'.[61] Where the law recurs, however (Lev. 20:13), with the addition of the death penalty, the commentary is quick to list 'homosexuality' among the 'sins against family life'.[62] Elsewhere, too, the commentary is unambiguous in its outright condemnation: 'Homosexuality is a detestable sin before the Lord.'[63] Yet while there are tendencies in

[58] Elias K. Bongmba, 'Hermeneutics and the Debate on Homosexuality in Africa', *Religion and Theology*, 22:1–2 (2015), 69–99; Masiiwa Ragies Gunda and Jim Naughton (eds), *On Sexuality and Scripture: Essays, Bible Studies, and Personal Reflections* (New York: Church Publishing, 2017); Gerald West and Charlene van der Walt, 'A Queer (Beginning to the) Bible', *Concilium*, 5 (2019), 109–118.

[59] See Gerald O. West, 'Towards an African Liberationist Queer Theological Pedagogy', *Journal of Theology for Southern Africa*, 155 (2016), 216–224, for an argument about a liberationist theological hermeneutics more broadly.

[60] Tokunboh Adeyemo (ed.), *Africa Bible Commentary* (Nairobi: WordAlive Publishers and Grand Rapids: Zondervan, 2006).

[61] Ernestina Afriyie, 'Taboos', in Tokunboh Adeyemo (ed.), *Africa Bible Commentary* (Nairobi: WordAlive Publishers and Grand Rapids: Zondervan, 2006), 159.

[62] Felix Chingota, 'Leviticus', in Tokunboh Adeyemo (ed.), *Africa Bible Commentary* (Nairobi: WordAlive Publishers and Grand Rapids: Zondervan, 2006), 161.

[63] Barnabe Assohoto and Samuel Ngewa, 'Genesis', in Tokunboh Adeyemo (ed.), *Africa Bible Commentary* (Nairobi: WordAlive Publishers and Grand Rapids: Zondervan, 2006), 38. This quotation is from the commentary on Genesis 19, another clobber text. Here the demands of the citizens of Sodom to investigate the visitors of Lot, widely interpreted as a threat of male rape, are glibly identified with 'homosexuality'. The many problematic, including racist, underpinnings of such identifications are well expounded by Randall

African theologies and biblical studies to read the Bible in particular ways, the Bible itself does not speak with one voice but constitutes, to use Gerald West's expression, opportunities for a queer theological pedagogy and a site of struggle.[64] Our objective in this book is to explore these opportunities for a queer interpretation. Building on the hermeneutical methodologies outlined above with regard to gender and HIV, our proposal is for queer African biblical hermeneutics to take a narrative form and to read the Bible with, and from the perspective of, LGBTQ+ communities.

Many of the scholars discussed above work with local communities – faith communities, women's groups, people living with HIV, and so on – to develop community-based and contextually relevant readings of biblical texts. Much of this work is indebted to the methodology of Contextual Bible Study (CBS) as developed at the Ujamaa Centre, directed by Gerald West, at the University of KwaZulu-Natal in Pietermaritzburg, South Africa. Originally developed with a view to reading the Bible for liberation in the context of apartheid South Africa, CBS has been popularised and expanded for transformative, socially engaged, and community-based biblical scholarship in a wide range of contexts.[65] It is a distinctive practice of 'reading with', whereby the Bible is read by 'ordinary readers', above all readers from poor and marginalised communities, in collaboration with socially engaged biblical scholars and theologians.[66] It emerged in the last years of the apartheid regime when CBS constituted a subversive act of liberation theology and political resistance. The practice continues to this day and has included among ordinary reader participants a variety of persons who are vulnerable and marginalised, such as survivors of rape and gender-based violence, unemployed youth, persons living with HIV, and LGBTQ+ persons.[67] They are encouraged to read the Bible from their own per-

---

C. Bailey, 'Why Do Readers Believe Lot? Genesis 19 Reconsidered', *Old Testament Essays* 23:3 (2010), 519–548.

[64] West, 'Towards an African Liberationist Queer Theological Pedagogy', 216, 222.

[65] For a full explanation of CBS and the Centre's history, see 'The Ujamaa Centre for Biblical and Theological Community Development and Research', http://ujamaa.ukzn.ac.za/Homepage.aspx (accessed 16 December 2020).

[66] Gerald O. West, *The Academy of the Poor: Towards a Dialogical Reading of the Bible* (Sheffield: Continuum, 1999).

[67] The CBS on LGBTQ+ issues developed by the Ujamaa Centre focuses on one of the so-called clobber verses, that is, a biblical passage often used to condemn same-sex relationships (in this case, the story of Sodom and

spective, plumbing it for resources that can help to alleviate suffering and to empower participants. The method has also been used as part of sensitisation strategies: for instance, to engage men on issues of sexual violence, and faith leaders on issues of sexual diversity.

The CBS methodology also underlies the Tamar Campaign, in which the biblical story of the rape of Tamar (2 Samuel 13) is used to address issues of gender-based and sexual violence in communities in South Africa and far beyond.[68] It has also been adopted by the South African organisation Inclusive and Affirming Ministries to read the Bible with faith communities around LGBTQ+ issues.[69] Our project, too, has been inspired by CBS methodology. Particularly valuable for our purposes has been the emphasis of CBS on, first, how both discrete local contexts and the circumstances and experiences of individuals and communities have impact on reading and interpreting the Bible; and second, on collaboration between persons from different backgrounds – in this case, Ugandan refugees and UK-based academics – in service of a common purpose. We gave our own twist to CBS, however, as we made use of The Nature Network's existing format for group activities, and built on their expertise in undertaking creative work, such as drama. The latter resulted in a particular focus on re-storying the Bible in the contemporary context.

Re-storying the Bible through community-based research

Building on the traditions of liberatory, contextual, and community-based readings of the Bible in Africa as outlined above, in the research underlying this book we engaged in reading select biblical stories with Ugandan LGBTQ+ refugees and in dialogue with their life experiences. The project was developed with The Nature Network (TNN), the Nairobi-based community-based refugee organisation described briefly in the Introduction and mentioned by several of the storytellers. The way in which the project

---

Gomorrah). Likewise, the booklet *The Bible and Homosexuality* (Cape Town: Inclusive and Affirming Ministries, 2008), addresses the clobber verses. In our project, we deliberately chose not to use the clobber verses but to work with different texts, which had been identified by our participants as meaningful to them (see below).

[68] Gerald O. West and Phumzile Zondi-Mabizela, 'The Bible Story that Became a Campaign: The Tamar Campaign in South Africa (and Beyond)', *Ministerial Formation*, 103 (2004), 5–13.

[69] *Reading Together: A Bible Study Method* (Cape Town: Inclusive and Affirming Ministries, 2019).

was designed and carried out was inspired by emerging methodologies (or, methodological orientations) of community-based participatory and activist research.

Community-based research

There is a vast body of literature about community-based, participatory, and activist research methodologies, although sometimes using different terminology and emphases. Inspired by feminist, queer, and decolonial scholarly practices, the bottom line is that this is an approach to research not just *about*, but *with* the community centred in it, based on principles such as relationality and co-production of knowledge, and characterised by a commitment to community empowerment and social justice.[70] This approach is reflected in the present project in various ways.

First, the idea for the project was born out of a relationship of several years between one of the academic leads (Adriaan) and the TNN community, as narrated in the Introduction. It was TNN leader Raymond Brian who, at some point, suggested to Adriaan undertaking research together, and in the discussion about possible ideas, a comment was made about TNN's commitment to 'telling our stories'. Combining this with the organisation's interest in faith and in drama, the contours of the present project were collaboratively developed.

Second, in the coordination of the project, the academic leads (Adriaan and Johanna) and the local research coordinators (Hudson and Raymond) worked closely together as a team. We deliberately invested in building a collegial relationship; for instance, by having project meetings over food and drinks, and by enjoying leisure time together, in addition to consulting about the work. In this team, the local coordinators had major responsibilities: they coordinated the on-the-ground work, conducted most of the individual interviews, facilitated the workshops, transcribed the audio-recordings of interviews and focus group discussions, and translated several texts from Luganda into English. Adriaan and Johanna gave guidance and feedback where appropriate; they also played a prominent role in the methodological design of the project, and in the analysis and writing up of the collected data.

Third, Raymond and Hudson actively involved community members in the project. Members of TNN assisted in the process of transcribing

---

[70] For a helpful overview, see Margaret R. Boyd, 'Community-Based Research: Understanding the Principles, Practices, Challenges, and Rationale', in Patricia Leavy (ed.), *The Oxford Handbook of Qualitative Research* (Oxford: Oxford University Press, 2014), 498–517.

interviews, planning and facilitating the focus group discussions, directing the drama play, and editing the video recording. Members of the wider Ugandan LGBTQ+ refugee community in Nairobi were invited to participate in the project activities. Fourth, and importantly, for the workshops we made use of group-work methodologies developed and used by TNN in recent years, which they describe as 'family-based therapy', referring to the notion of TNN as a queer family. Thus, the focus group discussions and drama sessions were strongly relational and community-based, with plenty of time for sharing food, chatting and laughing, song and dance. Attentive to the needs of the participants, breakfast (chapatis, hard boiled eggs, and strong tea with hot milk) was served as participants arrived in the morning, and a warm lunch (*matooke* – cooked bananas – with vegetables, chicken, rice, and chapatis) was served half-way through the day-long programme.

The sessions would typically start with a funny warming-up exercise. For instance, one day participants had to introduce their neighbour to the group, by stating their name and hobby. The hobbies, initially, covered things such as reading, dancing, music, and going to church, but when one person introduced their neighbour saying, 'he likes lots of sex', sex became a recurrent theme. The exercise brought with it lots of laughter, freeing up the mood before moving on to the more serious work. The latter would start with a round in which participants would share their expectations of the day, and also collectively set rules. Expectations were various. Some very practical: 'to receive a travel expense refund', 'good food and refreshments'; others, experiential: 'to learn', 'to form connections and make new friends', 'to read the story anew'. The rules agreed on pertained to respecting and listening to one another, to speaking one at a time, keeping to time, turning phones on mute, and to everyone's active participation. There was some discussion about imposing penalties – but this was mostly jocular and quickly abandoned. Apart from the odd ringing or beeping phone in the course of the day and a few late arrivers who did not participate actively, mostly the rules were followed and the energy and mood were great throughout the day.

What is noteworthy about this is not only the strong community-based approach, but also the democratic spirit in which each participant was made and held responsible for the day. Moreover, spirituality was naturally integrated in these group activities, for instance by the day being opened and closed with a prayer, and with the discussions being interrupted by singing a song, usually with a religious theme. Thus, the family-based therapy methodology was deeply holistic, as it attended to participants as physical, emotional, and spiritual beings. This is typical of the way in which TNN operates, and the research benefited enormously from their experience in facilitating group sessions and making participants feel truly at home. As a result of this approach followed in the research, the knowledge produced in the process and presented in this book was co-produced.[71] Co-creation here does not just refer to the collaboration between Adriaan and Johanna as academic researchers and Raymond and Hudson as community-based activists and research assistants, but more fundamentally to the way in which the community as a whole was actively involved in, made responsible for, and became invested in the process of producing knowledge in the form of storytelling, drama performance, and creative biblical interpretation.

Sometimes, community-based participatory research can be concerned with very tangible and immediate objectives of social change, for instance in projects with a public health focus. In the case of our project, the objectives were slightly less tangible, but we do believe – for reasons outlined earlier in this chapter – that the focus on life storytelling is of vital importance for the marginalised voices of LGBTQ+ refugees to be heard. Indeed, as several participants testified, they found their participation in the project to be therapeutic. The project has helped in enhancing the visibility of the Ugandan LGBTQ+ refugee community, among other ways through this book, but also through the drama films that were recorded, shared on YouTube, and even screened at an international online film festival.[72] The creative, communicative, social, and technical skills developed by participants, through activities such as life storytelling, focus group discussions, drama, recording, and editing, are useful for the future.[73] In these various ways, the project helped enhance the social well-being of the participants and contributed to empowerment for further social change.

Re-storying the Bible stories

As outlined in the Introduction, the research was carried out in two stages: first, individual life story interviews, and second, group work and creative drama about selected Bible stories. In the individual interviews, all participants were asked about their favourite story or character from the Bible (or the Qur'an, in the case of the Muslim interviewee). We put the question

---

[71] See Christina Horvath and Juliet Carpenter (eds), *Co-Creation in Theory and Practice: Exploring Creativity in the Global North and South* (London: Polity Press, 2020).

[72] The Changing the Story international online film festival, 1–5 June 2020.

[73] Within the stringent expenditure rules of the project grant, these activities also legitimated payment of participants, thus adding an economic benefit.

like this, in order to avert from the so-called clobber passages (the biblical verses often used to condemn homosexuality), and instead to invite biblical texts they could identify with in a positive way, or that otherwise were part of their memory and/or spoke to their imagination and were meaningful to them. While the clobber passages, or 'texts of terror', require a hermeneutics of suspicion, our participants generally demonstrated a hermeneutics of trust towards the Bible as a whole.[74] Although they were aware of certain passages that are used to condemn same-sex relationships, participants tended to dismiss these texts as irrelevant to them, privileging instead their personal faith in and love for God. The unconditional love of God was widely deemed the central message of the Bible. In that sense, their hermeneutics of trust, which acknowledges that biblical texts, in the words of Cameroonian-American theologian Alice Yafeh-Deigh, 'have a *potentially liberating* force', was reflective of a deep-rooted hermeneutic of love and healing.[75] Intuitively, participants also reinforced a key insight of queer Bible reading strategies, as captured by the queer biblical scholars Robert Goss and Mona West in their book *Take Back the Word*:

> The whole Bible is a text of terror because of the ways in which our abuse has been justified by the misinterpretation of a few obscure passages. We believe the point of reference for a queer reading of scripture is the notion that the Bible is our friend. When we approach the Bible as a friendly text, as a text that 'does not harm,' the terror of the Scriptures is transformed into the life-giving Word of God.[76]

---

[74] The term 'texts or terror' was originally coined by Phyllis Trible, *Texts of Terror: Literary-Feminist Readings of Biblical Narratives* (Minneapolis: Fortress Press, 1984); the term 'hermeneutics of suspicion' is associated with Elisabeth Schüssler Fiorenza, *But She Said: Feminist Practices of Biblical Interpretation* (Boston: Beacon Press, 1992), 57–62. About hermeneutics of trust, especially in the context of (Southern) Africa, see Gerald West, 'Negotiating with "the White Man's Book": Early Foundations for Liberation Hermeneutics in Southern Africa', in Emmanuel M. Katongole (ed.), *African Theology Today* (Scranton: University of Scranton Press, 2002), 27–28.

[75] Alice Yafeh-Deigh, 'Rethinking Paul's Sexual Ethics within the Context of HIV and AIDS: A Postcolonial Afro-Feminist-Womanist Perspective', in Madipoane Masenya (ngwan'a Mphahlele) and Kenneth N. Ngwa (eds), *Navigating African Biblical Hermeneutics: Trends and Themes from Our Pots and Our Calabashes* (Newcastle: Cambridge Scholar Publishing, 2018), 34–35.

[76] Robert E. Goss and Mona West, 'Introduction', in Robert E. Goss and Mona West (eds), *Take Back the Word: A Queer Reading of the Bible* (Cleveland: The Pilgrim Press, 2000), 5.

Engaging the Bible as their 'friend', participants came up with the following stories:

- The story of Adam and Eve (OT)
- The story of Joseph (OT)
- The story of David and Goliath (OT)
- The story of Daniel in the lions' den (OT)
- The story of Job (OT)
- The story of Jesus and Zacchaeus (NT)
- The parable of the prodigal son (NT)
- The story of Jesus and his twelve male disciples (one of whom slept on Jesus's chest) (NT)
- The story of Jesus and the woman caught in adultery (NT)
- Surah Ad-Duhaa and Surah Al-Baqarah (Qur'an)

The ease with which most interviewees came up with stories, were able to narrate them with quite some detail, and to connect them to their own life experiences, illustrates their overall familiarity with the Bible. The above list of stories offers an interesting insight into the queer biblical archive of our participants and into the hermeneutics through which they engage the Bible. The Old Testament (OT) stories invoked by interviewees are stories of facing and overcoming ordeals and challenges: Adam and Eve evicted from the Garden of Eden (Story 9, Shamuran); Joseph thriving after abduction and imprisonment (Story 11, Kennedy); the small David defeating the giant Goliath (Story 1, Raymond Brian); Daniel surviving the lions' den (Story 2, Tigan; Story 10, Julius); Job being restored and vindicated after tremendous suffering (Story 8, Doreen). The interviewees identified with the main characters in these stories and appropriated them to narrate also their own experiences of suffering and struggle, and of God's help in overcoming these. A similar way of reading sacred scripture is represented by Dhalie when they cite Surah Ad-Duhaa and Surah Al-Baqarah from the Qur'an (Story 6). They invoke these passages to emphasise their belief that whatever challenges one faces in life, God is there as a source of support.

The New Testament (NT) stories invoked are slightly more diffuse. The story of Jesus and Zakayo, or Zacchaeus (Cindy and Drake, Stories 4 and 7), and the story of Jesus and the woman caught in adultery (Cindy and Kennedy, Stories 4 and 11), are invoked as stories of affirmation and comfort, with Jesus in these stories presenting a model of inclusion and love that contrasts with attitudes of judgement in society. The parable of the prodigal son is not explicitly mentioned as a favourite Bible story but is paraphrased by Drake when he narrates the relationship to his father. The ending of his story is rather different from the ending of the parable, with Drake implicitly contrasting the expulsion by his father with the loving and forgiving father-figure in the parable (who is usually seen as representing God, the heavenly father). Two interviewees (Kyle and Keeya, Stories 3 and 12) make reference to Jesus and his twelve male disciples, specifically pointing to the biblical verse that speaks about one disciple resting on Jesus's chest (John 13:23).[77] They do not go as far as claiming that Jesus was gay, but they do draw attention to the level of homo-sociality and homo-intimacy in the Gospel accounts of Jesus's life, and to the queerness of Jesus not following societal norms of masculinity closely linked to marriage and procreation. The Bible itself, they suggest, renders the sexuality of (one of) its most central character(s) ambiguous, thus creating a space for queerness within Christianity.

After consultation with TNN members, we decided to take two stories forward to the next stage of the project: the story of Daniel in the lions' den (Daniel 6), and the story of Jesus and the woman caught in adultery (John 8:1–11). We chose these for several reasons. Both are relatively concise stories (unlike the stories of Joseph, or Job), making it possible to read and discuss them in group sessions. They come from the two main parts of the Christian Bible: the Daniel story from the Old Testament, and the story of Jesus and the woman caught in adultery from the New Testament. They also speak to the experiences of the Ugandan LGBTQ+ refugees in different ways: the Daniel story relates to experiences of persecution and socio-political homophobia, while the Jesus story relates to experiences of stigma and community judgement.

The next stage centred around group work on these two stories, aiming at a retelling of the biblical stories in the contemporary context. The indigenous queer studies scholar Qwo-Li Driskill, in hir book about Cherokee stories about two-spirit people and their relevance for queer people today, uses the term 're-storying'. By this, s/he means 'a retelling and imagining of stories that restores and continues cultural memories'.[78] Our research envisaged a somewhat similar re-storying of the select Bible stories, not so much in order to restore and preserve cultural memory, but

---

[77] For a discussion of this, see Theodore W. Jennings, *The Man Jesus Loved: Homoerotic Narratives from the New Testament* (Cleveland: The Pilgrim Press, 2003).

[78] Qwo-Li Driskill, *Asegi Stories: Cherokee Queer and Two-Spirit Memory* (Tucson: University of Arizona Press, 2016), 3.

Figure 1 Group work during a Contextual Bible Study session; 18 January 2020 (© The Nature Network)

to appropriate the Bible and generate new sacred queer stories. Earlier, we quoted Melissa Wilcox stating that 'personal stories react to and interact with sacred stories, but they also create them'.[79] Thus, the group process in stage two was designed to facilitate such a process, where participants could engage and interact with the biblical stories, in dialogue with their own life experiences, in order to engender a re-storied version of the original narrative. The aim was for this new version to be recognisably inspired by the original biblical story but allowing for creativity and freedom in its appropriation and narration.

The group process

The group process of re-storying evolved in two phases. The first phase centred around reading and engaging the biblical story, while the second phase centred around retelling and dramatising the story. In the case of the Daniel story, this process occurred over two days, which was necessary because of the length of the story and the size of the group. In the session

---

[79] Melissa M. Wilcox, *Queer Religiosities: An Introduction to Transgender and Queer Studies in Religion* (Lanham: Rowman & Littlefield 2020), 55.

about the story of Jesus and the 'adulterous woman', both phases were combined in one day, which was possible as the story is much shorter, and the number of participants was considerably smaller (15 compared to 28).

The phase of reading and engaging the biblical story, unfolded in a number of steps. As a warm-up, participants were asked to talk to their neighbour about what they remembered of the story, and to write this down together on paper. Everyone was then handed a printed copy of the Bible story, which was read aloud in small groups, everyone taking a verse in turn.[80] Each participant was asked to use three coloured markers to highlight the parts of the story they liked, they did not like, and they did not understand. The facilitator in each group initiated a conversation about this, and each group was asked to summarise key points of their discussion on a flipchart. On another large piece of paper, they were asked to identify the main characters of the story, and to list their characteristics. This then developed into a small group conversation about which character they identified with, and how the other characters could be linked to their own life situations. The flipchart papers were put on a wall in the main room, where the whole group gathered for a plenary discussion in which each small group shared their findings. The lead facilitators identified the commonalities and differences in terms of what the various groups had come up with and worked with the group towards a consensus about the overall message of the story, and how it linked to the shared situation and life experiences of participants.

The second phase built on the conclusions and on the points of consensus that had been reached. It began with brainstorming, in the plenary group, about the possible ways in which the story could be creatively re-told. With both stories, the group felt most comfortable with, and excited about, creating a piece of drama, enacting the story in a familiar contemporary context. The drama script was developed, with input from all participants, and the roles were democratically assigned, with all participants being given some responsibility – acting, directing, filming, or otherwise assisting. Each of the scenes was rehearsed one by one, after which the whole drama play was performed and filmed on video camera. Basically, in the course of an afternoon, the group produced a creative piece of drama re-storying the Bible

---

[80] We used the translation from the Good News Bible. One reason was that while other translations (e.g. the New Revised Standard Version) are recommended in higher education settings, and while the King James Version may be beloved in many church settings, the Good News Bible is written in clear, everyday language and particularly accessible and suitable for those for whom English is a non-primary language.

story in a contemporary context. The video recordings were later edited by Josh, a TNN member with relevant technical skills, and uploaded on the TNN YouTube channel from where it was shared on social media. We asked Tom Rogers Muyunga-Mukasa, another TNN member (introduced earlier in this book), who is known for writing poetry, to write a poem for each of the two stories we had worked with. These poems, which present another form of re-storying, are included in this book. A week or so after the group sessions, follow-up interviews were conducted with a small number of participants (five after the Daniel story, and four after the story about Jesus and the woman caught in adultery). The purpose of these individual interviews was for participants to have digested the story and the process of re-storying and to share their reflections.

The next two chapters offer a detailed analysis of the process of re-storying the two Bible stories in contemporary contexts, and of inter-reading the Bible stories with the participants' life stories. In addition to the individual interviews conducted in stage one of the project, the materials produced in the second stage of group work – flipchart papers, recordings of group discussions, the video-recorded drama piece, the poems, and the follow-up interviews – form the data on which these chapters are based.

2

Daniel in the Homophobic Lions' Den

If the number of paintings, children's books, and cartoon films about the story of Daniel in the lions' den is anything to go by, then this Old Testament story of the righteous Daniel, saved from a violent death and vindicated, speaks to the imagination and is widely known.[1] This is true for Western contexts where the story has a rich reception history, but also for contemporary African contexts, at least for the Ugandan LGBTQ+ refugees participating in our project.

As mentioned in the previous chapter, participants in the life story interviews came up with a range of Bible stories, which they were often able to narrate with quite some detail and to connect to their own life experiences. Both Tigan and Julius named Daniel in the lions' den as their favourite story in the Bible (Stories 2 and 10). Working with this story in the second part of the project, which focused on contextual and creative Bible study, turned out to be a rich and stimulating process.

The present chapter examines how this ancient biblical story provided a rich interface, or a collective 'reflective surface', with the life experiences of Ugandan LGBTQ+ refugees.[2] Many of the specific narrative elements

---

[1] E.g. see Hugh S. Pyper, 'Looking into the Lions' Den: Otherness, Ideology, and Illustration in Children's Versions of Daniel 6', in Caroline Vander Stichele and Hugh S. Pyper (eds), *Text, Image, and Otherness in Children's Bibles: What is in the Picture?* (Atlanta: Society of Biblical Literature, 2012), 51–72.

[2] About the Bible as a 'reflective surface' in contemporary African communities, specifically in dialogues about homosexuality, see Charlene van der Walt, 'Is "Being Right" More Important than "Being Together"? Intercultural Bible Reading and Life-giving Dialogue on Homosexuality in the Dutch Reformed Church, South Africa', in Ezra Chitando and Adriaan van Klinken (eds), *Christianity and Controversies over Homosexuality in Contemporary Africa* (London and New York: Routledge, 2016), 137. We prefer the term 'interface' over 'surface' to highlight the dialogical nature of the process of inter-reading life and Bible stories.

of the Daniel story resonated with participants' experiences of vulnerability, struggle, and hope. In particular the story proved to map closely on to one of the most tragic socio-political events in their lifetime: the passing of the Anti-Homosexuality Bill in their home country, Uganda, which forced many of them to leave for Kenya. The character with whom they readily identified was Daniel. The lions' den was variously linked to the situation back home in Uganda, but also to the perilous state of affairs as refugees in Kenya. The character of God in the biblical story inspired participants' faith that God would come to *their* rescue, too, as he did to Daniel. What follows in this chapter is an account of the process of inter-reading and dramatising Daniel in the lions' den vis-à-vis participants' lives, and of the new sacred and queer story that was engendered as a result. Thematically speaking, this chapter reconstructs the hermeneutics of LGBTQ+ liberation that emerged from this process.

The story of Daniel

The Bible's book of Daniel consists of two quite different parts. The first (chapters 1–6) contains court tales of Daniel and his friends, all pious Judeans living in exile. This portion is written mostly in Aramaic. The book's later part (chapters 7–12) consists of Daniel's visions. These chapters belong to a genre called apocalyptic prophecy and are mostly in Hebrew, the primary original language of the Old Testament. Interestingly, it has recently been suggested that the two parts of the book can be seen as 'a meaningful whole' when understood as a portrayal of the 'psychological and spiritual reactions of the Jewish people to their experiences of trauma, exile and loss'.[3]

The story of Daniel in the lions' den (chapter 6) is the final story in the first part and is set in the court of King Darius the Mede. Darius elevates Daniel to high office, which incites the jealousy of the other courtiers (referred to as 'governors' and 'supervisors' in the translation of the Good News Bible). Knowing of Daniel's devotion to the God of Israel, the courtiers trick Darius into issuing an order that prohibits the worship of anyone other than the king. As the courtiers knew he would, Daniel continues to pray to his God, as usual. Forced by his own unalterable royal decree, Darius has to follow the order and impose its punishment. Daniel is thrown into the lions' den, leaving Darius distraught. But God sends an

---

[3] Stewart Gabel, 'The Book of Daniel: Trauma, Faith, and the Resurrection of the Dead', *Trauma and Memory*, 4:1 (2016), 67–81.

angel to protect Daniel and close the lions' mouths. The next morning, Daniel is found unharmed. The king commands that all who conspired against Daniel be thrown into the den, together with their wives and children, and that all should fear and worship the God of Daniel.

This is a pious tale of devotion overcoming adversity and of God protecting and rewarding his faithful servant. It has similarities with the story of Daniel 3, where again, jealous courtiers conspire, this time against three friends of Daniel. In this story God also rescues his loyal servants, this time from a fiery furnace. How can such pious tales be read from queer and African perspectives?

The book of Daniel from queer and African perspectives

One queer purpose of this book is to combine and interface the life stories of Ugandan LGBTQ+ refugees in Nairobi with Bible stories. As mentioned in the previous chapter, there are some precursors that use life stories in the service of queer theology. Furthermore, the book of Daniel, too, has been identified as a queer text. Hence, US biblical scholar Mona West, writing in *The Queer Bible Commentary,* comments that, queerly, the book of Daniel is in two different languages (Hebrew and Aramaic) and has Greek additions. Moreover, it thematically centres on 'the politics of resistance and the indeterminacy of identity'.[4] Notably, West points out, it features eunuchs, whom she characterises as 'gender go-betweens', in starring roles and, thereby highlights the possibilities 'that queer people offer to today's society … "gifts of creativity, originality, art, magic, and theater"'.[5] We only consulted West's chapter of the commentary after recording the Daniel drama in Matasia and the refugees were unaware of it. In hindsight, however, 'gifts of creativity, originality, art, magic, and theater' reads as almost prophetic.

There have been suggestions that Daniel himself and his friends were eunuchs or 'gender go-betweens'. In Daniel 1:3–4, the king orders the head-*saris* to bring him some Israelites of royal descent, 'youths without blemish, handsome, proficient in all wisdom'. The word *saris* can refer either to a high official, or a eunuch, or both: that is, a eunuch who is *also* a high official.[6] Whether 'eunuch' refers to someone who was castrated,

---

[4] Mona West, 'Daniel', in Deryn Guest, Robert E. Goss, Mona West and Thomas Bohache (eds), *The Queer Bible Commentary* (London: SCM, 2006), 427.

[5] Ibid., 429, 430 (here West is quoting Nancy Wilson).

[6] The origin of the word *saris* is disputed. It appears to be of Semitic language origin and may originally be Old Aramaic or Assyrian.

or unable to father children, or to someone we might today call either 'intersex' or 'gender-queer', is impossible to establish. But there is reference to Israelites of royal descent who (like Daniel) served in Babylon (2 Kings 20:18), as well as to eunuchs who returned from exile and who, as faithful servants of God, shared in restoration and great honour (Isaiah 56:4–5). Daniel might indeed be a character legitimately claimed as queer, as is explored in scholarly speculations.[7] In a post on the QSpirit website, Daniel appears as part of a series on LGBTQ+ saints.[8] Alongside this queer potentiality, Daniel was also much renowned: he is listed elsewhere in the Bible alongside two other greats, Noah and Job, as an exemplar of righteousness (Ezekiel 14:14).

The book of Daniel has been the focus of some African-centred interpretations but not prominently so. Interpretations of Daniel by African scholars tend to focus not on sexuality or queerness but on either politics of governance or on migration. Regarding the first, for Tokunboh Adeyemo 'the book powerfully demonstrates that believers can serve with distinction under ungodly regimes without compromising their convictions. Daniel offers the church in Africa a model of servant leadership that is desperately needed today'.[9] Mourna Esaie de-Sia Lawman, in his doctoral thesis, uses the first six chapters of Daniel to reflect on leadership and corruption in both South Africa and Chad.[10] The ongoing research of Blessing Nyahuma, meanwhile, examines the genre of apocalyptic

---

[7] See for instance: Joshua H. Miller, '"Until Death Do We (Queers) Part": (Queer) Biblical Interpretation, (Invented) Truth, and Presumption in Controversies Concerning Biblical Characters' Sexualities', *QED: A Journal in GLBTQ Worldmaking*, 4:1 (2017), 42–67; and Brian C. Di Palma, *Masculinities in the Court Tales of Daniel: Advancing Gender Studies in the Hebrew Bible* (Oxford, New York: Routledge, 2018).

[8] Kittredge Cherry, 'Daniel and the Three Young Men: God Rescues Biblical Eunuchs, Affirming LGBTQ People of Faith', QSpirit, 21 July 2020. https:// qspirit.net/daniel/three-young-men-eunuchs (accessed 16 December 2020).

[9] Tokunboh Adeyemo, 'Daniel', in Tokunboh Adeyemo (ed.), *Africa Bible Commentary* (Nairobi: WordAlive Publishers and Grand Rapids: Zondervan, 2006), 989. The two topics Adeyemo singles out in text boxes are 'Dreams' (with both the book of Daniel and many African traditions recognising dreams as channels of communication between human and spiritual worlds, p.993) and 'Christians and Politics' (where he stresses the need for Christians to participate in politics, like Daniel and his friends do, p.1001).

[10] Mourna Esaie de-Sia Lawman, 'Reading the Book of Daniel in an African Context: The Issue of Leadership' (DTheol. thesis, University of South Africa, 2013).

biblical literature (including Daniel 7–12, although primarily focusing on the New Testament) as a lens to probe political chaos in Zimbabwe.[11] Concerning migration and migrant status, biblical scholar Andrew M. Mbuvi, a Kenyan immigrant to the US, expresses affinity with Daniel and his companions: 'In parallel fashion to the story in Daniel, the beginning [for me] meant something of a social dislocation and a loss of privilege.'[12] Mbuvi is also sensitive to xenophobia in the book of Daniel. He notes that Daniel's friends are first referred to as 'young men' (1:17) and 'friends' (2:13) but are racially designated as *yehudai* ('Judeans') by their Babylonian accusers (3:8). In the story of Daniel and the lions' den, too, the zealous courtiers report Daniel for being unpatriotic, adding that he is 'one of the exiles from Judah' (6:13). For Mbuvi this recalls '[m]any Arabs in the United States today' who also 'find themselves in the "lion's den" simply for, among others, their profiles, religion and heritage, which link them to the events of 9/11.'[13] Political machinations, particularly while negotiating marginal migrant status, is the topic that draws African biblical interpreters to the book of Daniel.[14]

As outlined in the previous chapter, African queer interpretations of the Bible are scarce, and as far as we know, they do not exist for the book of Daniel. As will emerge below, the participants in our project most often experienced the Bible as a tool of condemnation and judgement. Tellingly, after watching the recording of their dramatisation of the Daniel story, one

[11] Nyahuma is a PhD candidate at the University of Bamberg in Germany.

[12] Andrew M. Mbuvi, 'Daniel', in Hugh R. Page, Jr. (ed.), *The Africana Bible: Reading Israel's Scriptures from Africa and the African Diaspora* (Minneapolis: Fortress Press, 2010), 274.

[13] Ibid., 277.

[14] For an insightful postcolonial reading of the text, showing how Daniel and his fellow exiles turn their hybrid identity towards effective resistance, see the chapter by Hong Kong postcolonial critic Philip Chia, 'On Naming the Subject: Postcolonial Reading of Daniel 1', in R. S. Sugirtharajah (ed.), *The Postcolonial Biblical Reader* (Oxford: Blackwell, 2006), 171–185. African biblical interpreters have made similar points about subversive hybrid identities challenging imperialism, focusing on the biblical book of Esther. See Joseph Quayesi-Amakye, 'In the Citadel of Susa was a Jewish "Troublemaker": A Sociopolitical Reading of Esther 3 and 4', *Ghana Journal of Religion and Theology*, 7:1 (2017), 51–63; Tsaurayi K. Mapfeka, 'Empire and Identity Secrecy: A Postcolonial Reflection on Esther 2:10', in Johanna Stiebert and Musa W. Dube (eds), *The Bible, Centres and Margins: Dialogues Between Postcolonial African and British Scholars* (London: T&T Clark, 2018), 79–95.

of them said, 'this is the first time the Bible was not used against me' – which was met with nods of agreement. As such, our sacred queer story of Daniel offers a distinctive and empowering voice of liberation, building on existing traditions of African biblical hermeneutics of liberation but expanding their scope by explicitly applying them to communities marginalised on the basis of their non-conforming sexuality and gender identity.

Meeting Prophet Daniel at The Nature Network

While neither a queer reading of Daniel, nor an African reading of Daniel is a new thing, a queer African reading of Daniel 6 by LGBTQ+ refugees in Kenya for restorative and liberating purposes, *is* novel.

The initial impetus for selecting Daniel 6 was that two of the participants, Tigan and Julius, referred to the story of Daniel in the lions' den in their life story interviews. Tigan begins by apologising, saying 'I'm not really a Bible person'. But then he mentions this story and says, 'I would connect to that story in the way that the homophobic people in Uganda, our families … threw us into the lions' den' (Story 2). Although Tigan, on being exposed as gay, was rejected by his family (as he recounts movingly), the Bible story nonetheless makes him hopeful: 'By the time [our families] will come to check on us, we shall be prosperous, we shall still be here, we shall be alive, because God loves us.' Tigan sees 'a very big ray of hope' and recognises divine love for LGBTQ+ persons in God blessing them. He asserts:

> if … they throw us into the lions' den because of that, I believe that no, we shall not be eaten. We shall not. Like Daniel, we have survived a lot, and we are still around, we are surviving, we didn't die when we went through persecution, blackmailing, sex work – and now we are here.

Along similar lines, Julius also says:

> as an LGBTIQ person here in Kenya, I connect my life to that of a man called Daniel, in the Bible. Daniel, too, went through a lot of problems; he got thrown into a lion cage or something. It was a terrible moment for him; he had to look at how to get out of that lions' cage but he couldn't manage it. It was because of God's strength that Daniel survived that very difficult situation. That is like the kind of situation that a gay person refugee is facing. (Story 10)

Both Tigan and Julius spontaneously inter-read the story from Daniel 6 with their own experiences in a way that both acknowledges hardship *and* offers optimism and hope. The story reaffirms their hope, or faith, that with the help of God they and fellow LGBTQ+ refugees will survive their struggle, and not just survive but prosper.

Having agreed on taking Daniel 6 forward for group inter-reading, Raymond and Hudson as local research coordinators conducted the first meeting, which they called 'Meeting Prophet Daniel at The Nature Network.'[15] At the conclusion of this meeting, one participant, Tom, asserted the significance and relevance of the Bible to the queer refugee community, saying, 'there's something in the Bible for us. But we also need to be empowered to be able to energise what's in the Bible for us.' Further unpacking and revealing this 'something' through creative expression became the focus of the second meeting.[16] Here the Bible story was re-storied in the contemporary context, and the new story was dramatised and video recorded.[17] This session began by again reading and briefly discussing in small groups the text of Daniel 6, in order to remind participants of the details of the story and to recapture the discussions from the first meeting. It was striking how earnest everyone became when reading the text of the Bible, which was done going around in a circle, with each person reading a verse in turn. This time, the brief was not just to read the story but to relate it to life experience in a new and creative way. After a short discussion in the smaller groups, everyone came together to pool ideas and collectively to develop and act the drama. This happened over the course of one very full day. Josh, who served as videographer during the day, said in a follow-on interview that he had not felt quite sure about whether people would be interested in such an activity but that to his surprise the energy was tremendous and sustained: 'it was like – boom! – it was a full day!'[18]

Of special focus in the first session about the story were three questions: 'What did you like?', 'What did you not like?', and 'What did you not understand?' The purpose of this was first to ensure that participants

---

[15] The meeting took place at The Nature Network in Matasia on 16 November 2019 and had 22 participants.

[16] The second meeting took place at The Nature Network in Matasia on 12 January 2020. In total, almost 30 persons registered and about 20 of them participated actively throughout. This second meeting was again led by Raymond and Hudson but this time Adriaan and Johanna were also present. Tina gave a précis of what had transpired at the first meeting, referring to detailed charts covering the walls of the meeting room that summarised the collectively produced findings.

[17] *Daniel in the Homophobic Lions' Den*, produced by Josh (Nairobi: The Nature Network 2020), www.youtube.com/watch?v=-0j9xq6xX8c (accessed on 16 December 2020).

[18] Interview with Josh, Matasia on 15 January 2020.

familiarised themselves with the story and understood it, and second to reflect on the story in a way that validated personal perspectives and assessment. In terms of what the participants liked about the story, most prominent were the characters of Daniel and God. They liked Daniel because he was 'different', 'hard-working and prayerful', 'respectful', 'loyal', 'God-fearing', 'better than the others', 'courageous' in 'rebelling against the wrongful law' and in 'sticking to his principles'. They liked God because of his love, being 'a living God' and rescuing Daniel, because he 'performs wonders and miracles' and 'sent his angel to shut the mouth of the lions'. They did not like that the king signed the order, the 'rigid law', and that Daniel was cast into the lions' den. Above all, they had a general dislike for the governors, on account of their 'accusation', 'jealousy', 'envy', 'discrimination', 'conspiracy' and 'corrupting the king's mind'. In terms of the third question, the bulk of confusion centred on the king's order: why could it not be changed? Why did Darius, who clearly liked Daniel and admired his God, sign the order? Why did he submit to casting Daniel into the den of lions and then also rejoice when he survived? One other matter that raised some confusion was why, at the end of the story, the governors' wives and children were thrown into the den along with the governors.

From the deliberations a consensus emerged that the story had applicability to the participants' circumstances, as well as a message for them. Josh took from the story that it is important 'always being persistent to what you think is right, your freedom, your rights'. Tina, too, identified a message urging persistence and motivation: 'Maybe if you're a gay, it's not the end of the world: you should continue to fight, people shouldn't judge your appearance but should judge you by the services you provide.' Israel also felt heartened and inspired: 'People should be open to try new things, because, as you see, Daniel was in a foreign country but still it didn't stop him from working.' For one unnamed participant the take-home message was an affirmation of faith: 'I stand with God.' Faith in God came up often. Tigan said, 'The message that I've gotten from this is being humble. Daniel was humble, he still went ahead and prayed.' Another participant drew the following lesson:

> Be courageous. Daniel was prayerful during his toughest times ever, you know! And God helped him, so, as a gay refugee, however much they postpone you at UNHCR or the Embassy, you should not lose hope. So keep holding on there and don't lose hope!

The story of God coming to Daniel's rescue was taken as a sign that 'God has a reason why he created Daniel, and God has a reason why he created us LGBTQ+I. It means he wants us to live.' For another participant, too, the story's purpose was to show any detractors, such as the family or community who rejected you on the grounds of your sexual orientation: 'Show them a godly heart, you can help them, show them a heart of God in you. That will make them cry.'

Taken together, these responses demonstrate two points very clearly. First, participants' readiness and enthusiasm for accepting the book of Daniel as meaningful and authoritative. This is no surprise, given our discussion of the status of the Bible in contemporary African societies in the previous chapter. However, it is significant in a context where the Bible is widely used in African sexual politics, not only by Christians but also by Muslims, that LGBTQ+ people do not necessarily reject the Bible as sacred scripture but willingly engage and mine it.[19] Second, in engaging and mining the biblical text, our participants demonstrated considerable dexterity in terms of making the ancient story relevant to their own circumstances and experiences. Tigan and Julius did so spontaneously in the life story interviews, drawing meaningful connections between the story and their own life situations (Stories 2 and 10). Participants in the group process enthusiastically followed up on this by further exploring the multiple ways in which the Bible story speaks to their life stories, and vice versa.

Raymond and Hudson reported in their reflection on the process that the highlight for them was how 'the participants connected their situations with the story and the way people felt conversant with sharing their personal experiences'. They clearly felt energised by this, saying:

> The outcomes were so real, and right there before our own eyes. The sessions allowed us to like the Bible again. There were remarks among some who said they did not know the Old Testament had something that could relate with them. But the session allowed us to think deeply about the different causes of divisions among people, which most times are based on prejudice and unfounded conclusions. The community needs sessions like these ones about the Bible and other religious books. Participants found hope and strength. They were able to turn around and find meaning from the scriptures often used for preaching hate about them. They left knowing there are rays of hope. The session gave back to participants the keys to use to analyse scripture.

[19] See Kapya Kaoma, '"I Say, We Must Talk, Talk, Mama!" Introducing African Voices on Religion, *Ubuntu* and Sexual Diversity', *Journal of Theology for Southern Africa*, 155 (2016), 19–21.

Multiple identifications and associations

Throughout the process during the two sessions, characters and events in the biblical story were associated and identified with the refugees' experiences in a variety of ways. In Tom's poetic words, 'In Daniel's story is revealed, / many mysteries, / and many dens of lions' (see the poem, 'The Company of Men', following this chapter).

Daniel

The participants generally identified themselves with Daniel, because 'like Daniel we know the rules are wrong and that what we are doing and feeling is right and true to ourselves and our God' and because 'we too are seeking justice'. Dhalie stood out, saying they identified *not* with Daniel but instead with 'guys that were supporting Daniel'. Dhalie explained that this was because, especially while in Uganda, it was easier to be a human rights defender than an 'out' and outspoken gay rights advocate.[20] Affinity with Daniel's vulnerable status as an exile and refugee was acknowledged by several participants. Isaac expressed the pathos of this status vividly:

> It's so disheartening to be a refugee and asylum seeker. You lack proper documentation; you can't have an account in the bank; you can't involve yourself in an economic activity without proper documentation. You can't access health care or insurance. It's like you're an orphan.[21]

Above all, however, Daniel was appropriated as signifying the queer community. Probably, this was because discrimination on account of sexual orientation or non-conforming gender identity was experienced even more acutely than discrimination on account of poverty or refugee status. Dhalie captures this in their life story interview where they emphasise that LGBTQ+ refugees are particularly unsafe:

> Trust me, no one is trying to kill a pregnant Somali woman here in Kenya but a trans woman is not going to be safe to just move freely. Other refugees are also escaping trouble back home but when they are here, no one is trying to kill them. (Story 6)

The suggestion here is that a non-conforming sexual and gender identity – maybe in particular being trans – adds an extra layer of vulnerability to the insecurities and risks that come with being a refugee. The reference to the possibility of being killed is not illusionary, as there are numerous stories

[20] Interview with Dhalie, Matasia, 15 January 2020.
[21] Interview with Isaac, Matasia, 15 January 2020.

of violent physical attacks on LGBTQ+ people, both in Uganda and in Kenya, sometimes resulting in death.[22]

In the drama, Daniel is cast as an LGBTQ+ activist in Uganda who serves as a human rights advisor to the president but becomes the first victim of the law signed by the president. The virtues that participants had identified in the biblical Daniel – respect, loyalty, a courageous, determined, and God-fearing manner – are embodied by the actor in the drama when he emphasises being a loyal, tax-paying citizen and good Christian, while simultaneously strongly protesting against the bill his fellow advisors are pushing for. In Tom's poem, 'The Company of Men', Daniel describes himself as 'a companion of a steadfast God'. This captures the belief of participants more generally that Daniel – both in the biblical narrative, and in the contemporary retelling – is on the side of God, and God is on the side of Daniel.

King Darius

King Darius in the Bible story evoked mixed feelings among participants. As a leader, he is described with words such as 'clear-minded', 'visionary', and 'powerful'. Descriptors such as 'gullible', 'proud', 'authoritarian', and 'manipulative' were used to refer to the king allowing himself to be talked into signing the egocentric decree that no one but he should be worshipped in his empire. Yet other descriptors, such as 'friendly', 'loving', 'caring', 'charitable', and 'trustworthy', were also used to capture the king's sympathetic disposition towards Daniel, his trusted advisor, who became the victim of his own decree. Darius is further described as 'hot tempered' and 'ruthless', which probably relates to the ending of the story where he orders all his governors, their wives and children, to be thrown into the lions' den.

In the group discussions, the character of the king in the story was associated with the government of Uganda in general, but more specifically with Uganda's president, Yoweri Museveni. In the dramatisation, the king indeed became the president, although the president wears a crown, and the first lady seated next to him is dressed in a regal robe and calls herself 'the mother of the nation'. Certainly, this president has a somewhat royal appearance, which perhaps mirrors the fact that Museveni has been in office since 1986 and by his critics is seen as increasingly nepotistic and

---

[22] One of the most well-known and brutal cases, referred to by some of our participants, is the murder of Ugandan gay activist, David Kato, in his home near Kampala, in 2011. See also note 52.

autocratic.[23] Like King Darius, the president in the drama gets talked into signing a new law by his advisors, in this case the Anti-Homosexuality Bill (AHB). He does so reluctantly, referring the first draft of the bill back to parliament. This reflects events in Uganda, where Museveni 'sought to restrain enthusiasm for the AHB' and 'maintained a studied ambivalence' towards it, 'in an attempt to court both an evangelical Christian constituency opposed to homosexuality and an international donor community committed to LGBT rights'.[24] This ambivalence is reflected in the drama, where the president first reluctantly gives in to signing the bill, but later nullifies it on formal grounds – however, without questioning the intentions of the bill as such. In the dramatisation, as in Uganda's recent past, Museveni is more temperate than some of his more zealously homophobic MPs, notably David Bahati. As in the dramatisation, Museveni, too, made recourse to 'medical experts' and also attempted to achieve a compromise that softened some of the more fervent voices in his government.

Governors

The governors scheming against Daniel were seen by participants as the real culprits, the 'bad guys', both in the Bible story and in the dramatisation. Their collective character in the biblical story is described as 'jealous' and 'envious'. Additionally, they are called 'traitors', and associated with 'dishonesty' and 'conspiracy', and blamed for 'corrupting the king's mind'. These characteristics were applied to the contemporary context, where participants associated the governors with the forces campaigning against the LGBTQ+ community. They identified them partly with abstract realities, such as 'African culture' or 'religion', but more often with particular groups of people, such as 'pastors' and 'MPs', or 'maybe just some MPs – not all MPs'. David Bahati, the Ugandan MP who initiated the AHB and relentlessly lobbied for it to pass through parliament, was mentioned specifically here, as was Pastor Martin Ssempa, a religious leader who has been very vocal in the anti-homosexuality crusade in Uganda. The fact that not only politicians, but also religious leaders are associated with the governors in the Bible story can be seen as an acknowledgement of the prominent socio-political role that religious leaders play in Uganda, as in other parts of Africa, effectively blurring

---

[23] Deborah Kintu, *The Ugandan Morality Crusade: The Brutal Campaign against Homosexuality and Pornography under Yoweri Museveni* (Jefferson: McFarland, 2018).

[24] Rahul Rao, *Out of Time: The Queer Politics of Postcoloniality* (New York: Oxford University Press, 2020), 4.

the boundaries between religion and politics, and between church and state. Many religious leaders are, indeed, spearheading the campaigns against homosexuality and LGBTQ+ rights in Africa.[25]

The royal decree

In the Bible story, King Darius is persuaded by his governors to sign a decree stipulating that whoever, for a duration of thirty days, petitions any god or man except the king, shall be cast into the den of lions. Once signed by the king, this decree – according to the ancient law of the Medes and Persians – becomes unalterable.

The dramatisation depicts the presentation of the 'Kill the Gays Bill', later renamed the Anti-Homosexuality Bill, to the president. This recalls directly the bill considered by the Ugandan parliament, which became known informally by the former name on account of its proposal of the death penalty for same-sex sex acts. Several participants such as Raymond, Kyle, Doreen, and Julius, refer in their life stories to the heightened and dangerous tensions of the time around the passing of the AHB (Stories 1, 3, 8, and 10). Doreen, for instance, describes how the bill was everywhere – in the tabloids and in everyday conversation. She describes trying to escape attention and dropping out of schooling because of the oppressive homophobia all around, which made her yearn as follows: 'I wanted just to explode everything away. To just be me' (Story 8).

The dramatisation is at its most vivid and impassioned in the scene where Daniel and his supporters, on the one hand, the condemners on the other, make their respective cases for and against the bill. On one side are heartfelt cries of 'we have done nothing wrong', 'we are your subjects, voting for you and paying our taxes', 'we want to live and love in peace', 'we were born this way'. The discursive strategy here is that Daniel and his friends make a claim towards political citizenship and sexual respect-ability: the latter in Ugandan society being a condition for the former.[26] On the other side are angry cries of 'it's not African', 'it's a vice', 'stop

---

[25] See Kevin Ward, 'Religious Institutions and Actors and Religious Attitudes to Homosexual Rights: South Africa and Uganda', in Matthew Waites and Corinne Lennox (eds), *Human Rights, Sexual Orientation and Gender Identity in The Commonwealth: Struggles for Decriminalisation and Change* (London: Institute of Commonwealth Studies, 2013), 410–428.

[26] Joanna Sadgrove, Robert M. Vanderbeck, Johan Andersson, Gill Valentine, and Kevin Ward, 'Morality Plays and Money Matters: Towards a Situated Understanding of the Politics of Homosexuality in Uganda', *Journal of Modern African Studies*, 50:1 (2012), 103–129.

recruiting the young', 'it's a Western import', 'the Bible says'. These echo the popular religio-political discourses in Uganda and other African countries, in which homosexuality is framed as imported and, therefore, non-autochthonous.[27] This notion was firmly rejected by several of the participants, including Kyle: 'It's certainly not white people who taught me to be homosexual. ... I didn't see any white person in my young age' (Story 3). Yet this notion is widely embraced in Uganda, one consequence being that sexual minorities have been denied citizenship and excluded from the body of the nation.[28] Hence, the play clearly expresses intimate familiarity both with discrimination from multiple sides and with the arguments that make the counter case.

Where the royal decree in the Bible story is unalterable, the Anti-Homosexuality Act in Uganda was, in fact, nullified by the Constitutional Court on procedural grounds. In the dramatisation, the president quotes the same reason as the court did for its decision: the lack of quorum when the bill was passed through parliament. In announcing this nullification, the president stresses that this was the first ever Anti-Homosexuality Act in Africa. While seemingly succumbing to pressure from Western countries, he tries to save face, emphasising that Ugandans are not 'vassals and servants of the Western world' but, instead, citizens of a democracy. Following this, Daniel is released and there is a jubilant celebration by his supporters and disgruntlement from his enemies. The dramatisation thus ends on a high, with Daniel being granted freedom, and the governors defeated. Yet in reality, although the act was nullified, the effect of nullification on the LGBTQ+ community in Uganda was negligible. This is evidenced by the fact that most of our participants fled the country at a time when the act was no longer in place: the climate of politicised homophobia persisted in making their lives unbearable.

---

[27] These discourses certainly can be and have been challenged. Two recent examples are the contributions in Ezra Chitando (ed.), *Engaging with the Past: Same-Sex Relationships in Pre-Colonial Zimbabwe* (Geneva: WCC Publications, 2015) and an article by S. N. Nyeck, 'African Religions, the Parapolitics of Discretion and Sexual Ambiguity in African Oral Epics', *Journal of Theology for Southern Africa* 155 (2016): 88–103.

[28] See Adriaan van Klinken and Ebenezer Obadare, 'Christianity, Sexuality and Citizenship in Africa: Critical Intersections', *Citizenship Studies*, 22:6 (2018), 557–568.

Figure 2 Daniel in prison. Video still from 'Daniel in the Homophobic Lions' Den'; 12 January 2020 (© The Nature Network)

The lions' den

In the process of unpacking the story, interesting conversations emerged about the place of the lions' den, and about the associations with the lions. The den was 'how society makes you feel', and it was related not only to Uganda – the place they escaped from – but also to Kenya, where they currently find themselves. Although the refugees had left Uganda in search for a safer environment, Kenya, in the understated words of Tigan, 'is not like heaven' either (Story 2).

The lions in the Bible story were reminiscent of realities in their own lives in multiple ways. For some, the lions symbolise family and community members – 'they can do harm, but they don't always', as one participant put it. Poignant among accounts of family rejection are those of Tigan (particularly the point during his expulsion from home, when he turns to his mother to whom he always felt very close: 'she didn't look at me'; Story 2) and also Henry and Keeya who suffered threats and violence from family members (Stories 5 and 11). In terms of the community, the lions could be neighbours, landlords, employers, teachers, and classmates – anyone involved in the everyday policing of the norms of gender and sexuality in society.

Interestingly, it was suggested that lions could also be found within the LGBTQ+ community: the community 'contains enemies who blackmail, deny, divide: they too are lions'. Kennedy and Keeya both relate how they were reported to the police by persons within the LGBTQ+ community (Stories 11 and 12). Plenty of reference was made by others to jealousy, division, sexual violence, and blackmailing, which can make the community itself a toxic and dangerous environment. Blackmailing refers to the practice where certain LGBTQ+ persons coerce money from fellow LGBTQ+ people by threatening to disclose their sexual identities or to make public sensitive information.[29] Tigan's story about his boss making him work for free, and demanding sexual favours from him, is a case in point.

In the dramatisation, however, the lions are the police. Police brutality and corruption – both in Uganda and in Kenya – were recurrent themes in the stories of participants. Moreover, police violence was not only familiar but unanimously and unequivocally condemned, whereas characterising either family or factions within the LGBTQ+ community as the enemy both raise more complex and more conflicted emotions. Hence, family, while often a locus of disappointment and rejection, is nonetheless prominently associated with love and residual loyalties. Similarly, while there is acknowledgement of conflicts, tensions, and betrayals within LGBTQ+ communities, these are also relied on for support, solidarity, and the formation of new families. In the dramatisation, the lions' den is represented as a prison – something of which several of the refugees have concrete experience, both in Uganda and in Kenya. Doreen and Shamuran were both arrested (Stories 8 and 9); Kennedy was beaten and tortured in police custody (Story 11); Kyle was arrested and kept in prison without charge (Story 3); Cindy spent thirty days in prison where she was 'mocked, teased, and bullied', and 'would sleep in terror, in fear' (Story 4).

But the lions' den was also associated with the precarity of life in Kenya more generally. Julius says in his life story that he feels 'like a prisoner' in Kenya (Story 10). Henry, too, refers to Kenya as 'so bad' and as 'homophobic' (Story 5). Several reported unsympathetic treatment even from RAS (Dhalie, Story 6), guards outside UNHCR (Kyle, Story 3) and UN officials (Henry, Story 5). Most disturbing of all was Tina's disclosure in a one-to-one interview a few days after the dramatisation, when she recalled working in a group of dance performers.[30] A man posing as a client pretended to hire them but kidnapped them instead. Tina recounted, 'We were beaten and had to be hospitalised for a week. All our property was stolen. Kenya is our host country but it is also a den.'

---

[29] See Austin Bryan, 'Kuchu Activism, Queer Sex-work and "Lavender Marriages," in Uganda's Virtual LGBT Safe(r) Spaces', *Journal of Eastern African Studies*, 13:1 (2019), 98.

[30] Interview with Tina, Matasia, 15 January 2020.

God

Participants in the group session identified God as one of the characters in the story, using descriptors such as 'faithful', 'trustworthy', 'miraculous', 'powerful', 'rescuer', and 'a living God'. In the Bible story, God sends an angel to shut the mouth of the lions, which is interpreted in terms of the belief that 'God uses people to help us, the LGBTQ+ refugees'. The way in which God comes to Daniel's rescue is also regarded as a confirmation that 'no matter what challenges we go through, God will see us through'.[31] Although the Bible story puts great emphasis on Daniel's piety and commitment to God, Isaac took from the story that 'whether you're a Christian or not, there is God who will look after you wherever you'll be'.[32]

In the dramatisation, God is present but not particularly active: instead, God is a voice-over. At the beginning, God states that he is love, a living God, omnipresent; at the end, God's voice states that he rules forever, saves and rescues. The final words of the drama play are God's: 'I saved Daniel from prison.' God's power and presence are acknowledged but the events of focus are those in the human realm where God's actions are less visible. Perhaps this reflects the way in which participants themselves experience God: they firmly believe in the existence and goodness of God but do not express strong expectations of miraculous divine interventions in their day-to-day lives. Instead, God appears to be present in the background of their lives, as a source of comfort and care. God's intervention is believed to occur through other people and organisations supporting them. For instance, elaborating on the angel, Tina refers to UNHCR saying, 'Even when governments have disowned us, for the UNHCR we are still people, they see us as human beings. Even when the government says they do not want us, the UNHCR advocates for us.'[33] Yet such mediators, or divine instruments, do not detract from the abiding and dominant role of God, albeit in the background. As Ghanaian theologian Mercy Oduyoye puts it, 'God is always present in human affairs, as in the rest of creation, as judge, healer, and the one who takes the side of the weak and the vulnerable'.[34]

In the dramatisation, when Daniel is arrested, he cries out defiantly, 'God is my witness!', and when he is finally released, he shouts, 'God has helped me!' In between these two scenes, as Daniel suffers in prison, a stirring song, 'Gwasembayo' by Gabie Ntaate, offers words of comfort

---

[31] Interview with Sulah, Matasia, 15 January 2020.

[32] Interview with Isaac, Matasia, 15 January 2020.

[33] Interview with Tina, Matasia, 15 January 2020.

[34] Mercy A. Oduyoye, *Introducing African Women's Theology* (Cleveland: The Pilgrim Press, 2001), 50.

and hope.[35] The lyrics of this Luganda gospel song (which may well be inspired by the biblical book of Job) state that 'he [God] feels whatever we feel; God never tries us beyond what we can do or manage'. The suggestion of this song, at this moment in the play, is that God may test believers through challenges in life – and that the harassment and persecution on the basis of one's sexuality might be one such challenge. But the song also reassures that such tests will not become fatal, as God is in charge and offers support. Thus, the song exemplifies one of the characteristics of gospel music, both in its original black American and its contemporary East African forms: offering spiritual comfort in situations of hardship and distress.[36] The lyrics, together with the song's location in the film, also stress once more the trust that God is in control and ever present, even in the midst of suffering and even when his actions are inscrutable.

(Un)happy ending?

There was not much interest among participants in the rather dramatic ending of the Bible story, where not only the governors but also their wives and families are killed. Although this element was noted, in the group sessions it was not generally identified as a problematic aspect, possibly reflecting a hesitance to engage with a biblical text – part of sacred scripture – critically, negatively, or to question it. Only one participant, Josh, explicitly expressed his discomfort during the group session. Elaborating on this further in the one-to-one follow-up interview, he compared it with a situation in his own life where, when he was challenged and rebuked by his family on account of being gay, his father and brothers were vociferous but his mother not.[37] Josh said, 'My brothers were so much into my business, so I feel like those were the governors of my story.' But his mother, he said, just kept quiet. Josh described that she 'had this look that wasn't an "I hate you" look', and that her eyes said she felt sorry. For Josh, his mother was like the governors' wives and children: she was quiet. Showing his understanding of gender roles in marriage in their culture, he suggests that

---

[35] Gabie Ntaate is a Ugandan gospel artist. Her song 'Gwasembayo' was released on YouTube on 3 May 2019, www.youtube.com/watch?v=K_EwVs-OVHrM (accessed 16 December 2020). The Luganda word *gwasembayo* translates as 'you are the last option'. Raymond explains that if God says 'yes' then no one and nothing can put up resistance.

[36] Damaris Parsitau, 'Gospel Music in Africa', in Elias Bongmba (ed.), *The Wiley-Blackwell Companion to African Religions* (Malden: Wiley-Blackwell, 2012), 489–502.

[37] Interview with Josh, Matasia, 15 January 2020.

as a woman, she could not openly oppose her husband; but he emphasises that she did not actively condemn him either. For Josh, sending the wives and children to the den of lions was wrong: 'What did they do? They did nothing.' The other person to comment on this story element, also in a follow-on one-to-one interview, was Sulah.[38] Asked about it, Sulah said he was particularly unhappy with the killing of the children: 'Why would the children fall victim like the governors and wives? If it was my Daddy who did something wrong, it was him to suffer the consequences and not me.'

In the dramatisation, the element of vengeance on the governors and their families was left out entirely; instead, the story ends on a note of joyful celebration. Vengeance is also absent in the interviews with the refugees. For all the many accounts of suffering and menace – at the hands of family, laws, police, church leaders, and others – there are no expressions of desire for exacting suffering in return. Instead, over and over again, the refugees yearn for lives free from discrimination and, occasionally, for seeing their family members again and making themselves understood. Hence, Sulah said:

> I really want to sit down with my uncle and we talk about things. I feel I have not had closure on these issues. Yes, we talk about things and for them to accept me the way I am. They are still my family, I love them. I would love to meet with the people who inflicted pain on me. I want a sit down and talk, not like preach hate to them because I do not believe that hate should be given back. Hate should be given back with love.[39]

Maybe something Tina said can account for this lack of vengeance and instead the emphasis on love and (in the dramatisation) celebration: 'Most of the times LGBTI are the people who have a kind heart. We are kind-hearted people who love to help, people who love to share.'[40]

The happy and indeed celebratory ending of the drama – Daniel being freed – is striking, especially in the light of the current circumstances of the participants, who generally agreed that Kenya for them is like another lions' den. As mentioned above, the Anti-Homosexuality Act may have been ruled invalid but its long-term effects continue to define the lives of Ugandan LGBTQ+ refugees. The significance of the chosen ending of the dramatisation is threefold. One, it allows the refugees to rewrite history in a way in which they are not just victims of socio-political queer-phobia, but agents and indeed victors. Two, it captures

[38] Interview with Sulah, Matasia, 15 January 2020.
[39] Ibid.
[40] Interview with Tina, Matasia, 15 January 2020.

their current situation in Kenya – a country recalling the lions' den, but where nevertheless they have managed to create safe spaces, in the form of community-based organisations where refugees encourage, support, and nourish one another. Indeed, the joy at the end of the dramatisation reflects the genuine happiness, warmth, and love that we ourselves experienced in The Nature Network's Matasia house and that is attested by several of the storytellers in Part I of this book. Three, partly, the happy ending is aspirational, reflecting the hope that true freedom to live a life of dignity, safety, and respect will come after being resettled in a third country. In the one-on-one interviews following the group session, several participants associated Daniel's rescue with resettlement. In Tina's words:

> That is the moment when you feel yeaaaahhh! I am going where I can do anything I want. I am going where I shall be free. That is the victory that Daniel had. When Daniel was freed by the king, I take that to mean he was resettled.[41]

Likewise, Isaac meditates,

> Personally, the best rescue mission is when you're given the opportunity to leave the lions' den. It feels like one day waking up and being resettled to a country where you are given another chance to breathe, maybe to get married and have a family together. Also, to have a second chance in life to smile, because we are always happy but internally there is always fear because we are still in the lions' den. But one day you wake up and they say you're being resettled to a particular country where there is protection, there are laws that protect you and allow you to have a private life that is enjoyable; and maybe for those who are interested in politics also to engage in law-making and law implementation. So, for me seeing Daniel leave the den, I can say even me at one point I will be out.[42]

The politics of reclaiming

One of the main reasons why the Daniel story offers such a rich interface with the life experiences of participants is that they could read one of the most traumatic socio-political events in their lifetime – the passing of the Anti-Homosexuality Bill – into the story. Popular support for the bill

---

[41] Ibid.
[42] Interview with Isaac, Matasia, 15 January 2020.

by claiming that homophobia is justified by all of 'African culture', the church, the Bible and Islam, was very familiar to them. In academic literature anti-homosexuality legislation such as in Uganda is sometimes called 'protective homophobia', which is also described as uniting disparate religious groups and even credited with 'aiding inter-faith and ecumenical relationships'.[43] The actors playing representatives of these various factions were not short of hateful things to say; in follow-up interviews with Dhalie and Sulah, who played a government minister and a preacher respectively, this came up, too.[44] Dhalie admitted having initial misgivings about playing one of the homophobic parliamentarians: 'I don't like what these people do and now I'm going to be doing this!' Dhalie went on to say, however, that the experience was also poignant: 'When it was coming through my mouth, when I was acting there, I felt like, "oh, these people really feel like this"'. Sulah also reflected on his character:

> It gave me that power of understanding that we should be very careful with what one says. You see, the Bible is a holy book, which people have been using. Be careful with what you utter out. Think about what you say, it could be hurting other people.

Sulah's observation was based on his own experience of being on the receiving end of what is called proof-texting: that is, of plucking excerpts from the Bible out of their context to authorise a particular agenda. Interestingly, the dramatisation was clearly construed by both as empowering: Dhalie came to know the enemy and Sulah refers explicitly to receiving 'that power of understanding'. Possibly, even though the words both actors used in their characterisations were familiar, hateful, and homophobic, it was empowering to externalise, rather than internalise them.

One moment in the dramatisation caused particular hilarity. As Daniel was being abused by police officers, he cried out in indignation, asking why he was being arrested and handcuffed. One of the actors playing a police officer said, 'you're a homo' – which prompted spontaneous outbursts of laughter. Again, rather like with Dhalie and Sulah's roles, here the term of abuse ('homo') was detoxified through drama – to the extent that it provoked humour. This, too, is empowering, and reminiscent of the relexicalisation or reclaiming of terms of abuse or insult as an act of subversion or protest. An example of such is, for instance, the reclaiming of the word 'slut' (formerly exclusively an insult) in women's protest

---

[43] Kaoma, "'I Say, We must Talk'", 22.

[44] Individual interviews with Dhalie and Sulah were conducted in Matasia on 15 January 2020.

marches (called 'slut walks') and the previously derogatory words 'gay' and 'queer' and even – although controversially so – 'faggot' in parts of the queer community.[45] The destructive power of these words is removed both through reclaiming them and through humour, thereby stripping them of toxicity.

Reclaiming also happens through resisting dominant discourses of religion, the Bible, or culture. Regarding the church, Raymond said in his interview, 'you can't handle church, because of the hate', while Henry reported that church says only 'bad things about gays', which is why he would 'rather sit and pray on [his] own' (Story 5). Dhalie, meanwhile, described Islamic communities as similarly discriminatory and being publicly forced out of the mosque (Story 6). The voice of 'culture' (understood to be 'African culture' or 'Ugandan culture'), meanwhile, as Keeya summarises it, states that 'a man is supposed to marry a woman' (Story 12). The Bible, too, is experienced in predominantly hostile ways. Doreen said of the Bible and what is taught in church, '70 per cent was against my flow of life, against my nature, against my being, against my experience' (Story 8).

But participants demonstrated resistance and opposition to these discourses, which in the dramatisation is articulated by the character of Daniel. The life stories and follow-up interviews also provide counter voices. Concerning 'culture', Raymond reported that he came to discover aspects of Buganda history and culture, such as the story of Kabaka Mwanga, the king in the early days of missionary and colonial encounter, that were 'confusing and challenging' in the light of what he was taught about the alleged heteronormativity of African culture (Story 1).[46] Keeya, too, referred to Kabaka Mwanga and said, there is 'nothing new about being trans' (Story 12). Thus, both invoke the contested story about the 19th century Buganda king, who reportedly was involved in same-sex relationships, in order to claim belonging.[47] Kyle, moreover, identified the

---

[45] See Penelope Eckert and Sally McConnell-Ginet, *Language and Gender*, 2nd ed. (Cambridge: Cambridge University Press, 2013), 224.

[46] Raymond captured well the ambivalence of both the Bible and Ugandan culture. As he says in his life story: 'The Bible, it's condemning and loving at the same time. And when you come to culture, there's also love and condemnation.'

[47] For a detailed account of this history and its role in contemporary memory in Uganda, see Rahul Rao, 'Re-membering Mwanga: Same-sex Intimacy, Memory and Belonging in Postcolonial Uganda', *Journal of Eastern African Studies*, 9:1 (2015), 1–19.

tradition of Buganda indigenous religion, according to which all human beings (or at least, all Baganda), including males, are wives of Ndawula, whom he refers to as 'a small god' (Story 3). Ndawula is known as a deity associated with fertility among the Baganda.[48] Kyle associates Ndawula with gender nonconformity, and hence he concludes that 'homosexuality was in our tradition too'. Buganda tradition is clearly treasured by these and other participants. They are not rejecting their heritage; they are respectfully pointing to their rightful place within their tradition. Just as finding queer prototypes in the Bible is important for affirming sacred queer identity and for empowerment, so is the identification of queerness in Buganda culture.

While participants reported that there was considerable hostility directed at them from churches and church leaders, they also mentioned supportive church figures, such as the aforementioned priest, and the retired Anglican bishop, Rt Rev. Dr Christopher Senyonjo.[49] As with Buganda traditions, they expressed affection and yearning for the church and especially for God. Cindy, for instance, acknowledged the damaging things taught in church but maintained nonetheless: 'It's really important for me to go to church, because I need to be connected to God' (Story 4). Similarly, Tina emphasised her Catholic faith: 'I go for Mass every Sunday, unless I am busy. But when I am not, I go to Mass to thank God.'[50] Julius, too, said, 'I keep my faith in God' (Story 10), and Raymond, 'I love God so much' and '[t]he Lord sees the thing that is in you, the pure you' (Story 1). Kennedy feels sure that 'God has planned this for me' (Story 11), and Drake states, 'God loves me most' (Story 7). Dhalie explained that the more they study Islam, the more they love it (Story 6). Keeya, meanwhile, is a pastor, and said: 'Being gay doesn't make you leave God' and 'God himself is the one who knows why I'm gay. I believe that God has called me' (Story 12). It appears, therefore, that participants' belief in a God who accepts, loves, and supports them provides them with a basis for critiquing and resisting the church for its politics of exclusion, while at the same time claiming a space within it. This paradox is reminiscent of the way in which African feminist

---

[48] See Immaculate N. Kizza, *The Oral Tradition of the Baganda of Uganda: A Study and Anthology of Legends, Myths, Epigrams and Folktales* (Jefferson: McFarland, 2009), 201.

[49] About the ministry of Senyonjo, see Adriaan van Klinken, 'Changing the Narrative of Sexuality in African Christianity: Bishop Christopher Senyonjo's LGBT Advocacy', *Theology and Sexuality*, 26:1 (2020), 1–6.

[50] Interview with Tina, Matasia, 15 January 2020.

theologians relate to the church in Africa: as much as they critique it for its sexism and patriarchy, they 'hope that God will liberate the church from gender dualism and make all [human beings] real participants in this household of God.'[51]

Conclusion

The process of collectively reading the story of Daniel in the lions' den, inter-reading it with personal and communal life experiences, and creatively re-storying it through dramatisation, was experienced by participants as profoundly uplifting, inspiring, and empowering. This was revealed most explicitly a week after the second session, when there was another gathering at Matasia for the purpose of reading and dramatising the second biblical text, from the New Testament. At this gathering we watched the film, now edited by Josh and entitled 'Daniel in the Homophobic Lions' Den', all together. As we watched, there was complete absorption and much delight, some laughter, some humming along with the song accompanying Daniel's imprisonment. Afterwards, there was a feeling of satisfaction, pride, and accomplishment in the room. Next, the responses tumbled forth: 'I feel *good* about myself', 'the film is about us', 'it's educative', 'it made us come together', 'it has an equality message', 'it is emotionally attaching – especially the bit with Daniel in the den', 'the story becomes ours', 'laws are made and can be changed by people – we must keep on fighting, like Daniel', 'reach out to God, no matter how bad', 'this film shows our reality – I hope others will watch it', 'always consider God: He will fight for us', 'how much we did in a short time!', 'our ability is what we tell ourselves – our limits are in our head – we can do so much more – the film shows this', 'stand up for our rights!', 'it's art with a vision', 'the story transformed me', 'this is the first time the Bible was not used against me'.

The follow-on one-to-one interviews with several participants, conducted in the week following the group session, amply confirmed this positive response: the new story, interweaving biblical and life stories, had made the Bible more personal and more relevant and the collective refugee story more elevated. Classicist scholar Helen Morales writes of classical mythology reimagined in modernity: 'Seeing a character or person through a kind of dual vision, as [them]self and in the role of a figure from myth, gives the reader an enhanced prism through which to understand them.' Analogously, recasting the story of Daniel in the court of King Darius in the context of

---

[51] Oduyoye, *Introducing African Women's Theology*, 83.

events surrounding the Anti-Homosexuality Bill of Uganda had a similar effect of an 'enhanced prism'.[52] Like Morales, although substituting 'Bible stories' for 'myths', we, too, can say: 'Telling new stories is, of course, essential, but viewing our worlds through the lens of the old myths is also meaningful.'[53] This is particularly the case in the context of our project and given the status of the Bible as sacred scripture, which has allowed participants to understand themselves in the light of the biblical narrative of God as a liberator of those who are marginalised and oppressed.

The story of Daniel in the lions' den turned out to be a particularly rich resource in this project. Not only could participants easily read their personal experiences of struggle, survival, hope, and liberation into the story, they could also map a highly critical socio-political event in Uganda – the passing of the Anti-Homosexuality Bill and its related institutionalisation of queer-phobia in Ugandan society – which had profoundly affected their lives, directly on to the text. Thus, the story allowed for an inter-reading at both a personal and a socio-political level. Feeding back at the end of the process, participants reported that 'it was so amazing [because] it was one of those stories that apply to our community', and:

> The story has brought a much more different meaning. It was more motivating for me. To me the story in the Bible, such as about Daniel, was about ancient things. But when we applied it to our daily experiences it made more sense. And it also showed me that, no matter what the challenges we go through, God will see us through. To me, I feel the story of Daniel fits my life.[54]

The collective process of inter-reading and dramatising the new story represented, in Musa Dube's words, 'a moment of community writing or interpretation of life'.[55] Several participants testified to the significance of this. Josh, for instance, reflected:

---

[52] Helen Morales, *Antigone Rising: The Subversive Power of the Ancient Myths* (London: Wildfire, 2020), xi–xii. Morales goes on to describe 'The Odyssey Project', where the story of the Greek hero Odysseus' errors and trials is taught to a class of incarcerated youths. Morales summarises: 'Using myth to enlarge their lives gives the students a different sense of who they are and what they can achieve' (xii). In our situation, the retelling of the biblical story achieved something comparable.

[53] Ibid., xvii.

[54] Concluding discussion, creative bible study about Daniel in the Lions' Den, Matasia, 12 January 2020.

[55] Musa W. Dube, Introduction', in Musa W. Dube (ed.), *Other Ways of Reading: African Women and the Bible* (Atlanta: Society of Biblical Literature, 2001), 3.

We all know Daniel's story but we rarely connect those stories to our personal stories and that kind of connects to our stories. Yeah, for everyone who was there on Sunday [for the dramatisation], they kind of get to know that it can be me: Daniel can be me. It was really outstanding. It really connects so well. It's like the perfect story to reference when I am talking about my life.[56]

Isaac explained that the experience gave him 'two feelings':

One is relating to Christianity, because I'm Christian. Two is the way it related to my journal of life. Most of the churches here are homophobic, so it was so nice to review the Bible. It was a nice experience. I loved it. Then, on the other side, it brought emotions, trying to relate our own personal lives as the LGBTIQ, or the queer, in Kenya.[57]

These various responses capture the spiritual and political significance of re-appropriating the Bible from a largely homophobic church and reading it through the lens of personal and communal experiences and perspectives as LGBTQ+ refugees. The ancient, sacred story of Daniel's struggle and his rescue by God mirrored the everyday struggles that participants find themselves in, but also reflected and reinforced their own experience of, and hope for, liberation. Along the way, participants as 'ordinary readers' developed a new, African queer interpretation of the story of Daniel, building on existing hermeneutics of liberation but applying this explicitly to sexuality and refugee status.

What this inter-reading has shown, above all, is, in Adichie's words, that 'stories matter'. The Bible and its stories have indeed been used 'to dispossess and to malign' the Ugandan LGBTQ+ refugees in Nairobi seeking resettlement. But the stories of the Bible, including the story of Daniel in the lions' den, are also versatile and can be used to affirm and to repair 'broken dignity'. The process of story sharing, inter-reading, and creative re-storying has clearly been meaningful, restorative, liberatory, and allowed participants to momentarily 'regain a kind of paradise'.[58]

---

[56] Interview with Josh, Matasia on 15 January 2020.

[57] Interview with Isaac, Matasia, 15 January 2020.

[58] Chimamanda Ngozi Adichie, 'The Danger of a Single Story', TED Global 2009, www.ted.com/talks/chimamanda_ngozi_adichie_the_danger_of_a_single_story (accessed 16 December 2020).

The Company of Men

Tom Rogers Muyunga-Mukasa

In Daniel's story is revealed
many mysteries
and many dens of lions,
of love and purpose of life:
that in being with men,
I fulfil in me
my authentic calling.

I shall always
enjoy the companionship
of men,
of women;
it is through this companionship
that so much about God is revealed.

Together we are instruments,
we can be of service
to enrich God's kingdom.
Companionship reminds us
to seek counsel
in the deep of the night
or broadness of day;
there we are assured of security,
safety and assurance;
we gain revelations
that there is a God,
a greater one,
who confers longevity,
who knows the changes of the times,
who knows what is in the darkness,
who understands the thought of our minds,

who can make our troubles disappear,
like chaff on the threshing floor,
crumbled and blown away
by winds without trace.
Daniel witnessed this
in the company
of Azariah,
Hananniah,
Shadrach,
Meshach,
Abednego.

Companionship is a preparation:
it sets the grounds for leadership,
companionship strengthens steadfastness,
knees never bend in fear,
heads bow in humility only before God,
the body is made worthy,
when our fears are,
only because we fall short of trust,
only because we fall short of faith.
Companionship of men
leads to a companionship that
bestows favours.

In Daniel we saw all this:
companionship with God
comes with favours.
Daniel possessed an extraordinary mind,
that explained enigmas,
that solved difficulties,
that broke through insolence,
that expands the greatness of kingdoms,
that elevates the gloriousness of majesties.

In the company of men,
I am not any lesser a being;
In enjoying the company of men
in bed or boardroom;
I am at no fault
or held in any neglect of duty;

however there are,
dens of lions lurking:
I may be ridiculed,
but I shall heal;
even when I am pulled away
from my high ranks;
even when my purple robes
are torn from me,
I shall get them back;
even when
some get in my way;
even when
some use the law,
to pull me down
from my high positions
I shall still
get the very positions back;
they will watch me get re-instated;
I am not finished,
I prevail,
Just because
I am
a companion of a steadfast God,
the everlasting,
and ever present One!

3

Jesus and the Guys Charged with Indecency

I am the woman caught in adultery
I was brought to the marketplace
they were ready to stone me
my sins, they said, were many.
I wept.[1]

The story from the Gospel of John, about Jesus and the woman caught in adultery, is a popular one. It is said to be 'so widely known, so widely quoted, and so often alluded to in art, literature, film, and public discourse of all sorts that "throwing stones" serves as a cliché'.[2] Against that background, it may not be a surprise that two of the storytellers in Part I of this book, Cindy and Kennedy (Stories 4 and 11), mention it as their favourite story in the Bible, and that the story proved such a productive interface with their and other refugees' life experiences.

The story, found in the Gospel of John 8:1–11, is a relatively short one.[3] It narrates that Jesus, when visiting the temple in Jerusalem, is confronted with a woman who had been caught in the act of adultery, and he is pressed to judge her on the basis of the Law of Moses.[4] The people

---

[1] Rose Teteki Abbey, 'I Am the Woman', in Musa W. Dube (ed.), *Other Ways of Reading: African Women and the Bible* (Atlanta: Society of Biblical Literature, 2001), 23–26.

[2] Jennifer Knust and Tommy Wasserman, *To Cast the First Stone: The Transmission of a Gospel Story* (Princeton: Princeton University Press, 2019), 8.

[3] Some Bible translations have arranged the verses slightly differently. Here, the story is found in John 7:53–8:11.

[4] The Law of Moses, also known as the Mosaic Law, refers to the Pentateuch, the first five books of the Hebrew Bible (for Christians, the Old Testament), and is the basis of religious law in the Jewish tradition, where it is called the Torah.

bringing the woman to Jesus are described as 'the teachers of the Law and the Pharisees'.[5] These terms refer to two (largely indistinct) groups in Palestinian Jewish society of the time: both were knowledgeable about, and concerned with, religious law and tradition, and consequently scrutinised Jesus, his behaviour and teaching carefully.[6] According to this story they bring the woman to Jesus in an attempt to find a reason to accuse him of transgressing the Law of Moses, which stipulates the death penalty for the crime of adultery.[7] The story narrates how Jesus responded to their challenge: initially he kept quiet, bent down and wrote on the ground with his finger (no details are given about what he wrote); when they kept pressing him, he said: 'Let any one of you who is without sin be the first to throw a stone at her' (John 8:7). The accusers then disappear one by one, and Jesus is left alone with the accused woman, to whom he says: 'Is there no one left to condemn you? Well, then, I do not condemn you either. Go, but do not sin again' (John 8:10–11).

There is strong evidence that the story was not included in early manuscripts of the Gospel of John, but only was added in the third century.[8] Some feminist scholars have suggested that the story was deliberately excluded because it was seen as too controversial in the light of the patriarchal early church and its conservative sexual ethics.[9] Yet for all its textual instability, the story has proven to be enormously popular. This popularity extends to contemporary Africa, and the present chapter further adds to the story's rich reception history. In what follows, we first give a brief overview of contextual readings of this story from African and queer perspectives. Next comes a major section that offers a detailed analysis of the identifications of participants with the various characters in the story, and the subsequent re-storying of the narrative. We then specifically focus on the dismissal with which Jesus sends the woman away, which was creatively rephrased by participants to reflect that homosexuality, in their opinion, is not a sin.

---

[5] Quotations are from the translation of the Good News Bible, as that was the version used in the group sessions. Other translations use the word 'scribes' for 'teachers of the Law'.

[6] Jaroslav Jan Pelikan and E. P. Sanders, 'Scribes and Pharisees', *Encyclopaedia Britannica*, www.britannica.com/biography/Jesus/Scribes-and-Pharisees (accessed 16 December 2020).

[7] See Leviticus 20:10 and Deuteronomy 22:22.

[8] Chapter 2 in Knust and Wasserman, *To Cast the First Stone*.

[9] Luise Schottroff, *Lydia's Impatient Sisters: A Feminist Social History of Early Christianity* (Louisville: Westminster John Knox Press, 1995), 180.

African and queer readings of the story

The epigraph of this chapter is a part of the poem, 'I Am the Woman', by Ghanaian theologian Rose Teteki Abbey. The 'I'-figure in this long and powerful poem identifies with several female characters in New Testament stories about Jesus's interactions with women: the Samaritan woman at the well, Mary, the sister of Martha, and the woman caught in adultery. In line with African feminist biblical hermeneutics (see Chapter 1), Abbey foregrounds the female characters, elaborates on their experiences, and retells their stories in a way with which she herself, and African women more generally, can identify. The concluding sentence of her poem – 'Religion that enslaves us is false. True religion gives us freedom!' – reflects a dominant tradition in African women's theology in which gospel stories are appropriated in the struggle for women's liberation, and in which Jesus Christ is presented as a liberating figure for African women today.[10] The story of Jesus and the woman caught in adultery is one of the most popular ones in this tradition; it does not only feature in Abbey's poem but also in several writings of other African theologians and biblical scholars concerned with issues of gender. More recently, the same story has also been used in African biblical hermeneutics concerned with HIV and AIDS.

The 'I'-figure in Abbey's poem retells the story in a way that draws attention to an ironic absence in the narrated events:

> I wept for the so-called religious men
> Who used religion to abuse me and condemn me to death.
> 'Caught in the act of adultery,' they said. I smiled to myself.
> How does one commit adultery alone?[11]

Biblical scholar Musa Dube, in her discussion of the gospel story, also draws critical attention to the fact that only the woman, and not the man involved in the act of adultery, is brought to Jesus. For her it illustrates the way in which society polices women's sexual morality much more closely than men's, not only in biblical times but also in her contemporary Botswana culture. In her interpretation, Jesus in this story 'debunks yet another gender stereotype' as he 'shows that violence against women is unacceptable' and 'that the law should not be interpreted so as to

---

[10] For an overview, see Mercy Oduyoye, *Introducing African Women's Theology* (Sheffield: Sheffield Academic Press, 2001), chapter 4.

[11] Abbey, 'I Am the Woman', 24.

discriminate against women, but should rather be applied equally to men and women'.[12]

Several other biblical scholars have developed similar interpretations, using the story of the woman caught in adultery to address and interrogate issues concerning women's position in contemporary African societies: women's unequal treatment under the law and cultural customs, women being subjected to moral scrutiny, women being silenced and dehumanised, and their bodies being violated.[13] The Kenyan scholar Julius Kiambi, however, has been more critical about the potential to use this story for a liberating gender politics. Adopting a postcolonial feminist lens, he argues that although Jesus does indeed rescue the woman, he does not dismantle 'the imperial and patriarchal systems that have colonised this and other women'.[14] The woman, in his reading, is merely used to achieve male means – first by the teachers of the Law and the Pharisees, for their moral zealotry, and second, by Jesus who performs his moral superiority vis-à-vis them. Kiambi suggests the story's liberating potential can only be achieved when the othering of the woman, and of women more generally, on the basis of patriarchal and imperial gender norms, is interrogated, so that the story may come to advocate for 'ethical coexistence between men and women'.[15]

Some other scholars have read the same story in the context of the HIV epidemic, specifically interrogating the issue of stigma towards people living with HIV on the basis of the societal association between HIV and sexual immorality and sin. Ezra Chitando and Lovemore Togarasei, from Zimbabwe, interpret Jesus's strategic move through which he reminds the

---

[12] Musa W. Dube, 'Grant Me Justice: Female and Male Equality in the New Testament', *Journal of Religion and Theology in Namibia*, 3:1 (2001), 82–115, 94–95.

[13] For instance, see Elijah M. Baloyi, 'A Re-reading of John 8:1–11 from a Pastoral Liberative Perspective on South African Women', *HTS Teologiese Studies/Theological Studies*, 66:2, art. #838; James Lungu, *Socio-cultural and Gender Perspectives in John 7:53–8:11: Exegetical Reflections in the Context of Violence against Women in Zambia* (MA thesis, University of Stellenbosch 2016); John Arierhi Ottuh, 'Reading Deuteronomy 22:22 in John 8:1–11: A Contextual Reading from an African-Urhobo Perspective', *Scriptura*, 118:1 (2019), 1–19.

[14] Julius Kithinji Kiambi, 'Divining John 7:53–8:11 for Textual Gender-motivated violence: A Postcolonial Approach' (unpublished paper, 2012), https://papers.ssrn.com/sol3/papers.cfm?abstract_id=2017643 (accessed 16 December 2020).

[15] Ibid., 11.

accusers of their own sinfulness, and his refusal to condemn the woman, as a model for destigmatisation in the church and wider society.[16] From a Contextual Bible Study with a group of people living with HIV, Tanzanian theologian Elia Shabani Mligo observes that participants in his session directly identified themselves with the woman accused of adultery, while they identified the teachers of the Law and the Pharisees in the text with their church leaders and fellow Christians who point fingers at them for being 'sexually immoral people':

> They say that we are HIV positive because we were adulterers and fornicators. They see us as being different from them. In fact, what the woman faced is similar to what we face, even though our communities do not throw physical stones to kill us, as the woman was likely to face.[17]

Thus, this group of people living with HIV identified with the woman, because of a shared experience of stigmatisation on the basis of codes of sexual morality, resulting in a somewhat similar repercussion: where the woman risked being stoned to death, they experience symbolic stoning through abusive language, negative attitudes, and exclusion. Interestingly, the mostly female group with whom Mligo read the story also identified with the gendered aspect: like the woman in the text, they too narrated that they were more likely to be blamed for contracting HIV as a result of 'sexual looseness' than their male counterparts. Jesus, to this group, was a liberating figure, as he rescued the woman from her accusers, demonstrated the latter's hypocrisy, and sustained the woman's life by rejecting her stigmatisation and restoring her to the community. They interpreted the story as meaning that Jesus today would critique the church for stigmatising people living with HIV and would affirm their dignity and life.

The above review demonstrates that there is a tradition of Africa-centred contextual readings of the story of Jesus and the woman caught in adultery. The story has been widely used to address and interrogate those prevailing cultures of gender and sexuality in the church and in society that lead to stigmatisation, marginalisation, and dehumanisation. In these contemporary readings of the story, Jesus is generally reclaimed as a liberating figure who is on the side of those victimised, who counters their

---

[16] Ezra Chitando and Lovemore Togarasei, '"Woman, Where Are They?" John 7:53–8:11 and Stigma in the Context of HIV and Aids', *Missionalia*, 36:1 (2008), 4–15.

[17] Elia Shabani Mligo, *Jesus and the Stigmatized: Reading the Gospel of John in a Context of HIV/AIDS-Related Stigmatization in Tanzania* (PhD thesis, University of Oslo, 2009), 266.

stigmatisation, and restores them to life. A similar reading is offered by US queer theologian Robert Goss, who in his contribution to *The Queer Bible Commentary* argues that the story 'provides a powerful indictment of condemning attitudes toward sexuality and a double-standard patriarchal culture that targets the woman for punishment and not the male participant'.[18] In Goss's account, the story narrates how the religious elites of the time use the woman to catch Jesus in a trap, but 'Jesus demonstrates his moral authority and thus widens the gap between himself and the religious fundamentalists'. The story for him indicates that 'Jesus neither was obsessed with sex nor regulated the sexual lives of people', and that instead, he 'tackled the far more pressing issues of social injustice and exclusion'.[19] Along the same lines, US scholar Theodore Jennings, in his book about homoerotic narratives in the New Testament, argues that the story reveals that 'Jesus takes an anti-ascetic attitude toward sexuality', and that 'sexual irregularity is [not] an especially egregious form of sinful behavior'.[20]

Although the Ugandan LGBTQ+ refugees participating in our project are unlikely to be familiar with the academic literature reviewed above, most of them were familiar with the story itself and could easily relate it to their own life experiences. Two of the interviewees in the first stage of the project mentioned the story as their favourite story in the Bible. Kennedy clearly referenced it when he said, 'about that woman – I don't remember whether she was a prostitute or I think she was adulterous – that story where they were going to throw stones' (Story 11). Cindy referenced a story about 'a situation where people sent away a prostitute but Jesus welcomed the prostitute' (Story 4). This seems to refer to the above story from the Gospel of John, but might also relate to another biblical story, from the Gospel of Luke (7:36–50) about Jesus being anointed by a 'sinful woman' who is popularly described as a prostitute. In any case, in response to the question about their favourite Bible story, both Kennedy and Cindy chose a story from the gospels about Jesus in relation to a woman who faced stigma and exclusion because of her association with sexual sin, and they identified themselves with her. Hence, we decided to use this story for the second group session of a contextual and creative Bible study, which took place on 18 January 2020.

---

[18] Robert E. Goss, 'John', in Deryn Guest, Robert E. Goss, Mona West, and Thomas Bohache (eds), *The Queer Bible Commentary* (London: SCM Press, 2016), 556.

[19] Ibid.

[20] Theodore W. Jennings, *The Man Jesus Loved: Homoerotic Narratives from the New Testament* (Cleveland: The Pilgrim Press, 2003), 61.

For this session we deliberately kept the number of participants relatively low by inviting less widely. We ended up with a group of fifteen participants, about half of them being residents of TNN's Matasia house, complemented with other members of the refugee community. Because this story is much shorter than the Daniel story, and the group smaller, we also decided to do the Bible study and the creative session in one day, rather than over two days. It made for a full and intensive day programme, but thanks to everyone's serious involvement and active participation, we managed to complete the process before sundown.

The title of the resulting drama play, 'Jesus and the Guys Charged with Indecency', was inspired by the Kenyan Penal Code concerned with 'indecency between males' (art. 165, see below).[21] In this play, a group of young LGBTQ+ folk are dancing in a club called Little Temple. The name of the club is a reference to the opening of the Bible story, which states that Jesus 'went back to the temple', but is also the actual name of a one-time club in downtown Nairobi known to be frequented by queer people (the club changed its name a few years ago). In the play, the club is raided by police (something similar, incidentally, happened at Little Temple in Nairobi). The partying youth are arrested and subjected to forced anal examination (a practice to which men accused of same-sex practices have been commonly subjected in Kenya, and which was ruled to be unconstitutional by the Court of Appeal in Mombasa in 2018).[22] The arrested youths are taken to the Matasia Village Court, where prosecutors accuse them of public indecency. The judge then points the accusers to a list of things that can all be considered as offences of 'our religion, our culture, and our constitution', saying that if any of them has not made themselves guilty of any of these, they can throw the first stone at the accused. The court members back down and leave, after which the judge, being left with the accused, advises them: 'Go, enjoy your life, but responsibly.'

After the group session, one participant, Tom, engaged in another creative form of re-storying by writing a poem, 'Accused of a Sodomy Act'. This poem, which follows the present chapter, is set in a village somewhere in East Africa. The 'I'-figure, who describes himself as a man

---

[21] *Jesus and the Guys Charged with Indecency*, produced by Josh and Mandrine (Nairobi: The Nature Network, 2020), www.youtube.com/watch?v=9f-1JD9tQew (accessed 16 December 2020).

[22] Joackim Bwana, 'Mombasa Court Declares Anal Tests on Homosexual Suspects Illegal', *The Standard*, 23 March 2018, www.standardmedia.co.ke/article/2001274237/mombasa-court-declares-anal-tests-on-homosexual-suspects-illegal# (accessed 16 December 2020).

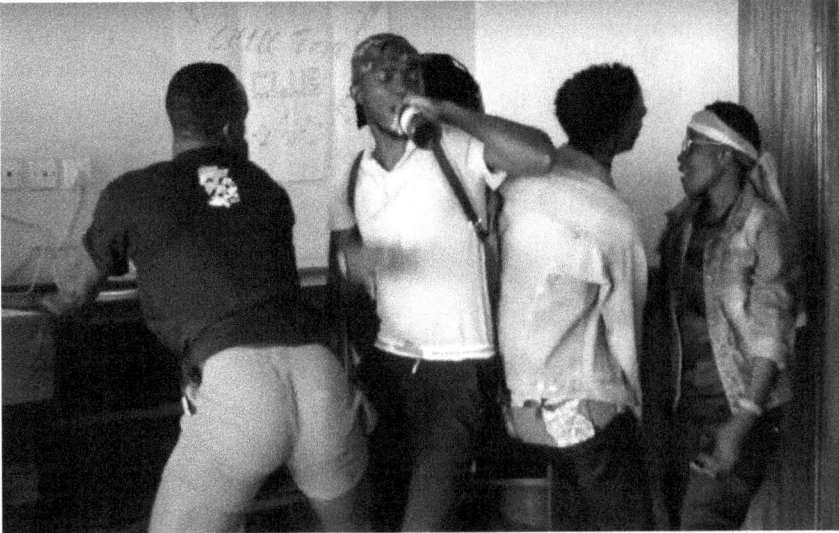

Figure 3 Clubbing at Little Temple, a Nairobi club popular among LGBTQ+ folk. Video still from 'Jesus and the Guys Charged with Indecency'; 18 January 2020 (© The Nature Network)

who lies with fellow men, imagines the village elders and family relatives accusing and shaming him, but Jesus turning against them and setting him free. Both the drama play and Tom's poem exemplify the same point that Dube makes about Abbey's poem: these contemporary retellings of the biblical story 'show that the encounter with Jesus brought a new world' – in Abbey's case, liberation from patriarchy, and in Tom's case, liberation from heteronormativity. This liberatory element is then reclaimed as a basis for empowering groups that are currently marginalised in African societies, such as women and sexual and gender minorities.[23]

Identifications with the story

Throughout the process, participants, divided into two sub-groups, identified and discussed the main characters in the story, reflected on the narrated events, and drew parallels with their own life experiences. This, in the end, resulted in a retelling of the story in the contemporary context, as captured in the drama play. The following section analyses the ways in

---

[23] Musa W. Dube, 'Introduction', in Musa W. Dube (ed.), *Other Ways of Reading: African Women and the Bible* (Atlanta: Society of Biblical Literature, 2001), 5.

which participants inter-read the Bible story and their own life experiences, organised around the four main characters they identified: the teachers of the Law and the Pharisees, the Law of Moses, the woman, and Jesus.

The teachers of the Law and the Pharisees

The characteristics with which participants associated the teachers of the Law and the Pharisees in the story were not very complimentary: words such as 'accusers', 'authoritative', 'conservative', 'discriminating', 'irrational', 'judgemental', and 'shaming' were used. They were considered irrational because they brought only the woman to Jesus, but not her male counterpart. They were seen as conservative, because of their use of the Law of Moses to persecute the woman. They were described as 'law-abiding citizens', but of the kind who use the Law to showcase their own piety but then judge and shame fellow citizens. One group included a slightly more positive note, describing the teachers of the Law and the Pharisees as 'patient' and as 'respectful to Jesus', on the basis that they addressed Jesus as 'teacher', and invited and waited for him to give his verdict on the case. The other group was more suspicious: having noted the comment in the story that the accusers were trying to trap Jesus so they could accuse him, they observed that these religious leaders saw Jesus as a competitor and problem.

Participants had no difficulty in linking the teachers of the Law and the Pharisees to characters in their own context. The first association, as by Kennedy (Story 11), was to see them as representatives of the church – pastors and fellow Christians – who show a similarly judgemental attitude to LGBTQ+ people today as the Jewish legal experts had towards the 'adulterous woman'. A second association was with community leaders, including, but not limited to, religious leaders. In his poem, Tom uses the term 'elders', which refers to senior men (and possibly women) who in traditional African village-life are the custodians of cultural laws and customs. The third and broadest association was to identify the teachers of the Law and the Pharisees with everyone in society who adopts negative attitudes and uses abusive language towards LGBTQ+ people. As Rodgers puts it:

> I am seeing the people who are judging us today, I am seeing them like those Pharisees who brought that woman. So, I think these modern people would come and tell Jesus, 'We have caught this guy. This guy is a paedophile. He wears pampers. He teaches our children bad things'. Like, they bring that narrative that the kind of life I am living is not meaningful.[24]

---

[24] Interview with Rodgers, Matasia, 23 January 2020. The reference to 'wearing pampers' reflects a popular way in East Africa of ridiculing men who have sex

Thus, against this broad understanding, the accusers in the story can be linked to teachers and classmates, employers and colleagues, parents, siblings and other relatives, and so on. In the drama play developed out of the story, the teachers of the Law and the Pharisees were replaced by the Matasia Village Court, comprising a legal prosecutor but also Christian and Muslim community elders charging the accused on the basis of the law, and calling for them to be killed by burning or stoning.

The Law

The Law of Moses was identified by participants as a character in the story. This identification acknowledges the agency of laws, not only in the biblical story but also in their own lives. Participants generally expressed astonishment about the fact that according to the Law of Moses, as invoked by the accusers, adultery should be punished by stoning to death. In one of the small groups, the Law was described as 'brutal', 'condemning', 'uncalled for', and even 'ungodly'. When referred to the relevant biblical texts about adultery in Leviticus and Deuteronomy, participants were quick to realise that the same Law of Moses also contains the infamous clobber verses often used against same-sex loving people (Leviticus 18:22 and 20:13), which also stipulate the death penalty (Leviticus 20:13). They were also reminded of the initial version of Uganda's Anti-Homosexuality Bill which, inspired by biblical notions of 'sodomy', included a death penalty clause for 'aggravated homosexuality'.[25] Although this clause was later removed, the penal codes of both Uganda and Kenya severely penalise same-sex sexual practices – referred to as 'unnatural offences' and 'carnal knowledge against the order of nature'.[26] In Uganda, the penalty is

---

with men and of mocking the supposed perversity of anal sex – see George Paul Meiu, 'Underlayers of Citizenship: Queer Objects, Intimate Exposures, and the Rescue Rush in Kenya', *Cultural Anthropology*, 35:4 (2020), 575–601. Likewise, the reference to paedophilia and to 'teaching our children bad things' echoes a widespread concern in East Africa that gay people present a particular threat to children and youth (see Joanna Sadgrove et al., 'Morality Plays and Money Matters: Towards a Situated Understanding of the Politics of Homosexuality in Uganda', *Journal of Modern African Studies*, 50:1 (2012), 121). The accusation of 'recruiting the young' was also levelled at the LGBTQ+ community in the Daniel dramatisation (see Chapter 2).

[25] The word 'sodomy' comes from the biblical story of Sodom and Gomorrah (Genesis 19), which is one of the 'clobber' texts often used against same-sex sex acts and relationships. See Chapter 1, note 63.

[26] Ugandan Penal Code, art. 145; Kenyan Penal Code, art. 162.

imprisonment for life, while in Kenya it is incarceration for up to fourteen years. The Kenyan Penal Code has an additional article about 'Indecent practices between males' (art. 165), with a penalty of imprisonment of five years. Thus, participants knew only too well, from their own experience, that a law, whether enshrined in sacred scripture or in a penal code, can be excessive and indeed ungodly because it transgresses what they perceive to be God's character of justice, love, and forgiveness.

In addition to the existence of formal legislation against homosexuality, participants were very much aware of the religious, cultural, and social laws, as well as moral codes, on the basis of which they experience harassment and persecution. As one interviewee put it dramatically but certainly not unrealistically, 'we go through different homophobic attacks, different prosecutions and imprisonment, and even death itself.'[27] Thus, the Law of Moses in the Bible story for them represented not just the legal but also the written and unwritten religious, cultural, and social laws to which they are subjected as LGBTQ+ people, and through which they are constantly judged, policed, and persecuted by the wider community. In fact, these various categories of law – legal, religious, cultural, and social – are difficult to separate in their context. In East Africa, homosexuality is, after all, popularly seen as un-natural, un-African, un-Christian, and un-Islamic, and these notions are perpetuated by a range of groups in society.[28] The multiple faces of the law used against them were represented in the dramatisation by the variety of figures serving as members of the Matasia Village Court: not only a legal prosecutor, but also community elders (male and female) citing the Bible, the Qur'an, and cultural customs, respectively, to argue for the accused to be convicted and, indeed, killed.

The woman

The woman in the Bible story is nameless and, apart from a few words at the end, speechless. She appears mostly as a mere object in the hands of her accusers, who bring her to Jesus and make her stand in front of the

---

[27] Interview with Isaac, Matasia, 15 January 2020.

[28] Robert W. Kuloba, '"Homosexuality is Unafrican and Unbiblical": Examining the Ideological Motivations to Homophobia in Sub-Saharan Africa – The Case Study of Uganda', *Journal of Theology in Southern Africa*, 154 (2016), 6–27; Hassan J. Ndzovu, '"Un-natural", "un-African" and "un-Islamic": The Three Pronged Onslaught on Undermining Homosexual Freedom in Kenya', in Adriaan van Klinken and Ezra Chitando (eds), *Public Religion and the Politics of Homosexuality in Africa* (London and New York: Routledge, 2016), 78–91.

crowd. Participants drew attention to this when describing her as 'quiet', 'scared', 'defenceless', 'vulnerable', 'humiliated', 'isolated', 'inferior', and 'victim'. Her apparent lack of agency in the story was perhaps best captured in the descriptor 'bait', which refers to the point that the woman is being used instrumentally by the teachers of the Law and the Pharisees in their attempt to entrap Jesus. Noting that the male partner is absent in the story, participants pointed at the unequal and unfair treatment that women often experience, both in biblical times and today.

Virtually all participants automatically identified with the woman in the story. The parallels they drew between the woman and themselves as LGBTQ+ persons and refugees were multiple: the experience of being judged for their gender and sexual activity; community leaders and religious elites mobilising against you; being publicly defamed, humiliated, and victimised; being exposed to community violence and harassment; the law turning against you; facing unequal treatment. Psychologically projecting themselves into the woman, participants also recognised and identified with her feeling powerless and vulnerable, her low self-esteem, and her self-blame for what had happened. In short, what they shared with the woman was an experience of profound stigmatisation and a suffering from the emotional effects. As the following interviewees put it when reflecting on the Bible study session:

> I found myself in the same situation as the woman in the Bible who is being condemned, whereby in my case it was my family who condemned me. I was condemned by my family and community, so I had to leave my country that is, Uganda, and seek refuge in another country. So, I link this story to myself as a person who was condemned just like the lady in the Bible.[29]

> This story talks about the condemnation, about the victimisation. Me being involved in the LGBTI, I experience the same, also here in Kenya. One time I was in church and the pastor was giving a sermon, it was about the LGBTI. The pastor is someone I looked up to, a person of authority whom I trusted and whom I knew was not out to hurt me personally. But still, he started preaching against us, and it hurt me. The stigma exists and it is on the ground. The stigma comes from way back in time with the people we grew up with, when they got to know and label us, saying we were engaged in 'vices', and other words that they put on us.[30]

[29] Interview with Nita, Matasia, 23 January 2020.
[30] Interview with Rover, Matasia, 31 January 2020.

In addition to their sexuality, participants narrated experiencing further stigmatisation because of their refugee status, and, in several cases, also their non-conforming gender performance, their HIV status and/or their involvement in sex work. Indeed, their narratives exemplify the intersectionality of stigma experienced by LGBTQ+ refugees in East Africa.[31]

Referring to the story, one participant, Francis, explained that the reason why the woman was not given a chance to offer her account of what had happened can be captured in one word: bias. As he put it: 'Everyone was so biased and wanted to kill her or do anything bad, because what she had done was seen as bad to the public, to society.' [32] A similar bias, he continued, is faced by LGBTQ+ people like himself:

> The story speaks a lot to our entire life. What happens in this story is exactly the stuff that happens in the community and it happened to me personally, because I was tortured, I was not given chance to speak, back in Uganda. Whenever I said something, they would say, 'Aaaah that's a homosexual person, he doesn't have anything to say because he was taken in sin.' They see us as a mess.

Thus, the bias Francis refers to is about prejudice that reduces a person, or a group of people, to one negatively perceived aspect of who they are or what they do, which then comes to define the attitude with which they are approached by the community. Thus, the woman in the Bible story is reduced to being adulterous, while Francis in his own story is reduced to his sexuality and 'girly' gender performance. In both cases, the community defines them by the apparent sin with which they are associated, and subsequently negates their humanity and denies their voice. Socially speaking, they are already considered dead, which then results in calls for them to be expelled from the body of the community or the nation, and indeed for them to be killed (as with the 'Kill the Gays Bill' in Uganda).[33] Yet our participants had sought to escape the fate of social exclusion and death, by seeking refuge in Kenya and applying for resettlement in a country that will recognise them as fully human. As refugees, they have learned to speak back to power – for instance, the

---

[31] About this multiplicity and intersectionality of stigma, see for instance chapter 3 in Chi Mgbako, *To Live Freely in This World: Sex Worker Activism in Africa* (New York: New York University Press, 2016).

[32] Interview with Francis, Matasia, 27 January 2020.

[33] Achille Mbembe describes 'social death' as certain groups of people, such as slaves, facing 'expulsion from humanity altogether'. See Achille Mbembe, 'Necropolitics', *Public Culture*, 15:1 (2003), 21.

power of UNHCR – and to engage in a struggle for recognition, for their voices to be heard, and their dignity and rights to be respected.

In the process of retelling the story, participants insisted that the woman's lack of agency needed to be counter-balanced in the drama, with the accused being given an opportunity to speak. Thus, being charged with indecency (a term derived from the above-mentioned Kenyan Penal Code) in the Matasia Village Court, the spokesperson of the accused group retorts by saying that they were 'just having fun' while partying in a club. This is an ostensibly simple response, but it normalises and therefore humanises them. It can also be seen as implicitly interrogating double standards, whereby queer youth are penalised for 'having fun' while straight folk are not, in a way that is reminiscent of how the *woman* is accused of adultery while her male counterpart goes free. In a hetero-patriarchal society, misogynistic double standards are detrimental to the well-being of women, while heteronormative double standards are damaging to LGBTQ+ people.

As much as participants identified with the woman's experience of being silenced and stigmatised, and being subjected to social prejudice and community judgement, they also took inspiration from the ending of the story. As one of them put it, 'the adulterous woman, she was the victim, she did not have a voice, but at the end of the story she became the victor'.[34] This victory is based on her finding her voice, when she responds to Jesus's question by saying that not one of her accusers is left to condemn her. Thus, with the woman's voice, also her dignity and humanity are affirmed and restored through her encounter with Jesus. The few words she speaks – 'no one, sir' – for the participants illustrate how she reclaims the moral integrity and human dignity that her accusers had tried to take away from her. Taking inspiration from this, Francis concludes:

> Actually, the Bible tells us a lot and tells a lot to the society, because we as LGBTIQ people are also human beings in the community, we breathe the same breath, we have the same blood. Some people think we can't do anything in life but being LGBTIQ doesn't stop us from being who we are.[35]

Thus, having grown up, and still living, in a society that calls them all kinds of derogatory names and that denies them their potential, the character of the woman in the Bible story reassured participants that they are valuable, and their humanity recognised.

---

[34] Interview with Nita, Matasia, 23 January 2020.
[35] Interview with Francis, Matasia, 27 January 2020.

Jesus

Participants contrasted Jesus's character with that of the teachers of the Law and the Pharisees. Where the latter attempted to entrap Jesus, illustrating their mean character, his response to them was described with terms of praise, such as 'wisdom', 'discerning', and 'patience'. And where the teachers and Pharisees were ready to condemn the woman on the basis of the Law of Moses, illustrating their judgemental attitude, Jesus, on the contrary, was 'kind', 'merciful', 'forgiving', and 'non-judgemental' towards her, proving himself a 'listener', 'protector' and 'defender'. The way in which he dealt with the appeal to the Law of Moses was interpreted as 'unpredictable', 'creative', and 'authoritative', revealing his status as a 'teacher' and a 'leader'. Interestingly, Jesus was also described as a 'parent'. Although this was not further elaborated, the suggestion might be that in comparison to their own parents, who in several cases rejected them, Jesus for them presents an image of unconditional parental love, care, and guidance.[36] As Keeya puts it when narrating his life story: 'Human beings disappoint and may dump you but the Lord doesn't disappoint you … I love him so much' (Story 12). Clearly, participants identified with the woman in the text, applying Jesus's attitude towards her to themselves in their own situation. In one of the group discussions it was even concluded that 'Jesus in the story is like an activist for the minorities', the suggestion being that this includes sexual minorities today.

Participants pointed at several aspects of Jesus's attitude to the woman, and his response to the teachers of the Law and the Pharisees, that they considered affirming and liberating. Some drew attention to the fact that Jesus did not engage in a scriptural discussion with the religious elites about the question of whether the act of which the woman was accused was sinful. Instead, his response that whoever is without sin may throw the first stone at her serves to undermine the moral high ground of her accusers, making them aware of the fact that they, too, have sinned under the Law of Moses. This response was welcomed by some participants, who were not so much interested in the question as to whether homosexuality is a sin according to the Bible; they simply argued that even if it is a sin, the story confirms that this does not affect their value in the eyes of God, and therefore does not provide society with a basis to condemn them. 'All sins are equal', one participant in the group discussion concluded, while

---

[36] About the image of Jesus as a parent, and specifically a mother, in Africa, see Diane B. Stinton, *Jesus of Africa: Voices of Contemporary African Christology* (Nairobi: Paulines, 2004), 175–183. About parental rejection, see the life stories of Tigan (2), Henry (5) and Keeya (12) in Part I of this book.

another one reacted to that by saying, 'every human being does do sin; it might be a little sin it might be a big sin but it is a same sin'. Either way, the point of both is that there is no moral ground for either the woman in the story, or LGBTQ+ people today, to be cast as sinners by fellow human beings who, after all, are sinners themselves. This take is of interest in the light of Kiambi's above-mentioned postcolonial feminist critique of the Jesus-figure in the story for not dismantling the systems of gender ideology and power. For these participants, Jesus's suggestion that all sins are fundamentally equal may not explicitly dismantle but does effectively undermine the workings of hetero-patriarchy against its victims, such as women and sexual and gender minorities.

By questioning the basis on which the religious elites cast the woman as a sinner deserving to be stoned, Jesus in the eyes of participants over-turned the stigma the woman was associated with by her accusers. His non-judgemental attitude was then utilised as a basis to criticise the stigma and condemnation that LGBTQ+ people today continue to face. As one interviewee, Kennedy, concluded while reflecting on the story: 'Everyone is a sinner. So, the magnitude of you measuring sin, you as a human being, and you judging another person, it is unfair. I believe that the way the church perceives the LGBTQ+ community is very ill and bad' (Story 11). As pointed out earlier, the woman was reduced to one negatively perceived aspect – her involvement in an act of adultery – and similarly, Kennedy and other participants narrate how they have been reduced by religious and social elites to their sexuality, refugee status, HIV status, or involvement in sex work, with their human dignity being denied and their potential of what they have to offer being overlooked. The Bible story confirms their hope that Jesus breaks the systemic culture of prejudice and stigmatisation that they experience in society, and recognises their full human person-hood. In the drama play this was expressed by the Jesus figure, the judge, asking the accused to speak and respond to the accusations. One of the actors commented later: 'The judge said, "Let the accused give a chance to defend themselves." Anyone should come out and defend themselves. It implies that the judge is so considering, he wanted to know more about us.'[37] Thus, participants felt that, like the woman in the story, and like the 'I'-figure in Abbey's poem, their silencing, stigmatisation, and dehu-manisation is interrogated by Jesus, with their voice and dignity being acknowledged, valued, and fully restored.

---

[37] Concluding discussion, creative bible study about Jesus and the 'adulterous woman', Matasia, 18 January 2020.

The fact that in the drama play, the Jesus figure of the story is cast as a judge is worth reflecting on. In the group process of developing the drama-tisation, this was not discussed at length but was rather quickly decided upon. Other options, such as casting the Jesus figure as a religious leader, or a community elder, were not considered. The identification of Jesus as a judge may have been inspired by other gospel stories, such as Luke 18:1–8 where Jesus seems to contrast himself with an unjust judge who is begged by a widow to speak justice, or by New Testament references to Jesus Christ as an eschatological judge (John 5:22; 2 Timothy 4:1). However, it may also reflect the way in which the struggle for LGBTQ+ human dignity in contemporary Africa to a significant extent has become a legal battle, with LGBTQ+ activists investing their hopes in the judiciary more than in politicians, as agents that will bring about change.[38] For instance, in Uganda it was the Constitutional Court that in 2014 annulled the Anti-Homosexuality Act, and in Kenya, at the time of this project, an appeal against the decision of the High Court not to decriminalise homosexuality had just been submitted to the country's Supreme Court. The limitation of this Bible story, in the light of these legal battles, is, of course, that Jesus does not explicitly question the Law itself, or call for its removal. Although one of the participants referred to Jesus as an activist, on the basis of this story he can hardly be cast as one advocating for decrimi-nalisation (of either adultery or homosexuality), any more than as a judge ruling in favour of a petition for decriminalisation. Participants did not seem bothered about this, apparently because in their reading Jesus does something that is at least as important as decriminalisation: he presents a model of destigmatisation and of humanisation.

Jesus's attitude towards the woman was widely described by partici-pants as welcoming, merciful, and forgiving. Thus, Cindy states: 'Jesus welcomed the prostitute. This was also a person, who can change. I think that really reflects on our lives, because the society sends us away; they don't want us; they don't want anything to do with us' (Story 4). The fact that Cindy, like some other participants, identifies the 'adulterous woman' as a prostitute is significant, not the least in the light of the fact that refugees themselves frequently engage in sex work. The key lesson taken from the story appears to be that God does not reject people because of their sexual lives. In the closing session after the drama performance,

---

[38] Ashley Currier and Joëlle M. Cruz, 'Civil Society and Sexual Struggles in Africa', in Ebenezer Obadare (ed.), *The Handbook of Civil Society in Africa* (New York: Springer, 2014), 337–360.

where participants were asked to feed back what they took away from the process, one of them stated:

> We serve a God who does not discriminate in terms of sexuality or nationality, and where you come from. So, while the world tries to prosecute us, the God we serve is one God who is loving and kind, and is a God of second chances. He says, 'Go back, enjoy your life, but responsibly.' God knows we are living in this world, you have to enjoy every bit of it, that's the nature of us.

Striking in this statement is the direct equation of the character of Jesus with the character of God (who is not mentioned in either the Bible story or the dramatised retelling). It exemplifies the grassroots understanding of our participants in which Jesus represents God. This association of Jesus with God is not so much dogmatic but rooted in experiential knowledge, informed by a lived spirituality: it is in the concrete and personal experience of being affirmed, loved, healed, and liberated by Jesus that they, like many other African Christians, recognise Jesus Christ as divine. Ghanaian theologian Mercy Oduyoye has stated that the biblical Jesus of Nazareth 'has become for us [African women] the Christ' through being women's companion, friend, and liberator in situations of poverty, disease, and marginalisation.[39] In the same way, it appears, LGBTQ+ folk experience Jesus as the Christ, a divine saviour whom they can relate to, and whose radical acceptance and love convinces them of the unconditional acceptance and love of God.

Jesus, in the above quotation, represents a 'God of second chances', as he was able to see the woman, not as a sinner, but in Cindy's words as 'a person who can change' (Story 4). Both participants appear to refer here to the words with which Jesus dismisses the woman: 'Go now and leave your life of sin.' We will return to this dismissal in more detail in the next section below. What matters here is that it was interpreted as words of forgiveness. Whatever sin the woman may have done, Jesus saw past it, not reducing her to being a sinner but recognising her human dignity and potential, and subsequently giving her another chance in life. As Francis put it, 'Jesus supported the woman, not just supporting her but I can say he

---

[39] Mercy A. Oduyoye, 'Jesus Christ', in Susan F. Parsons (ed.), *The Cambridge Companion to Feminist Theology* (Cambridge: Cambridge University Press, 2002), 166. About experiential Christology, especially from an African women's perspective, see Teresia M. Hinga, *African, Christian, Feminist: The Enduring Search for What Matters* (Maryknoll: Orbis, 2017), chapters 7–8; Stinton, *Jesus of Africa*.

was merciful and yeah he forgave her; he's the only person who forgives, who forgives us always when we commit sins'.[40] Interestingly, Francis directly applied Jesus's forgiveness of the woman to himself as a gay man, but while speaking realised a possible problem in doing so: adultery might be a sin that needs forgiveness, but homosexuality, in his opinion, is not. So, he corrected himself by adding, 'but personally I don't call homosexuality a sin'. Although most participants seemed to share this view, they still appeared to be encouraged by Jesus's attitude of forgiveness. As one participant in the group discussion put it: 'The woman was caught in the act. She is still forgiven. No matter how messed up life gets and how put down you are – there is room for forgiveness.' The encouragement taken from this may specifically apply to those who had been, or still were, involved in sex work. Several participants in the life story interviews spoke about their moral dilemma, feeling 'bad' and even 'terrible' about doing sex work but at the same time having neither a choice nor an alternative in their struggle for survival.[41] Although the question of sex work was not discussed at length in the group discussions about this Bible story, it was mentioned as one of the reasons why LGBTQ+ refugees experience stigmatisation and judgement in society. The story's message of acceptance, forgiveness, and new chances is likely to have reassured those participants struggling with the stigma, partly internalised, surrounding sex work.

As mentioned earlier, participants generally identified with the woman in the story, and thus positioned themselves on the receiving end of Jesus's – and, related to that, God's – acceptance, love, and forgiveness. However, one interviewee, Nita, explicitly stated identifying not with the character of the woman, but with Jesus:

> I would link this story to my life, and as an LGBTI person I would not relate to the woman but to Jesus. There are very many ways to understand the story. I would not call myself the adulterous woman. I would call myself Jesus. There is a way everyone understands the story. I would call myself Jesus. As we were learning about the character of Jesus, he was a teacher, a comforter, and he was authoritative. So, he had authority. I do not want to imagine myself as someone in trouble. Instead I imagine myself as a solver of problems. I imagine myself as a teacher of every skill that I have and I am ready to move it to anyone. I am not a victim. So, the adulterous woman is my fellow community member. I am not imagining myself as the victim. I am a problem solver. So many problems have come up, but few

---

[40] Interview with Francis, Matasia, 27 January 2020.
[41] See the life stories of Tigan (2) and Henry (5) in Part I of this book.

people have come out to solve them. I want people to come and they ask me, 'We have this problem, how do we solve it?' I would then say, 'Okay, you are condemning this person for being adulterous or having HIV?' That was an example from the story. I am comparing myself to Jesus. But I would show that condemning is not what solves problems.[42]

For Nita, the woman is the victim in the story. Although stating that at the end of the story she becomes the victor, Nita draws attention to the woman's lack of agency throughout the story: she does not become a victor through her own actions, but through the liberating interaction with Jesus; Jesus, on the other hand, holds a status of authority in the community and uses this position to share wisdom and solve problems. This account echoes images of Jesus as leader that can be found across Africa.[43] Yet where these images usually centre around traditional forms of leadership, such as of kings and chiefs, Nita presents a more grassroots image of community leadership with which, as a community activist himself, he can readily identify. Nita's identification with the character of Jesus is a way of claiming agency; it expresses his desire to be a problem solver, too, and, in particular, to fight cultures of exclusion and condemnation in society. Interestingly, during the session itself, the comment had been made that judgement does not only happen towards, but also among, members of the LGBTQ+ community. Examples of groups that may experience stigma within the community included trans people, effeminate and bottoming gay men, those who are HIV positive, and those engaged in sex work. Nita refers to this when saying: 'You could be condemned for so many things, not only by the community but also by fellow queer people about stuff.' Elaborating on that, he narrates his own experiences as a bisexual man, with bisexuals in his opinion not being seen as 'pure' enough by other groups under the LGBTQ+ umbrella: 'They see us as semi-straight and call us opportunists, frauds, and pretenders.' It is this experience that appears to inspire him to identify with Jesus and to commit himself to promoting a culture of acceptance and inclusion within the community.

Adapting the dismissal line

The gospel story concludes with a dismissal, the words with which Jesus sent the woman away: 'Go, but do not sin again'. Interestingly, the African biblical scholars discussed in the opening section of this chapter do not

---

[42] Interview with Nita, Matasia, 23 January 2020.
[43] Stinton, *Jesus of Africa*, 199–215.

reflect on these words, (possibly) conveniently overlooking them. Jennings makes a brief comment, suggesting two possible options:

> He [Jesus] either wants the woman to avoid the behavior that would result in her being stoned if he were not there to protect her in the future, or Jesus does disapprove of adultery but is not prepared to make a big deal about it.'[44]

For our participants, the dismissal was one of the most puzzling sentences in the whole story. It made them wonder whether and why Jesus considered adultery a sin, and how that might then relate to the question of homosexuality. When made aware of the Law of Moses which, as mentioned earlier, does indeed outlaw adultery, they understood why Jesus could not publicly contradict this. Yet, while agreeing that Jesus may have seen adultery as a sin (although not one worthy of a severe penalty), participants generally believed that homosexuality is not a sin. On the contrary, as reflected in the life stories in Part I, they claimed that LGBTQ+ people are created in the image of God, pointed at the homo-sociality and homo-intimacy of Jesus in relation to his male disciples, and even suggested that 'God is gay' (Story 5). Thus, during the session there was considerable discussion about how Jesus's dismissal of the woman could be read, or re-read, in relation to their own situation. At the end, all participants were invited to rephrase the concluding sentence in their own words, capturing how they imagine Jesus's words to them as LGBTQ+ persons. The resulting responses can be classified into two categories – pastoral affirmation and ethical imperative – although, arguably, in many cases these categories are blurred and mixed in the dismissals that participants came up with.

Pastoral affirmation

Pastorally affirmative dismissals are words through which Jesus affirms the LGBTQ+ person concerned – an affirmation of their fundamental embodied existence and of their fundamental humanity, not in spite of but including their non-conforming sexuality and gender identity. In the group session, such a pastoral affirmation is reflected in several dismissals that participants came up with, such as: 'Go, be yourself', 'Go, live your life', 'Go, be free – be you', and 'It is well, it is well, go in peace'. These dismissals reflect some of the key characteristics of queer personhood: to be authentic and independent, to enjoy freedom of self-expression and to be at peace with oneself and others. The desire for freedom and peace is echoed by many participants and is framed by some of them explicitly as

---

[44] Jennings, *The Man Jesus Loved*, 61.

something that, fundamentally, only God can give. For instance, Keeya, who insisted on concluding his life story interview with a prayer, prayed for all LGBTQ+ people who judge themselves because of their sexuality, who feel like giving up and may even think of committing suicide. His simple prayer is: 'Lord help them, set them free' (Story 12).

An example of a dismissal that blurs the lines of the category of pastoral affirmation and ethical imperative is, 'Go, love yourself and love the world'. This was linked by the participant, in a later interview, to the notion of the love that God has shown in Jesus to humankind, including to LGBTQ+ folk. If Jesus loves us as LGBTQ+ persons, they suggested, we should, and can, also love ourselves, which subsequently allows us to love others:

> Jesus is a loving man and I am sure he would tell me go out there and love. Love yourself, love your neighbour and love the world. Love does not condemn, love does not kill, love does not hate. Jesus would tell me, 'Love yourself and love the world.'[45]

The participant clearly invokes the second of the two great commandments that Jesus gives in the gospels: 'Love your neighbour as you love yourself' (Matthew 22:39; Mark 12:31).[46] But, interestingly, he appears to have changed the order, putting love for the self before love for the neighbour and the world at large. This may reflect the notion that, in a world where neighbours, friends, and family have too often turned directly against and expressed hatred towards him, self-acceptance and indeed self-love are of critical importance before one can even think of loving the possibly queer-phobic neighbour.

One participant, in their version of the dismissal, explicitly countered the idea of homosexuality as a sin, saying that Jesus would tell them: 'You're not sinning, you are just different, and being different is not bad.' The notion of difference was invoked by yet another participant, who believed that Jesus would say to them: 'You are just different, and you have value like any other human being.' This value was affirmed by two other participants who appeared to invoke the words of Psalm 139 in the Bible, which is a poetic text in which the author suggests, using intimate language, that God already knew them before they were born: 'You created every part of me; you put me together in my mother's womb.'[47] The following dismissal reclaims these words and puts them into Jesus's mouth as an affirmation of

---

[45] Interview with Nita, Matasia, 23 January 2020.

[46] The commandment cited by Jesus is from the Old Testament's Law of Moses (Leviticus 19:18).

[47] Psalm 139:13. Another possible text that may have inspired these participants

the queer self, with Jesus telling them: 'I love you, and I knew you before you were born.' In a later personal interview to conclude the Bible study session, one participant further elaborated on these words, paraphrasing the words of Psalm 139:

> I think Jesus would tell me: 'However, I created you, I loved you; if I did not love you, I would have killed you in your mother's womb. But I created you and I created with a reason, just find your reason, just live your life.' Yeah! I think that is how it would turn out.[48]

Theologically speaking, this quotation exemplifies the conflation of the Jesus of the gospels, and the creator God, which was quite common among participants. The just-quoted interviewee went on spontaneously to justify this equation by invoking the classic doctrine of the Trinity:

> So, when God was creating the world, He was with Jesus and the Holy Spirit. So, Jesus was there when God created me. He would tell me that because he was there when God was creating. He would tell me that.[49]

Thus, the creator God who, according to Psalm 139 formed each human person individually in their mother's womb is the same divine being as the Jesus who, in the gospel story, affirms the full humanity of the woman caught in adultery and who, in the experience of participants, affirms their humanity as LGBTQ+ people.

Ethical imperative

In addition to the pastoral affirmations, many of the dismissals that participants suggested also included a strong ethical imperative. That is, in these versions, Jesus did not only affirm the lives of LGBTQ+ people but sent them away with a directive for how to lead their lives.

In some cases, this takes the form of an imperative towards self-realisation, such as here: 'Don't do what people expect you to do, but do what your life tells you to. Fulfil your own life.' Or in another version: 'You are a human being; you were not born a sinner, but you were born a talent', the sub-text being that the person concerned has to realise their human potential and utilise their talents. Thus, instead of the seemingly negative instruction in the gospel story not to sin again, the dismissal in these versions is given a positive and constructive edge, not only in relation

---

is Jeremiah 1:5, where God says: 'Before I formed you in the womb I knew you, before you were born I set you apart.'

[48] Interview with Rover, Matasia, 31 January 2020.

[49] Ibid.

to the self but also in relation to others. Two participants captured this poignantly, with Jesus in their version telling them to go and live a 'productive' and 'meaningful' life. Elaborating on this in a later interview, one participant reflected:

> So, to me Jesus would tell that first of all, I should live a meaningful life. I should change the narrative of the people. Especially those who are so good at criticising homosexuality. Like criticising the LGBTI people in relation with religion and culture. I think he will tell me to lead a meaningful life. To be more productive. To engage in things that the people view as normal. If I can engage in that kind of stuff, really I can change the narrative.[50]

It appears that for them, the imperative of 'changing the narrative' refers to the popular perceptions of LGBTQ+ people that exist in society: that they lack morality and responsibility, are reckless and useless, and, in the words of one participant, 'use their body as a sex object'. In order to counter such narratives, LGBTQ+ folk feel that they must prove their value through making a meaningful contribution to the community and society. The earlier quoted pastoral affirmation, 'you are just different, and you have value like any other human being' was followed by an imperative, with the participant adding: 'It's your role to teach your value to other people.' These dismissals are somewhat paradoxical in that they affirm the intrinsic value of LGBTQ+ people, but at the same time appear to put pressure on LGBTQ+ folk to demonstrate this value for society at large to recognise it. One might argue that this ambiguity is also reflected in the original gospel story, where Jesus appears to accept the woman without judgement, while simultaneously suggesting that she was, in fact, involved in sinful behaviour. One might further argue that this ambiguity is perhaps at the heart of queer living, because even in societies that seemingly accept LGBTQ+ people and recognise their rights, there tend to be implicit (and sometimes explicit) expectations, if not requirements, of meeting certain standards of moral responsibility and social respectability.

The ending of Tom's poem, 'Accused of a Sodomy Act' (after this chapter), is a dismissal that weaves together a pastoral affirmation and an ethical imperative. Here, Jesus says to the accused:

> Go and treat yourself with love,
> you are as splendidly made as any,

---

[50] Interview with Rodgers, Matasia, 23 January 2020.

all the creatures are formidably made,
go and do not seek vengeance,
rather lead your life fully.

Interestingly, the instruction not to seek vengeance mirrors our findings
from the group process about the Daniel story (see previous chapter), with
participants leaving out the element of vengeance from the Bible story,
and also rendering it absent in their own life stories. The final line of the
poem, about leading life fully, echoes the quest for fullness of life that runs
through African theology, in particular women's theology – with fullness
of life being a state where human beings can flourish individually and
communally, unrestricted by the various death-dealing forces that continue to threaten life on the continent.[51]

Conclusion

The story of Jesus and the woman caught in adultery already has a long
reception history, worldwide and in Africa, to which our participants
have added another chapter. In the tradition of African appropriations
of this biblical story, Ugandan LGBTQ+ refugees read the story from
the perspective of their experience of social marginalisation, stigmatisation, and exclusion. They identified themselves with the woman who had
been caught in adultery, as they recognised her experience of community
justice and mob violence on the basis of certain norms of gender and
sexuality. The threat of being stoned figuratively or literally – by words,
whispers, and acts of violence – is all too real to them. Like the people
living with HIV in Mligo's study, our participants read the story as a
critique of the church and the community for silencing and objectifying
them, reducing them to sinners and refusing to recognise their human
dignity and potential. That is, the story becomes a means to address and
interrogate the dehumanisation they face. Jesus, for them, represents the
acceptance, affirmation, love, and care that they desperately missed in
their families and communities, but that they hope and believe to receive
from God. Where the woman in the story remains mostly silent and
allows herself to be sent away by Jesus with the instruction not to sin
again, our participants demonstrate their agency by categorically resisting the association of queer sexuality with sin, and by rephrasing the
dismissal in a way that they find life-giving.

[51] Mary N. Getui and Matthew M. Theuri (eds), *Quests for Abundant Life in
Africa* (Nairobi: Acton, 2002).

Mligo, in his study with people living with HIV in Tanzania, concludes that the image of Jesus that emerges from their re-reading of the story is one of a 'compassionate companion'.[52] Dube, too, has foregrounded the importance of compassion as a theological and ethical principle in the context of the HIV epidemic. However, she makes the crucial point that compassion is not just pastoral, but political:

> [Compassion] must move us to actively seek change, to end the pain, the suffering, and the hurt of those who are most affected. Compassion is not charity; it is revolution. Defining compassion as revolutionary means that compassion is justice seeking – it aims to tackle the root causes of suffering, not just the symptoms. ... Compassion, in other words, should always involve activism and liberation from all forms of oppression.[53]

The same point is echoed by our participants. They, too, read the figure of Jesus in the story as compassionate. Yet, as pointed out above, they suggest that Jesus's compassionate attitude effectively undermines the workings of hetero-patriarchy. Thus, the story of Jesus and the woman caught in adultery is not just a pastoral affirmation but reinforces their quest for justice as LGBTQ+ refugees – for gender justice, sexual justice, asylum justice, socio-economic justice – in order for them to experience life in abundance.

---

[52] Mligo, *Jesus and the Stigmatized*, 316ff.

[53] Musa W. Dube, *A Theology of Compassion in the HIV/AIDS Era* (Theology in the HIV/AIDS Era Series, module 7) (Geneva: World Council of Churches, 2007), 20.

Accused of a Sodomy Act

Tom Rogers Muyunga-Mukasa

At first it was whispered,
it became the rumour,
the teller added spices,
the listener inundated by stories.
Some listeners were taken aback,
shocked;
others went about doing their business,
less bothered.
The tale of the man at the corner.
It was where we had our water point,
the village water point;
the 'water-man' as we called him,
the man at the corner,
the man who oversees the point,
this man,
it was said,
sleeps with fellow men,
never with women.

In my village the older elders,
the frailest and gauntest of them all,
said this was common in their time,
it was never frowned upon,
it was never spoken about aloud.
They said it all changed later,
the ones who brought a certain Book,
also introduced laws
through which
this act was frowned upon.
The latter elders
now lead the teams
to frown upon the act.

Jesus, it was said,
was on his way to our part,
most likely
on the market day;
on that day
they were to report
the water-man.
Quietly the accusers laid traps,
but the water-man
escaped the traps;
at one time they lined up a girl
to the water-man,
the girl was sent,
to have him seduced,
she failed in all attempts;
next
they sent younger boys,
two,
three,
four young boys,
one after the other,
all failed to lure him.

Then some in our village
failed to pay their water bills;
the water-man
put down
every one of them
in a book of debts;
he sent the book
to the debt-collector;
they promised to pay,
they gave excuses,
they also
looked for ways
to bring a case
against the water-man,
any case,
a case that would stick,
so that
they could banish the water-man.

They connived
to have the water-man replaced.

I saw and heard all this
from my closeted corner;
I wondered
how my case would be,
when Jesus
were to come to our village.
This is how
my case would unfold:

I am similar
to the water-man
in almost all ways.
My family
took me
through a circle of shame.
It was during a funeral
of one of our clan members.
Funerals
are also communal rites of passage;
at a time like this
families resolve issues:
they disown
wayward daughters and sons;
they reconcile
over past misunderstandings;
newer plans are made,
name-giving is done,
wrongs are righted;
a blanket ostracisation betide
they who go against
the clan norms;
the norm is:
a man lies with a woman,
a woman lies with a man,
masculinity is the one half,
whose other half is femininity.

In my case
I lie with a fellow man;

I know of women too,
who lie with fellow women.
I am considered
a half who can never be whole.
Patriarchy draws hard lines,
in form of
masculinity and femininity.

In Jesus' presence,
with the accusers
having evidence against me,
with me all tied up,
bound and bruised,
emotionally and physically,
they would accuse me thus:
'we do not like him at all',
the elders would say;
'we have remedies for this kind of practice',
the elders would continue;
'he never lies with a woman',
this from fellow age-mates;
'he never shows us his children',
this from the immediate family;
'we offered medicinal herbs in case of a dysfunction',
this from the aunties;
'we are ready to give him our girls in marriage',
this from the match-maker families outshouting each other;
'the rains no longer come in their right seasons',
the farmers would shout;
'all our animals die in large numbers',
added the animal keepers.

Jesus would then look at each one of the accusers,
and would then look at me for a longer time.
Jesus would ask:
'How many of you have dug trenches to trap rain-water?'
'How many of you are not aware of the destruction of crop pests?'
'How many of you have rain-water storage tanks at their houses?'
'How many of you have a child for every sexual act they engaged
    in?'
'How many of you have not woken up in beds other than your
    marriage beds?

'How many fathers among you have not got children out of
    wedlock?'
'How many of you fathers pay for childcare for all your children?'
'Those among you who have not sinned at all, let them continue
    with any accusation.'

Jesus had drawn the people
around him,
he showed us our human limits;
they disappeared one by one,
they perceived a side of Jesus that was different,
Jesus would bend down again,
stand upright in his full height,
to ask where everyone had gone.
His godly nature
that stretches limitlessly.
At that moment I knew
about the other half in me,
a half of me I had buried so deep;
I reconciled myself to that other half,
Jesus drew it out of me;
my knees buckled,
I felt face down.
Jesus bent down to pick me up,
'Where are your accusers?'
he asked,
'Gone!'
said I,
'Go and treat yourself with love,
you are as splendidly made as any,
all the creatures are formidably made,
go and do not seek vengeance,
rather lead your life fully.'

4

Reflection: A Postcolonial and Self-reflexive Reading

As a key part of project activities, participants read two stories in the Bible and related these stories to their own perspectives and experiences. In the process, they spontaneously related the stories' characters and events with figures and experiences in their own day-to-day context and lives. In this concluding reflection, two of us, Adriaan and Johanna, as the lead authors of this book, turn the gaze briefly but explicitly towards ourselves, as white European academics who see ourselves as friends and allies – according to some of our participants 'members of the family' – of the Ugandan LGBTQ+ refugees we worked with together in this project.[1] How have the stories come to speak to us? What follows are some tentative thoughts emerging from postcolonial and self-reflexive readings of the Bible stories and inter-reading them with our own experience in this project.

We begin with what might seem to be a slight detour: political theorist Rahul Rao's recent conceptualisation of a 'queer politics of postcoloniality',[2] which he applies specifically to the Ugandan context of sexual politics as

---

[1] We each have written elsewhere about how our respective positionalities, identities and experiences in African contexts have shaped us and our research. E.g. see the auto-ethnographic interludes in Adriaan van Klinken, *Kenyan, Christian, Queer: Religion, LGBT Activism, and Arts of Resistance in Africa* (University Park: Penn State University Press, 2019) and Johanna Stiebert, 'Of Borders, Crossings, Colours and Botswana', in Johanna Stiebert and Musa W. Dube (eds), *The Bible, Centres and Margins: Dialogues Between Postcolonial African and British Biblical Scholars* (London: T&T Clark, 2018), 15–23. However, in this book, we deliberately foreground not our own stories but those of the refugees who participated in the project. We have tried wherever possible to present participants' experiences, perceptions and perspectives in their own words.

[2] Rahul Rao, *Out of Time: The Queer Politics of Postcoloniality* (Oxford: Oxford University Press, 2020).

crystallised in the discourse around the Anti-Homosexuality Bill (AHB). Rao argues that the AHB infamously

> sought to intensify and expand the realm of prohibition, creating a range of new offences related to the practice and 'promotion' of homosexuality out of a professed desire to protect the 'traditional family' and 'culture of the people of Uganda' from the putatively alien scourge of queer sex.[3]

In other words, from the point of view of the proponents of the AHB, queer sexuality and advocates of LGBTQ+ rights threaten the moral purity and cultural integrity of the 'pearl of Africa', as Uganda is popularly known, because they allegedly defy Ugandan culture and sell out the body of the nation by engaging intimately with 'the West' and copying its supposedly morally degraded sexual culture. In the eyes of these proponents, members of Ugandan LGBTQ+ communities are like the guys charged with indecency in the drama: sexually corrupted, comparable with adulterers, defiantly deviant, and deserving of imprisonment, even the death penalty.

But Rao goes further to observe: 'Faced with the claim that they were "unAfrican", Ugandan LGBTI activists responded by pointing to the remarkable internationalism of the AHB itself.'[4] With this action, the accusation was reversed, and it was now the proponents of the AHB who were accused of following a Western agenda, more particularly, the agenda of the US Christian Right that is seeking to export the culture wars over issues of sexuality to Africa, and targeting Uganda as its focal point.[5] Notably, in both these accusation narratives, Ugandans have little agency. Instead, they are (like the woman in the Gospel of John) accused of 'adultery': of sleeping with either a liberal or a conservative West as bedfellow. The criterion on the basis of which Uganda is accused is enmeshed with postcolonial independence, autonomy, and integrity, albeit interpreted and applied in opposite ways. Both narratives, however, reflect that the politics of queer sexuality in Uganda are defined by 'an unfinished struggle marked by the shadow of coloniality'.[6]

With this in mind, one might ask, 'who is the Jesus or the God character in the stories of Daniel and John? Who brings liberation?' Is it the people of Uganda? Is it the international community? Is it the Universal Declaration

---

[3] Ibid., 3.

[4] Ibid., 3.

[5] See Kapya Kaoma, *Globalizing the Culture Wars: U. S. Conservatives, African Churches, & Homophobia* (Somerville: Political Research Associates, 2009).

[6] Rao, *Out of Time*, 7.

of Human Rights, or the African Charter of Human and Peoples' Rights? Who can speak words of truth and justice in this highly volatile and politically charged situation where sexuality has become a battleground at the expense of many children of Uganda, including those whose testimonies can be found in Part I of this book? Our participants, in their reading of the story about the woman caught in adultery, simply left Jesus as Jesus, or directly identified him with God. Meanwhile, in their reading of the story of Daniel, God's protection and rescue of Daniel was praised, but God's allowing Daniel to be tested and endangered was not challenged. Where the Bible stories speak about Jesus and God, the question arises, whose Jesus and whose God is this? Is this the Jesus and the God brought to Uganda by white European missionaries with whose approval the colonial anti-sodomy laws were introduced? Or, is this the Jesus and the God of conservative evangelicalism, either of US or of African guise, in whose name the AHB was justified? Or, is this the Jesus and the God of human rights and LGBTQ+ activists in Uganda, elsewhere in Africa and worldwide, whose names are invoked to advocate a progressive sexual politics? Following the key principle of Contextual Bible Study and other liberation theologies, to read the Bible from the perspective of the marginalised and with the oppressed, we sympathise with our participants when they imagine and assert Jesus and God being on *their* side, accepting them the way they are, breaking with the cultures of stigma and discrimination that they face, and effectively undermining the workings of traditional, colonial, and postcolonial hetero-patriarchies. Yet for us, there is more to probe here.

Postcolonial feminist scholar Gayatri Spivak has famously captured the dynamics of colonial feminism as a case of 'white men saving brown women from brown men'.[7] Paraphrasing this, Rao has observed that in the global South today we see something comparable: 'the eagerness of white gays to save brown gays from brown homophobes'.[8] Where Africa, and specifically Uganda, have been framed in Western narratives as 'the world's worst place to be gay',[9] the 'white saviour' complex can be observed in attempts of human rights and LGBTQ+ activists and allies from the West trying to support and advocate for African LGBTQ+

---

[7] Gayatry C. Spivak, 'Can the Subaltern Speak?' in Rosalind Morris (ed.), *Can the Subaltern Speak? Reflections on the History of an Idea* (New York: Columbia University Press, 2010), 21–78.

[8] Rahul Rao, *Third World Protest: Between Home and the World* (Oxford: Oxford University Press, 2010), xx.

[9] Scott Mills, *Uganda: The World's Worst Place to Be Gay?* Documentary of the British Broadcasting Corporation, 2011.

communities.[10] This is obviously done with good intentions but not always with adequate knowledge, understanding, or sensitivities.[11] And so we find ourselves, uncomfortably, wondering to what extent this complex may be reflected also in us, as UK-based academics, undertaking the research project that resulted in the present book.

The latter question is inspired by the critique presented by the black South African scholar Gloria Kehilwe Plaatjie of the Contextual Bible Study (CBS) work of Gerald West of the Ujamaa Centre (which we discussed in Chapter 1).[12] Plaatjie acknowledges CBS as an approach 'recognized for its empathy and intentions of solidarity' with marginalised readers.[13] She draws critical attention, however, to the fact that West's focus is 'on reading with black ordinary readers, rather than with white ordinary readers', and she observes that this 'risks being seen as anthropological, or as a white male doing what other white males have always done – namely, writing about and becoming an authority on black people'.[14] As Plaatjie points out, race, class, and gender, and the dynamics between them, should not be underplayed. For Plaatjie, 'reading with' (the CBS

---

[10] The white saviour complex refers to white persons acting to help non-white persons in a way that is self-serving. It has been applied, for instance, to white celebrities (e.g. Madonna, Ed Sheeran, and Stacey Dooley) posting pictures of themselves alongside impoverished black children. Such is widely deemed as casting white celebrities as virtuous (and 'woke') helpers and poor black people as passive recipients of help, or mere accessories. However, these celebrity cases fit in a long colonial history and in a much broader social reality of charity and development work and the media representations thereof. The white saviour complex or saviour mentality is discussed with reference to development and activism by Jordan Flaherty, *No More Heroes: Grassroots Challenges to the Savior Mentality* (Chico: AK Press, 2016) and to textual analysis, by R. Straubhaar, in 'The Stark Reality of the "White Saviour" complex and the Need for Critical Consciousness: A Document Analysis of the Early Journals of a Freirean Educator', *Compare: A Journal of Comparative and International Education*, 45:3 (2015), 381–400.

[11] Robbie Corey-Boulet, *Love Falls on Us: A Story of American Ideas and African LGBT Lives* (London: Zed Books, 2019).

[12] Gloria Kehilwe Plaatjie, 'Toward a Post-apartheid Black Feminist Reading of the Bible: A Case of Luke 2:36–38', in Musa W. Dube (ed.), *Other Ways of Reading: African Women and the Bible* (Atlanta: Society of Biblical Literature, 2001), 114–142.

[13] Ibid., 118.

[14] Ibid., 118.

approach) is not enough: instead, she advocates for 'reading from' black, non-academic, marginalised readers.[15] Reading from, meanwhile, requires someone who is not 'a complete outsider to the political, social, economic, and cultural experiences that have molded the thinking and practice' of the non-academic readers.[16] We take on board Plaatjie's point and agree we could not have entered into or participated in the activities of this project without the introduction by and mediation and leadership of Raymond and Hudson who, as *both* TNN community members *and* co-researchers, provided important channels of communication and translation in both directions, and who played a vital role in the process of knowledge production during this project. Out of this awareness, the sessions of contextual and creative Bible study that were part of our project were fully facilitated by Raymond and Hudson, with the help of fellow TNN members. The first session was, in fact, held in our absence, and in the following sessions we took quite literally a backseat although participating in the group deliberations. In that sense, the project was not about *us* reading the Bible *with* the participating refugees but was about *them* reading *from* their own perspective. The community itself was facilitating the process, and we were participant-observers.

Yet the idea for this Bible reading project had come from us in the first place, although it had been developed together with TNN as a partner. Thanks to our position in UK academia, we had been able to secure the funding to make it happen. As white UK-based researchers, bringing the funding for project activities where we took 'a backseat' while the participating Ugandan refugees read the Bible from their perspectives, Plaatjie's point about 'the risk of being seen as anthropological' might well apply to us, perhaps more than to West who, by comparison, is considerably more immersed in, and knowledgeable about, the research settings of CBS activities.[17]

Thinking about this, we have further been inspired by the white, feminist biblical scholar Jayme Reaves.[18] Reaves reflects on the biblical narratives of Sarah and Hagar (in the Bible's book of Genesis), which have long

---

[15] Ibid., 119.

[16] Ibid., 120.

[17] We certainly do not want to disqualify the guild of anthropology. Plaatjie appears to allude to the tradition of ethnographic othering that has long haunted anthropology as a discipline that emerged during colonialism. We acknowledge that the discipline has increasingly practised internal critique of this tradition as well.

[18] Jayme R. Reaves, 'Sarah as Victim and Perpetrator: Whiteness, Power, and Memory in the Matriarchal Narrative', *Review and Expositor* (2018), 1–17.

been interpreted by womanist scholars in terms of power dynamics drawn along lines of racial supremacy.[19] If Hagar is the Egyptian (that is, African) slave, then Sarah is readily identified as the white slave owner. Reaves is one (surprisingly) rare example of a white biblical scholar engaging with womanist scholarship and examining her own white privilege.[20] She begins by acknowledging that,

> because of my position as a white woman, I have wittingly or unwittingly been in the role of Sarah more often than I have been in the role of Hagar. In this story between Sarah and Hagar, Sarah is the oppressor. In this story, I am Sarah. … white feminists like me look to Hagar and focus on her exploitation and abuse because we want to be on her side and show our 'wokeness' rather than focusing on the ways Sarah's part of the story questions us about our whiteness, use of power, and complicity in systems of oppression.[21]

Reaves' conclusion is a call to responsibility and heightened perception, which we welcome:

> Let us open our eyes to our privilege and the ways in which we read the biblical text that perpetuate injustice. Let us remember redemption and injustice in equal measure. Let us repair by acceding our power over, and assuming power with. Let us care. Let us know and speak each other's names.[22]

Also appealing for us about Reaves' reading is her self-critical reflection *into* the biblical text. This compels us to inter-read Daniel 6 and John 8 and ask, 'who are we here?' We are not Daniel in the lions' den or in prison, following arrest under a newly imposed Anti-Homosexuality Bill. Although we have experience in our own lives of being accused of 'indecency', in the context of this project we cannot identify with the woman

---

[19] See, for instance, Renita J. Weems, *Just a Sister Away: A Womanist Vision of Women's Relationships in the Bible* (Philadelphia: Innisfree Press, 1988) and Delores S. Williams, *Sister in the Wilderness: The Challenge of Womanist God-Talk* (Maryknoll: Orbis, 2013).

[20] The rarity of such approaches can to some degree be accounted for by the phenomenon called 'white fragility', whereby white people when challenged on account of their covert racism or biases behave with defensiveness or denial. For a full discussion, see Robin DiAngelo, *White Fragility: Why It's So Hard for White People to Talk About Racism* (Boston: Beacon, 2018).

[21] Reaves, 'Sarah as Victim and Perpetrator', 2, 9.

[22] Ibid., 17.

caught in adultery, or with the guys charged with indecency, as we respectfully leave it to our participants to identify their profound experiences of
stigmatisation and persecution in the story. Neither are we, we hope, the
governors or the accusers, except perhaps in a rather distanced way as
UK residents who are somehow implicated in what Rao conceptualises as
the global queer politics of postcoloniality. Obviously, we do not actively
identify with the divine figures (Jesus, God, the angel) in the stories and
imagine ourselves as 'saviours'. Yet, in the light of the (often unconscious)
white saviour complex, Julius Kiambi's earlier quoted postcolonial feminist criticism that 'Jesus saves the day for the woman [caught in adultery]
but does not dismantle the ideology that would seal a similar fate for other
women' resonates critically with us.[23]

Through this project, we have been able, albeit in comparatively small
ways, to 'save the day' for participants: the little pocket money they got
for participating in the interviews and group sessions helped them to get
through another day or two; the project money we were able to transfer
to The Nature Network helped them to pay the bills for rent and food for
several months. With the project coming formally to an end, we remain
committed to supporting the community where we can. Yet has this project achieved anything more for our participants and the community they
are part of? Has it improved in any way the situation in which LGBTQ+
refugees in Kenya find themselves? In any significant practical, let alone
structural, sense it has not. Maybe, however, it does not have to in order to
be meaningful and worthwhile – after all, we do not want to be the 'white
saviour', and that implies adopting an attitude of humility about our (in)
ability to make any substantial difference.

We are aware that praising the 'bravery' and 'resilience' of the poor
and black is part of the white saviour complex, and we know that suffering
deprivation has taken its toll – most starkly and distressingly, as mentioned
earlier, in the form of enduring physical violence and of committing suicide. It has been the case, however, that through this project we have been
continually and immensely impressed by the skills of survival, and more
than that, the joy and flourishing, that our participants exemplify. In the
midst of very difficult circumstances, the LGBTQ+ refugee community
we worked with demonstrates extraordinary tenacity, courage, and creativity. More than that, The Nature Network builds this community, through
a method of family-based therapy, around a praxis of love, demonstrating,

[23] Julius Kithinji Kiambi, 'Divining John 7:53–8:11 for textual Gender-motivated violence: A Postcolonial Approach' (unpublished paper, 2012), https://
papers.ssrn.com/sol3/papers.cfm?abstract_id=2017643, 13.

in Chisomo Kalinga's words, African queer communities' 'most important asset'.[24] The storytelling methodology of this project has enabled us to foreground and explore these characteristics, qualities, and virtues, thus counter-balancing the stereotypical representations of Ugandan LGBTQ+ people as either perverts (in popular Ugandan discourse) or victims (in mainstream Western narratives).

Although the idea of contextual and creative Bible study was introduced by us, this project has only succeeded because it could build on the already existing culture and structure developed by our partners of The Nature Network, and on the expertise and skills of the local coordinators, Raymond Brian and Fredrick Hudson. Yes, money plays a role in a project like this, and it is a legitimate question to ask what power relations such a flow of money – managed by UK-based researchers, flowing in the direction of local partner organisations – reflects and reinforces. In the design of our project, we have tried to address this question by adopting a broader notion of resources. We as UK-based academics secured the funding and, by the rules of our institution, were responsible for managing these financial resources. Yet Raymond and Hudson, and other partners at TNN, brought in a wealth of other resources – human capital, community knowledge, creative skills, and group-work expertise – that proved to be essential. As scholars, we brought in academic knowledge, but our TNN partners brought in complementary forms of knowledge that turned out to be at least as vital for this project: knowledge of community organising, facilitating group sessions, creative and performative arts, and of course the knowledge contained in the life stories themselves. On the basis of this notion of contributing diverse but equally important resources, we have sought to collaborate in a spirit of collegiality, mutuality, and reciprocity.

In the process, we have not only been touched by the deeply moving stories of the precarious lives of LGBTQ+ refugees, but also by the experience of being warmly welcomed and included into the queer family of The Nature Network, and we have learned from the situated knowledges, skills, and life experiences that participants brought into this project. Perhaps in the Bible stories we – like Dhalie – can best identify with the peripheral supporters of Daniel, who celebrate with him when he is freed, and with the not-present peoples who affirm and exonerate the guys charged with indecency, who are outraged by the accusations levelled at them. It might well be, too, that there is *no* room for us in these Bible stories, *no*

---

[24] Chisomo Kalinga, 'Love: An Ethnographic Inquiry into Queer, Christian Relationships in Kenya', *HAU: Journal of Ethnographic Theory*, 10:2 (2020), 624.

character to identify ourselves with. That in itself is a humbling thought. Interrogating the white saviour complex, after all, begins with decentring ourselves as white European academics working in an African context, and with foregrounding the agency of community members, however marginalised they may be. As this project and the work of community-organisations such as TNN demonstrate, they are more than capable of telling their stories themselves!

Conclusion

This book has centred around stories. Because, in the words of Chimamanda Ngozi Adichie, 'stories matter'.[1] In the quotation that serves as epigraph to the Introduction, Adichie captures the multiple possibilities, both negative and positive, opened up by storytelling and story sharing. Against the 'single story' of 'African homophobia', as well as 'religious homophobia', this book has foregrounded the stories through which Ugandan LGBTQ+ refugees narrate their life experiences, struggles, and hopes. Moreover, it has explored how their stories resonate with biblical stories, and how the latter can be creatively appropriated to signify their lives. The process of storytelling, of which this book has offered an account, and the stories that resulted from it, can be described as both sacred and queer. These stories are queer, in the sense that they boldly narrate non-normative sexualities and gender expressions, construe alternative forms of kinship and belonging, reflect precarious lives that are in transit, and demonstrate vulnerability, courage, and resilience. They are sacred, in that they narratively claim human dignity, effectively countering popular narratives and biblical interpretations that dehumanise or victimise LGBTQ+ lives and cast them as sinful. Moreover, this dignity is grounded in the belief in God's affirming love and is affirmed through the reading of canonised sacred scripture.

The main methodological contribution of this book is its appropriation of the Bible for the process of sacred queer storytelling by Ugandan LGBTQ+ refugees. Although it has been acknowledged that the Bible in contemporary Africa 'forms part of the problem because it is a site of struggle [in which] the debate on homosexuality is being fought',[2] this

---

[1] Chimamanda Ngozi Adichie, 'The Danger of a Single Story', TED Global 2009, www.ted.com/talks/chimamanda_ngozi_adichie_the_danger_of_a_single_story (accessed 16 December 2020).

[2] Masiiwa R. Gunda, *The Bible and Homosexuality in Zimbabwe: A Socio-historical Analysis of the Political, Cultural and Christian Arguments in the Homosexual Public Debate with Special Reference to the Use of the Bible* (Bamberg: Bamberg University Press, 2010), 22.

book suggests that it can be part of the solution, too. This suggestion is not based on the simple premise that sacred queer storytelling with the help of the Bible will solve the problem of the politics of homosexuality in African societies – these politics are far too complex and multifaceted for simple solutions. However, if the Bible is indeed 'a site of struggle', it is pertinent for this site not to be left to conservative religious leaders and other public opinion makers, who mobilise the authority of the Bible as a weapon for anti-LGBTQ+ politics. The notion of 'struggle', after all, presupposes (at least) two strugglers. Engaging this site of struggle, and opposing such conservative and homophobic voices, should also not be left to academically trained theologians and biblical scholars who can develop alternative, LGBTQ+-affirming interpretations – no matter how important a task this is. This book has shown that African LGBTQ+ communities themselves can engage the Bible as a site of struggle; as 'ordinary' but interested readers, they can read and interpret ancient sacred scripture through the lens of their own experiences. As the two inter-readings of specific biblical stories in Part II of this book have demonstrated, the resonance between biblical stories and the life stories of Ugandan LGBTQ+ refugees participating in this project are multiple, and the Bible turns out to be a rich interface and resource not only for participants to identify and recognise their own struggle but also to derive perspectives of affirmation, empowerment, and liberation. Thus, in response to the suggestion made by Cameroonian-American theologian Elias Bongmba, that 'it is time to read the Bible differently' in the context of African debates about homosexuality, because 'the Bible is a human product and invites a new appreciation, which should depart from protecting it as a text', we have engaged in a creative re-storying of biblical stories in order for the Bible to speak to the life experiences of LGBTQ+ refugees from Uganda, and vice versa, for their life experiences to speak to the Bible.[3]

Kenyan theologian Nyambura Njoroge has raised the critical question whether the Bible should be considered a curse or a blessing to Africa. Referring to the imperial history of Christianity, and the ongoing use of the Bible for socio-political oppression, she meditates:

What does this Bible, which in my Gikuyu language is called *Ibuku ria Ngai*, 'the Book of God,' have to offer in the midst of the bloodshed among the youth of Africa, of the prime ages of fifteen to forty? What can a book offer that is used to exploit its illiterate and ignorant listeners, the elderly

---

[3] Elias K. Bongmba, 'Hermeneutics and the Debate on Homosexuality in Africa', *Religion and Theology*, 22:1–2 (2015), 87.

women and men, who watch helplessly when their children and grand-children die, leaving no name behind to carry on life? What can a book offer that is interpreted to enrich the greedy preachers, the vultures, the crusaders who take advantage of the poor, deaf, cripples, and the dumb? What can a book offer that is used by the so-called messengers of the good news to stigmatize and ostracize those dying from HIV/AIDS? What can a book offer that has been used to keep Africans, women and slaves 'in their place'? No doubt, we know that this same book has also brought hope and life to people's lives and communities. So is this book a curse or a blessing to the weary and lamenting people of Africa?[4]

Sexual and gender minorities, and the detrimental effect that the Bible has had on them, are not explicitly mentioned here, but it is easy to include them in the point Njoroge makes. As one of our participants, Doreen, puts it in her life story interview:

> I grew up where everything I was reading in the Bible and everything I was taught in the church – or, let's say, 70 per cent – was against my flow of life, against my nature, against my being, against my experience. It was telling me what is expected of me to be a man: to marry and have children, leave a legacy, create a lineage, and all that. … And the preacher, the read-ers of the Bible, scholars, they use the Bible to tell you that you are doing the wrong thing. (Story 8)

Although Njoroge expresses deep concern about the role that the Bible has played, and continues to play, in legitimating situations of discrimination, exclusion, and marginalisation of certain groups of people, she does not simply conclude that the Bible is, indeed, a curse. She alludes to the possi-bility for the Bible to be 'life-giving, creative, healing, and authentic', if it is rescued from 'misuse and misinterpretation', and she refers to strategies of reading with 'ordinary readers' as a critical way to realise this potential.[5] In this book, we have adopted this method in our reading of select bibli-cal stories with Ugandan LGBTQ+ refugees, thus expanding the scope of African biblical studies which so far has not extensively engaged with LGBTQ+ communities, and of queer African studies, which so far has not engaged in depth with Christianity, or specifically the Bible, in the pro-cess of documenting and building queer African archives. Building on the

---

[4] Nyambura J. Njoroge, 'The Bible and African Christianity: A Curse or a Blessing?' in Musa W. Dube (ed.), *Other Ways of Reading: African Women and the Bible (Atlanta: Society of Biblical Literature*, 2001), 213–14.

[5] Njoroge, 'The Bible and African Christianity', 215.

status of the Bible as an influential and popular socio-cultural text in East Africa, and as sacred scripture for our participants, be they Christian or Muslim, we have explored the capacity of a particular African queer constituency – Ugandan LGBTQ+ refugees – to interpret the Bible through their eyes, and to reclaim it as affirming and empowering to them.

The feedback of our participants testifies that through this process, the Bible for them has changed, in Njoroge's words, from a curse into a blessing, as the stories we worked with (with which they had come up in the first place) turned out to be 'life-giving, creative, healing, and authentic'. The significance of reclaiming the Bible from a largely homophobic church, and appropriating it to affirm LGBTQ+ lives, was recognised by one of the participants, Nita, when at the end of the process he concludes:

> The person who came up with the idea of using the Bible to reflect on the life of the LGBTI is a genius and I am not over-praising anyone. And the word genius is an understatement. Because so many people have used different catalogues to write about the LGBTI. But to use the Bible as a source, to write something from the Bible, is great because it is respected. The Bible goes way back in time and it is credible. Using the Bible is a good way to respect and be respected. The Gospel is a book of life and we should use it to reveal life.[6]

Nita's words appear to suggest that the use of the Bible is strategic, given its status as an ancient book with sacred status, holding high esteem in society today. Using such a resource is a way for LGBTQ+ communities to gain respect, and it adds an important 'catalogue' or register to the discourse on LGBTQ+ lives, complementing other catalogues, such as of human rights and the law. However, Nita further suggests that the use of the Bible is not only strategic, but also qualitatively important, because 'the Gospel is a book of life' and thus holds great potential to reveal and promote life, especially with regard to those people whose lives are under threat, such as LGBTQ+ folk. Thus, it is the overall message of the Gospel, and of the Bible more generally, that is summarised here as life-giving. And it is this which makes sacred scripture so powerful and effective: both with a view to spiritually affirming and healing LGBTQ+ people of faith, and to bringing about change in religious circles and society more generally.

The affirming and healing effect of the process of inter-reading Bible stories and life experiences was captured powerfully by Isaac, in the

---

[6] Interview with Nita, Matasia, 23 January 2020.

individual interview with him after the session about the Daniel story. Isaac articulates the connection he came to feel with the Bible, as follows:

> The word that was written [in the Bible] can be compared to our day-to-day experience. It gives the authenticity of what the word in the Bible is and what we are going through in life. So, for me, it rejuvenated the other religious part of me where I feel like my God is passing a certain message through someone and there is that reaction from the word. That Sunday [of the dramatisation], I slept well. I slept well because it had been a while since I went to church and now I'm here acting and reflecting on God's Word. And I was like, 'Okay God: I think you can bless me through this.'[7]

What Isaac seems to be describing is a spiritual experience, of connecting to the Bible and with God. He explicitly confirms Njoroge's point that the Bible can become a blessing. He appears to feel some sense of vindication: that he has been part of interpreting the Bible in a way that is affirming, profound and persuasive. As he put it:

> Me having emotions with another man: it's God's creation. The people who regard themselves as staunch Christians who feel like the queer community shouldn't exist: I think they don't get it right. They should revisit every single part of the Bible.

What Isaac is expressing here is a new confidence in the Bible speaking to him, and in his ability to reclaim it for himself. This clearly has an empowering effect, as he, like other participants, now feel confident directly to interrogate 'staunch Christians' who use the Bible against them.

In Tina's resolute words, 'the religious people use the Bible wrongly'.[8] These quotations reflect the hermeneutics of trust discussed earlier in this book. Through the process of creatively reading and engaging with the biblical stories in the light of their own life experiences, the LGBTQ+ refugees participating in our project discovered the 'liberating force' that, in Alice Yafeh-Deigh's words, is at the heart of a hermeneutics of trust.[9] Doing so, they experienced, to quote Robert Goss and Mona West, that 'the Bible is our friend', not intending to harm LGBTQ+ persons but

---

[7] Interview with Isaac, Matasia, 15 January 2020.

[8] Interview with Tina, Matasia, 15 January 2020.

[9] Alice Yafeh-Deigh, 'Rethinking Paul's Sexual Ethics within the Context of HIV and AIDS: A Postcolonial Afro-Feminist-Womanist Perspective', in Madipoane Masenya (Ngwan'a Mphahlele) and Kenneth N. Ngwa (eds), *Navigating African Biblical Hermeneutics: Trends and Themes from Our Pots and Our Calabashes* (Newcastle: Cambridge Scholar Publishing, 2018), 35.

to affirm their dignity and their right to fullness of life.[10] And if the Bible is their friend, so is the God of the Bible, who they firmly believe is on their side. One of the empowering effects, as reflected in the just-presented quotations, is that participants feel confident to speak back to religious leaders who use the Bible to marginalise and oppress them. Engaging the Bible on this basis, a basis of trust, complements another strategy, of a hermeneutics of suspicion, which enables LGBTQ+ people to deconstruct the clobber verses in the Bible typically used against them.[11] Where the latter is concerned with 'disarming biblically based gay-bashing',[12] the former is concerned with changing the Bible from a curse into a blessing.

Both hermeneutical strategies, which are complementary, demonstrate in different ways the potential of the Bible as a resource for transformative activism and scholarship with regard to LGBTQ+ issues in contemporary Africa.[13] A hermeneutics of trust, however, might be particularly suitable in contexts where the Bible is generally held in high esteem and is indeed, trusted as the Word of God. Strategies based on trust, combined with a sense of criticality and contextuality, can stimulate ways of reading the Bible that 'lead to responsible creativity, healing, and wholeness'.[14] Future studies can further explore the differences, as well as the overlap, between these hermeneutical strategies, and their respective contributions to social and religious transformation.[15]

---

[10] Robert E. Goss and Mona West, 'Introduction', in Robert E. Goss and Mona West (eds), *Take Back the Word: A Queer Reading of the Bible* (Cleveland: The Pilgrim Press, 2000), 5.

[11] For an example of this in an African context, see Gerald West, 'The Bible and Homosexuality 2016', Ujamaa Centre, http://ujamaa.ukzn.ac.za/Libraries/manuals/Bible_and_homosexuality_1.sflb.ashx (accessed 16 December 2020).

[12] Ronald E. Long, 'Disarming Biblically Based Gay-bashing', in Deryn Guest, Robert E. Goss, and Mona West (eds), *The Queer Bible Commentary* (London: SCM Press, 2006), 1–18.

[13] E.g. see Masiiwa Ragies Gunda and Jim Naughton (eds), *On Sexuality and Scripture: Essays, Bible Studies, and Personal Reflections* (New York: Church Publishing, 2017); Gerald West and Charlene van der Walt, 'A Queer (Beginning to the) Bible', *Concilium*, 5 (2019), 109–118.

[14] Njoroge, 'The Bible and African Christianity', 233.

[15] We have discussed the question of a hermeneutics of trust versus suspicion in some more detail, in Adriaan van Klinken and Johanna Stiebert, 'Challenging Contexts from the Lions' Den: Reading Daniel with Ugandan LGBT Refugees in Nairobi', in Louise Lawrence, Peter-Ben Smit, Hannah Strømmen and Charlene van der Walt (eds), *Challenging Contexts: Biblical Texts Beyond Boundaries* (Oxford: Oxford University Press, forthcoming).

The two drama films that came out of this project, 'Daniel in the Homophobic Lions' Den', and 'Jesus and the Guys Charged with Indecency', were both selected for screening at the Changing the Story International Film Festival (online), 1–5 June 2020. The news of the selection was enthusiastically received by our participants in Nairobi, who saw it as an affirmation of the work undertaken in this project, and more than that, a validation of their stories which, through these films, would now have a global reach. In response to the Facebook post announcing the festival screening of the films, they made comments such as, 'This is so awesome, I am so thrilled. We can make change! Yes we are!' and 'This is wonderful; even God is remembering us as The Nature Network'. Thus, not only was the selection seen as a confirmation that they are change makers, but also as a sign that God is supportive of that change. Speaking at the festival's online Q&A session with other film makers, Raymond Brian – for this occasion fully and colourfully dragged up as Mother Nature – stated:

In these films one watches LGBT youths turning hateful rhetoric into a call for love, direction, inclusion, and respectful regard. This is just a sneak peek! I am sure you will come out after watching as a more refreshed person. Allow the youths to participate in life-long influencing activities. Empower them!

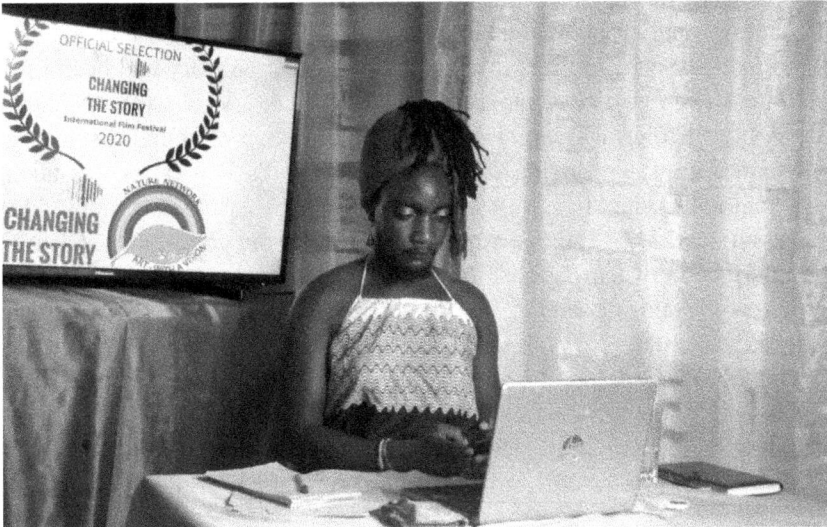

Figure 4 Mother Nature (aka Raymond Brian) presenting at an online panel of the Changing the Story film festival; 5 June 2020 (© The Nature Network)

This statement not only illustrates the level of ownership over the project, but also the belief in the power of storytelling to repair broken dignity and to bring about social change. Imagine the excitement when, at the end of the festival, it was announced that 'Daniel in the Homophobic Lions' Den' had been awarded the Platinum Audience Choice Award! Admittedly, our participants had been busy mobilising members of their own community to vote for the film, which in itself illustrates their level of investment in this project and its outcomes. The short video in which TNN members celebrate the news of the Award was shared on the TNN Facebook page, and vividly captures the sheer joy with which the news was received.[16] It serves as evidence that the Bible *can* become a blessing to marginalised LGBTQ+ refugee communities.

In the course of the year 2020, about ten months after we had conducted the final Bible study session at TNN as part of this project, a screenshot with a biblical passage was shared on the TNN Facebook page. It was in the midst of the COVID-19 pandemic, which greatly impacted the LGBTQ+ refugee community in Kenya as it reinforced and multiplied their already existing vulnerabilities. TNN had responded to this situation by setting up several activities to support refugees facing hardship, to sensitise them on the risks of the virus, and to educate them on prevention strategies. The Bible passage shared on Facebook was from the Gospel of Mark (3:7–12), and we learned that the story had been used as part of the TNN community prayer and Bible study meeting that week. Interestingly, this passage tells about Jesus healing people, and then about Jesus avoiding the crowds by seeking refuge on a small boat. In a creative way, the story had been used to address two questions that are critical in the context of COVID-19: the possibility of religious healing, and the importance of social distancing. This anecdote is worth sharing, as it demonstrates how TNN has taken ownership of Contextual Bible Study, continuing to use it as a method for addressing and reflecting on challenges faced by the community. Clearly, the interface between Bible stories and the life experiences of LGBTQ+ refugees is manifold and dynamic, allowing for new situations to be addressed in creative ways.

This book has mapped a new chapter in the long history of the Bible and its reception in Africa. Building on African biblical hermeneutics of liberation and on strategies of reading the Bible with 'ordinary readers', it has demonstrated how the Bible can be appropriated as a tool of

---

[16] The Nature Network, 'Changing the Story Film Festival 2020', 5 June 2020, www.facebook.com/kenaturenetwork/videos/vb.250366898682974/8763812 39524330 (accessed 16 December 2020).

liberation of communities that are marginalised on the basis of their sexuality and gender expressions. The work presented here hopefully serves as a stimulus to African biblical studies, especially outside of South Africa, to engage more explicitly with LGBTQ+ communities and develop queer contextual readings of biblical scripture. It further challenges the emerging field of queer African studies, to engage with religion in all its dimensions, including sacred scripture, as a potential site of LGBTQ+ empowerment and politics. Moreover, it demonstrates to African cultural studies that the Bible is an influential popular cultural text, the significance of which is not limited to the religious sphere narrowly defined, but extends to the realms of community organising, social activism, and creative and performative arts. Lastly, building on traditions of storytelling in feminist, postcolonial, and queer scholarship, this book has provided a methodology of life storytelling vis-à-vis the stories in canonised scriptures, thus exploring new ways in which storytelling can be utilised to signify marginalised lives and creatively to produce knowledges of resistance. Here's to more African sacred queer stories to be told!

Bibliography

Abbey, Rose Teteki. 'I Am the Woman', in Musa W. Dube (ed.), *Other Ways of Reading: African Women and the Bible* (Atlanta: Society of Biblical Literature, 2001), 23–26.

Adamo, David T. *Africa and Africans in the Old Testament* (Eugene: Wipf and Stock, 2001).

Adeyemo, Tokunboh (ed.). *Africa Bible Commentary* (Nairobi: WordAlive Publishers; Grand Rapids: Zondervan 2006).

——. 'Daniel', in Tokunboh Adeyemo (ed.), *Africa Bible Commentary* (Nairobi: WordAlive Publishers; Grand Rapids: Zondervan, 2006), 989–1012.

Adichie, Chimamanda Ngozi. 'The Danger of a Single Story', TED Global 2009, www.ted.com/talks/chimamanda_ngozi_adichie_the_danger_of_a_single_story (accessed 16 December 2020).

Afriyie, Ernestina. 'Taboos', in Tokunboh Adeyemo (ed.), *Africa Bible Commentary* (Nairobi: WordAlive Publishers; Grand Rapids: Zondervan, 2006), 159.

Akoto, Dorothy. 'Can These Bones Live? Re-reading Ezekiel 37:1–14 in the HIV/AIDS Context', in Musa W. Dube and Musimbi R. A. Kanyoro (eds), *Grant Me Justice! HIV/AIDS & Gender Readings of the Bible* (Maryknoll: Orbis, 2004), 97–111.

Amuke, Isaac Otidi. 'Facing the Mediterranean', in *The Gerald Kraak Anthology: African Perspectives on Gender, Social Justice and Sexuality*; Vol. II *As You Like It* (Auckland Park: Jacana Media, 2018), 1–19.

Ashcroft, Bill, Gareth Griffiths, and Helen Tiffin. *Post-Colonial Studies: The Key Concepts* (London and New York: Routledge, 2000).

Assohoto, Barnabe, and Samuel Ngewa. 'Genesis', in Tokunboh Adeyemo (ed.), *Africa Bible Commentary* (Nairobi: WordAlive Publishers; Grand Rapids: Zondervan, 2006), 9–86.

Awondo, Patrick, Peter Geschiere, and Graeme Reid. 'Homophobic Africa? Toward A More Nuanced View', *African Studies Review*, 55:3 (2012), 145–168.

Azuah, Unoma (ed.). *Blessed Body: The Secret Lives of Nigerian Lesbian, Gay, Bisexual and Transgender* (Jackson: CookingPot, 2016).

Bailey, Randall C. 'Why Do Readers Believe Lot? Genesis 19 Reconsidered', *Old Testament Essays* 23:3 (2010), 519–548.

Baloyi, Elijah M. 'A Re-reading of John 8:1–11 from a Pastoral Liberative Perspective on South African Women', *HTS Teologiese Studies/ Theological Studies*, 66:2, art. #838.

Bompani, Barbara, and Caroline Valois. 'Sexualizing Politics: The Anti-Homosexuality Bill, Party-politics and the New Political Dispensation in Uganda', *Critical African Studies*, 9:1 (2017), 52–70.

Bongmba, Elias K. 'Hermeneutics and the Debate on Homosexuality in Africa', *Religion and Theology*, 22:1–2 (2015), 69–99.

Boyd, Margaret R. 'Community-Based Research: Understanding the Principles, Practices, Challenges, and Rationale', in Patricia Leavy (ed.), *The Oxford Handbook of Qualitative Research* (Oxford: Oxford University Press, 2014), 498–517.

Bryan, Austin. 'Kuchu Activism, Queer Sex-work and "Lavender Marriages," in Uganda's Virtual LGBT Safe(r) Spaces', *Journal of Eastern African Studies*, 13:1 (2019), 90–105.

Bwana, Joackim. 'Mombasa Court Declares Anal Tests on Homosexual Suspects Illegal', *The Standard*, 23 March 2018, www.standardmedia.co.ke/article/2001274237/mombasa-court-declares-anal-tests-on-homosexual-suspects-illegal (accessed 8 May 2021).

Byamugisha, Gideon, and Glen Williams (eds). *Positive Voices: Religious Leaders Living with or Personally Affected by HIV and AIDS* (Oxford: Strategies for Hope Trust, 2005).

Cherry, Kittredge. 'Daniel and the Three Young Men: God Rescues Biblical Eunuchs, Affirming LGBTQ People of Faith', QSpirit, 21 July 2020. https://qspirit.net/daniel-three-young-men-eunuchs (accessed 16 December 2020).

Chia, Philip. 'On Naming the Subject: Postcolonial Reading of Daniel 1', in R. S. Sugirtharajah (ed.), *The Postcolonial Biblical Reader* (Oxford: Blackwell, 2006), 171–185.

Chingota, Felix. 'Leviticus', in Tokunboh Adeyemo (ed.), *Africa Bible Commentary* (Nairobi: WordAlive Publishers; Grand Rapids: Zondervan, 2006), 129–168.

Chirwa, Wiseman C. 'Dancing towards Dictatorship: Political Songs and Popular Culture in Malawi', *Nordic Journal of African Studies*, 10:1 (2001), 1–27.

Chisiwa, Zindaba. 'Using Theatre for Development to Engage Boys in Examining Masculinity and HIV in Two Malawi Schools', *Journal of Applied Arts & Health*, 10:1 (2019), 87–98.

Chitando, Ezra (ed.). *Engaging with the Past: Same-Sex Relationships in Pre-Colonial Zimbabwe* (Geneva: WCC Publications, 2015)

Chitando, Ezra, and Lovemore Togarasei. '"Woman, Where Are They?" John 7:53–8:11 and Stigma in the Context of HIV and Aids', *Missionalia*, 36:1 (2008), 4–15.

Chitando, Ezra, and Masiiwa R. Gunda. 'HIV and AIDS, Stigma and Liberation in the Old Testament', *Exchange: Journal of Contemporary Christianities in Context*, 36:2 (2007), 184–197.

Chitando, Ezra, and Sophie Chirongoma (eds). *Redemptive Masculinities: Men, HIV, and Religion* (Geneva: WCC Publications, 2012).

Chitando, Ezra, and Tapiwa P. Mapuranga. 'Unlikely Allies? Lesbian, Gay, Bisexual, Transgender and Intersex (LGBTI) Activists and Church Leaders in Africa', in Ezra Chitando and Adriaan van Klinken (eds), *Christianity and Controversies over Homosexuality in Contemporary Africa* (London and New York: Routledge, 2016), 171–183.

Corey-Boulet, Robbie. *Love Falls on Us: A Story of American Ideas and African LGBT Lives* (London: Zed Books, 2019).

Cornwall, Susannah. *Controversies in Queer Theology* (London: SCM Press, 2011).

Currier, Ashley, and Joëlle M. Cruz. 'Civil Society and Sexual Struggles in Africa', in Ebenezer Obadare (ed.), *The Handbook of Civil Society in Africa* (New York: Springer, 2014), 337–360.

Daymond, M. J. 'Self-Translation, Untranslatability: The Autobiographies of Mpho Nthunya and Agnes Lottering', in Michael Chapman (ed.), *Postcolonialism: South/African Perspectives* (New Caste: Cambridge Scholars Publishing, 2008), 84–105.

DiAngelo, Robin. *White Fragility: Why It's So Hard for White People to Talk About Racism* (Boston: Beacon, 2018).

Di Palma, Brian C. *Masculinities in the Court Tales of Daniel: Advancing Gender Studies in the Hebrew Bible* (London and New York: Routledge, 2018).

Diamant, Anita. *The Red Tent* (New York: Wyatt Books, 1997).

Dibia, Jude, and Olumide F. Makanjuola (eds). *Queer Men's Narratives* (Abuja: Cassava Republic, 2020).

Driskill, Qwo-Li. *Asegi Stories: Cherokee Queer and Two-Spirit Memory* (Tucson: University of Arisona Press, 2016).

Dube, Musa W. *A Theology of Compassion in the HIV/AIDS Era* (Theology in the HIV/AIDS Era Series, module 7) (Geneva: World Council of Churches, 2007).

——. 'Fifty Years of Bleeding: A Storytelling Feminist Reading of Mark 5:24–43', in Musa W. Dube (ed.), *Other Ways of Reading: African Woman and the Bible* (Atlanta: Society of Biblical Literature, 2001), 50–60.

——. 'Five Husbands at the Well of Living Waters', in Musimbi Kanyoro and Nyambura Njoroge (eds), *A Decade in Solidarity with the Bible* (Geneva: WCC Publications, 1998), 6–26.

——. 'Grant Me Justice: Female and Male Equality in the New Testament', *Journal of Religion and Theology in Namibia*, 3:1 (2001), 82–115, 94–95.

——. 'Introduction', in Musa W. Dube (ed.), *Other Ways of Reading: African Women and the Bible* (Atlanta: Society of Biblical Literature, 2001), 1–19.

——. *Postcolonial Feminist Interpretation of the Bible* (Nashville: Chalice Press, 2000).

——. *The HIV & AIDS Bible: Selected Essays* (Scranton: University of Scranton Press, 2008).

Dube, Musa W., and Musimbi R. A. Kanyoro (eds). *Grant Me Justice! HIV/AIDS & Gender Readings of the Bible* (Maryknoll: Orbis, 2004).

Dube, Musa W., and R. S. Wafula (eds). *Postcoloniality, Translation, and the Bible in Africa* (Eugene: Pickwick Publications, 2017).

Eckert, Penelope, and Sally McConnell-Ginet. *Language and Gender*, 2nd ed. (Cambridge: Cambridge University Press, 2013).

Ekine, Sokari, and Hakima Abbas (eds). *Queer African Reader* (Dar es Salaam: Pambazuka Press, 2013).

Ellison, Marvin M., and Kelly Brown (eds). *Sexuality and the Sacred: Sources for Theological Reflection*, 2nd edn (Louisville: Westminster John Knox Press, 2010).

Englund, Harri (ed.). *Christianity and Public Culture in Africa* (Athens: Ohio University Press, 2012).

Epprecht, Marc. *Sexuality and Social Justice in Africa: Rethinking Homophobia and Forging Resistance* (London: Zed Books, 2013).

Finnegan, Ruth. *Oral Literature in Africa*, rev. edn (Cambridge: Open Book, 2012).

Flaherty, Jordan. *No More Heroes: Grassroots Challenges to the Savior Mentality* (Chico: AK Press, 2016).

Fongang, Delphine. 'Autobiography's *Other*: The Untold Life Narratives from Sub-Saharan Africa', *a/b Auto/Biography Studies*, 32:2 (2017), 393–394.

Furniss, Graham, and Liz Gunner. 'Introduction: Power, Marginality and Oral Literature', in Graham Furniss and Liz Gunner (eds), *Power,*

Marginality and African Oral Literature (Cambridge: Cambridge University Press, 1995), 1–19.

Gabel, Stewart. 'The Book of Daniel: Trauma, Faith, and the Resurrection of the Dead', *Trauma and Memory*, 4:1 (2016), 67–81.

Ganzevoort, R. Ruard. 'Introduction: Religious Stories We Live By', in R. Ruard Ganzevoort, Maaike de Haardt, and Michael Scherer-Rath (eds), *Religious Stories We Live By: Narrative Approaches in Theology and Religious Studies* (Leiden: Brill, 2014), 1-17.

Getui, Mary N., and Matthew M. Theuri (eds). *Quests for Abundant Life in Africa* (Nairobi: Acton, 2002).

Gifford, Paul. 'The Ritual Use of the Bible in African Pentecostalism', in Martin Lindhardt (ed.), *Practicing the Faith: The Ritual Life of Pentecostal-Charismatic Christians* (New York: Berghahn Books, 2011), 179–197.

Goss, Robert E. 'John', in Deryn Guest, Robert E. Goss, Mona West, and Thomas Bohache (eds), *The Queer Bible Commentary* (London: SCM Press, 2006), 548–565.

Goss, Robert E., and Amy Adams Squire Strongheart (eds). *Our Families, Our Values: Snapshots of Queer Kinship* (Binghamton: The Haworth Press, 1997).

Goss, Robert E. and Mona West, 'Introduction', in Robert E. Goss and Mona West (eds), *Take Back the Word: A Queer Reading of the Bible* (Cleveland: The Pilgrim Press, 2000), 3–9.

——. (eds). *Take Back the Word: A Queer Reading of the Bible* (Cleveland: Pilgrim Press 2000).

Greenough, Chris. *Queer Theologies: The Basics* (London and New York: Routledge 2020).

——. *Undoing Theology: Life Stories from Non-Normative Christians* (London: SCM Press, 2018).

Guest, Deryn, Robert E. Goss, Mona West, and Thomas Bohache (eds). *The Queer Bible Commentary* (London: SCM, 2006).

Gunda, Masiiwa Ragies. 'African Christian Theology and Sexuality: Some Considerations', in Elias K. Bongmba (ed.), *The Routledge Handbook of African Theology* (London and New York: Routledge, 2020), 367–380.

——. 'Jesus Christ, Homosexuality and Masculinity in African Christianity: Reading Luke 10:1–12', *Exchange*, 42:1 (2013), 16–33.

——. *The Bible and Homosexuality in Zimbabwe: A Socio-historical Analysis of the Political, Cultural and Christian Arguments in the Homosexual Public Debate with Special Reference to the Use of the Bible* (Bamberg: Bamberg University Press, 2010).

Gunda, Masiiwa Ragies, and Jim Naughton (eds). *On Sexuality and Scripture: Essays, Bible Studies, and Personal Reflections* (New York: Church Publishing, 2017).

Gunda, Masiiwa R., and Joachim Kügler (eds). *The Bible and Politics in Africa* (Bamberg: Bamberg University Press, 2012).

Gutiérrez, Gustavo. *The Power of the Poor in History* (transl. from Spanish by Robert R. Barr) (Eugene: Wipf and Stock, 2004).

Healey, Joseph, and Donald Sybertz. *Towards an African Narrative Theology* (Maryknoll: Orbis, 1996).

Hendricks, Pepe (ed.). *Hijab: Unveiling Queer Muslim Lives* (Cape Town: The Inner Circle, 2009).

Hinga, Teresia M. *African, Christian, Feminist: The Enduring Search for What Matters* (Maryknoll: Orbis, 2017).

Horvath, Christina, and Juliet Carpenter (eds). *Co-Creation in Theory and Practice: Exploring Creativity in the Global North and South* (London: Polity Press, 2020).

Jackson, Michael. *The Politics of Storytelling: Variations on a Theme by Hannah Arendt*, 2nd edn (Copenhagen: Museum Musculanum Press, 2013).

——. *The Wherewithal of Life: Ethics, Migration, and the Question of Well-Being* (Berkeley: University of California Press, 2013).

Jennings, Theodore W. *The Man Jesus Loved: Homoerotic Narratives from the New Testament* (Cleveland: The Pilgrim Press, 2003).

Jordan, Mark. *The Invention of Sodomy in Christian Theology* (Chicago: University of Chicago Press, 1997).

Judge, Melanie. 'Navigating Paradox: Towards a Conceptual Framework for Activism at the Intersection of Religion and Sexuality', *HTS Theological Studies*, 73:3 (2020), 1–10;

Kalinga, Chisomo. 'Love: An Ethnographic Inquiry into Queer, Christian Relationships in Kenya', *HAU: Journal of Ethnographic Theory*, 10:2 (2020), 623–625.

Kaoma, Kapya. *Christianity, Globalization, and Protective Homophobia: Democratic Contestation of Sexuality in Sub-Saharan Africa* (New York: Palgrave Macmillan, 2018).

——. *Globalizing the Culture Wars: U. S. Conservatives, African Churches, & Homophobia* (Somerville: Political Research Associates, 2009).

——. '"I Say, We must Talk, Talk, Mama!" Introducing African Voices on Religion, Ubuntu and Sexual Diversity', *Journal of Theology for Southern Africa*, 155 (2016), 6–27.

Kaschula, Russell H. 'Introduction: Oral Literature in Contemporary Contexts', in Russell H. Kaschula (ed.), *African Oral Literature: Functions in Contemporary Contexts* (Claremont: New Africa Books, 2001), xi–xxvi.

Katongole, Emmanuel M. '"African Renaissance" and the Challenge of Narrative Theology in Africa', *Journal of Theology for Southern Africa*, 102 (1998), 29–39.

Kiambi, Julius Kithinji. 'Divining John 7:53–8:11 for Textual Gender-motivated violence: A Postcolonial Approach' (unpublished paper, 2012), https://papers.ssrn.com/sol3/papers.cfm?abstract_id=2017643 (accessed 16 December 2020).

Kintu, Deborah. *The Ugandan Morality Crusade: The Brutal Campaign against Homosexuality and Pornography under Yoweri Museveni* (Jefferson: McFarland, 2017).

Kizza, Immaculate N. *The Oral Tradition of the Baganda of Uganda: A Study and Anthology of Legends, Myths, Epigrams and Folktales* (Jefferson: McFarland, 2009).

Knust, Jennifer, and Tommy Wasserman. *To Cast the First Stone: The Transmission of a Gospel Story* (Princeton: Princeton University Press, 2019).

Kügler, Joachim, and Masiiwa R. Gunda (eds). *From Text to Practice: The Role of the Bible in Daily Living of African People Today*, 2nd edn (Bamberg: University of Bamberg Press, 2013).

Kuloba, Robert W. '"Homosexuality is Unafrican and Unbiblical": Examining the Ideological Motivations to Homophobia in Sub-Saharan Africa – The Case Study of Uganda', *Journal of Theology in Southern Africa*, 154 (2016), 6–27.

Lawman, Mourna Esaie de-Sia. 'Reading the Book of Daniel in an African Context: The Issue of Leadership' (DTheol. thesis, University of South Africa, 2013).

Lisanework, Zelly (ed.). *Tikur Eugeda: Queer Stories from Ethiopia* (Addis Ababa: House of Guramayle, 2019).

Long, Ronald E. 'Disarming Biblically Based Gay-bashing', in Deryn Guest, Robert E. Goss, and Mona West (eds), *The Queer Bible Commentary* (London: SCM Press, 2006), 1–18.

Lungu, James. 'Socio-cultural and Gender Perspectives in John 7:53–8:11: Exegetical Reflections in the Context of Violence against Women in Zambia' (MA thesis, University of Stellenbosch 2016).

Lynch, Gordon. *The Sacred in the Modern World: A Cultural Sociological Approach* (Oxford: Oxford University Press, 2012).

Macharia, Keguro. 'Archive and Method in Queer African Studies', *Agenda*, 29:1 (2015), 140–146.

Magesa, Laurenti. *What Is Not Sacred? African Spirituality* (Maryknoll: Orbis, 2013).

Maluleke, Tinyiko S. 'African "Ruths", Ruthless Africas: Reflections of an African Mordecai', in Musa W. Dube (ed.), *Other Ways of Reading: African Women and the Bible* (Atlanta: Society of Biblical Literature, 2001), 237–251.

Mapfeka, Tsaurayi K. 'Empire and Identity Secrecy: A Postcolonial Reflection on Esther 2:10', in Johanna Stiebert and Musa W. Dube (eds), *The Bible, Centres and Margins: Dialogues Between Postcolonial African and British Scholars* (London: T&T Clark, 2018), 79–95.

Marnell, John. *Seeking Sanctuary: Stories of Sexuality, Faith and Migration* (Johannesburg: Wits University Press, 2021).

Masenya, Madipoane. 'Proverbs 31:10–31 in a South African Context: A Reading for the Liberation of African (Northern Sotho) Women', *Semeia*, 78 (1997), 55–68.

Matebeni, Zethu. 'Introduction', in Unoma Azuah (ed.), *Blessed Body*: *The Secret Lives of Nigerian Lesbian, Gay, Bisexual and Transgender* (Jackson: CookingPot, 2016), 1–2.

Matebeni, Zethu, Surya Monro, and Vasu Reddy (eds). *Queer in Africa: LGBTQI Identities, Citizenship, and Activism* (London and New York: Routledge, 2018).

Mbembe, Achille. 'Necropolitics', *Public Culture*, 15:1 (2003), 11–40.

Mbiti, John. *African Religions and Philosophy*, 2nd edn (London: Heinemann, 1990).

Mburu, Elizabeth. *African Hermeneutics* (Carlisle: HippoBooks, 2019).

Mbuvi, Andrew M. 'Daniel', in Hugh R. Page, Jr. (ed.), *The Africana Bible: Reading Israel's Scriptures from Africa and the African Diaspora* (Minneapolis: Fortress Press, 2010), 273–279.

Meiu, George Paul. 'Underlayers of Citizenship: Queer Objects, Intimate Exposures, and the Rescue Rush in Kenya', *Cultural Anthropology*, 35:4 (2020), 575–601.

Mgbako, Chi. *To Live Freely in This World: Sex Worker Activism in Africa* (New York: New York University Press, 2016).

Miller, Joshua H. '"Until Death Do We (Queers) Part": (Queer) Biblical Interpretation, (Invented) Truth, and Presumption in Controversies Concerning Biblical Characters' Sexualities', *QED: A Journal in GLBTQ Worldmaking*, 4:1 (2017), 42–67.

Mills, Scott. *Uganda: The World's Worst Place to Be Gay?* Documentary of the British Broadcasting Corporation, 2011.

Mligo, Elia Shabani. 'Jesus and the Stigmatized: Reading the Gospel of John in a Context of HIV/AIDS-Related Stigmatization in Tanzania' (PhD thesis, University of Oslo, 2009).

Mohammed, Azeenarh, Chitra Nagarajan, and Rafeeat Aliyu (eds). *She Called Me Woman: Nigeria's Queer Women Speak* (Abuja: Cassava Republic, 2018).

Morales, Helen. *Antigone Rising: The Subversive Power of the Ancient Myths* (London: Wildfire, 2020).

Mtshiselwa, Ndikho. 'Re-Reading of 1 Kings 21:1–29 and Jehu's Revolution in Dialogue with Farisani and Nzimande: Negotiating Socio-Economic Redress in South Africa', *Old Testament Essays*, 27:1 (2014), 205–230.

Mwachiro, Kevin (ed.). *Invisible: Stories from Kenya's Queer Community* (Nairobi: Goethe Institut, 2013).

Nadar, Sarojini. 'Her-Stories and Her-Theologies: Charting Feminist Theologies in Africa', *Studia Historiae Ecclesiasticae* 35 (2009), 135-150.

——. '"Stories are Data with Soul" – Lessons from Black Feminist Epistemology', *Agenda*, 28:1 (2014), 18–28.

Nannyonga-Tamusuza, Sylvia A. *Baakisimba: Gender in the Music and Dance of the Baganda People of Uganda* (New York and London: Routledge, 2005).

'National Population and Housing Census 2014 – Main Report' (Kampala: Uganda Bureau of Statistics, 2016).

Naughton, Jake, and Jacob Kushner. *This is How the Heart Beats: LGBTQ East Africa* (New York: The New Press, 2020).

Ndzovu, Hassan J. '"Un-natural", "un-African" and "un-Islamic": The Three Pronged Onslaught on Undermining Homosexual Freedom in Kenya', in Adriaan van Klinken and Ezra Chitando (eds), *Public Religion and the Politics of Homosexuality in Africa* (London and New York: Routledge, 2016), 78–91.

Njoroge, Nyambura J. 'The Bible and African Christianity: A Curse or a Blessing?' in Musa W. Dube (ed.), *Other Ways of Reading: African Women and the Bible* (Atlanta: Society of Biblical Literature, 2001), 207–236.

Nyanzi, Stella. 'Dismantling Reified African Culture through Localised Homosexualities in Uganda', *Culture, Health and Sexuality*, 15:8 (2013), 952–967.

——. 'Queer Pride and Protest: A Reading of the Bodies at Uganda's First Gay Beach Pride', *Signs: Journal of Women in Culture and Society*, 40:1 (2014), 36–40.

Nyanzi, Stella, and Andrew Karamagi. 'The Social-political Dynamics of the Anti-Homosexuality Legislation in Uganda', *Agenda*, 29:1 (2015), 24–38.

Nyeck, S. N. 'African Religions, the Parapolitics of Discretion and Sexual Ambiguity in African Oral Epics', *Journal of Theology for Southern Africa*, 155 (2016): 88–103.

Nzimande, Makhosazana K. 'Reconfiguring Jezebel: A Postcolonial Imbokodo Reading of the Story of Naboth's Vineyard (1 Kings 21:1–16)', in Hans de Wit and Gerald O. West (eds), *African and European Readers of the Bible in Dialogue: In Quest of a Shared Meaning* (Leiden: Brill, 2008), 223–258.

Oduyoye, Mercy A. 'Biblical Interpretation and the Social Location of the Interpreter: African Women's Reading of the Bible', in Fernando F. Segovia and Mary Ann Tolbert (eds), *Reading from this Place: Social Location and Biblical Interpretation in Global Perspectives* (Minneapolis: Fortress Press, 1995), 33–51.

——. *Daughters of Anowa: African Women and Patriarchy* (Maryknoll: Orbis, 1995).

——. *Introducing African Women's Theology* (Cleveland: The Pilgrim Press, 2001).

——. 'Jesus Christ', in Susan F. Parsons (ed.), *The Cambridge Companion to Feminist Theology* (Cambridge: Cambridge University Press, 2002), 151–170.

Okpewho, Isidore. *African Oral Literature: Backgrounds, Character, and Continuity* (Bloomington: Indiana University Press, 1992).

Ombagi, Eddie. '"Stories We Tell": Queer Narratives in Kenya', *Social Dynamics*, 45:3 (2019), 410–424.

Ottuh, John Arierhi. 'Reading Deuteronomy 22:22 in John 8:1–11: A Contextual Reading from an African-Urhobo Perspective', *Scriptura*, 118:1 (2019), 1–19.

Otu, Kwame E. 'LGBT Human Rights Expeditions in Homophobic Safaris: Racialized Neoliberalism and Post-Traumatic White Disorder in the BBC's *The World's Worst Place to Be Gay*', *Critical Ethnic Studies*, 3:2 (2017), 126–150.

Parsitau, Damaris. 'From Victimhood to Creative Resistance: The Book that Tells Stories and Signals Other Ways of Being', *Religious Studies Review*, 46:3, 337-339.

——. 'Gospel Music in Africa', in Elias Bongmba (ed.), *The Wiley-Blackwell Companion to African Religions* (Malden: Wiley-Blackwell, 2012), 489–502.

Paszat, Emma. 'Why "Uganda's Anti-Homosexuality Bill"? Rethinking the "Coherent" State', *Third World Quarterly*, 38:9 (2017), 2027–2044.

Pelikan, Jaroslav Jan, and E. P. Sanders. 'Scribes and Pharisees', *Encyclopaedia Britannica*, www.britannica.com/biography/Jesus/ Scribes-and-Pharisees (accessed 16 December 2020).

Phiri, Isabel A., and Sarojini Nadar (eds). *African Women, Religion, and Health: Essays in Honour of Mercy Amba Ewudziwa Oduyoye* (Pietermaritzburg: Cluster, 2006).

Phiri, Isabel A., Beverley Haddad, and Madipoane Masenya (eds). *African Women, HIV/AIDS, and Faith Communities* (Maryknoll: Orbis, 2003).

Phiri, Isabel A., Devarakshanam Betty Govinden, and Sarojini Nadar (eds). *Her-Stories: Hidden Histories of Women of Faith in Africa* (Pietermaritzburg: Cluster, 2002).

Phiri, Lilly, and Sarojini Nadar. 'To Move or Not to Move! Queering Borders and Faith in the Context of Diverse Sexualities in Southern Africa', in Daisy L. Machado, Bryan S. Turner, and Trygve Eiliv Wyller (eds), *Borderland Religion: Ambiguous Practices of Difference, Hope and Beyond* (London and New York: Routledge, 2016), 74–86.

Pinnock, Kate. 'UNHCR and LGBTI Refugees in Kenya: The Limits of "Protection"', *Disasters*, 22 May 2020, https://doi.org/10.1111/ disa.12447.

Plaatjie, Gloria Kehilwe. 'Toward a Post-apartheid Black Feminist Reading of the Bible: A Case of Luke 2:36–38', in Musa W. Dube (ed.), *Other Ways of Reading: African Women and the Bible* (Atlanta: Society of Biblical Literature, 2001), 114–142.

Pyper, Hugh S. 'Looking into the Lions' Den: Otherness, Ideology, and Illustration in Children's Versions of Daniel 6', in Caroline Vander Stichele and Hugh S. Pyper (eds), *Text, Image, and Otherness in Children's Bibles: What is in the Picture* (Atlanta: Society of Biblical Literature, 2012), 51–72.

Quayesi-Amakye, Joseph. 'In the Citadel of Susa was a Jewish "Troublemaker": A Sociopolitical Reading of Esther 3 and 4', *Ghana Journal of Religion and Theology*, 7:1 (2017), 51–63.

Rao, Rahul. *Out of Time: The Queer Politics of Postcoloniality* (New York: Oxford University Press, 2020).

——. 'Re-membering Mwanga: Same-sex Intimacy, Memory and Belonging in Postcolonial Uganda', *Journal of Eastern African Studies*, 9:1 (2015), 1–19.

——. *Third World Protest: Between Home and the World* (Oxford: Oxford University Press, 2010).

Reading Together: A Bible Study Method (Cape Town: Inclusive and Affirming Ministries, 2019), http://iam.org.za/wp-content/uploads/2019/03/IAM_Reading-Together_v4.pdf (accessed 16 December).

Reaves, Jayme R. 'Sarah as Victim and Perpetrator: Whiteness, Power, and Memory in the Matriarchal Narrative', *Review and Expositor* (2018), 1–17.

'Refugee Law and Policy: Kenya', Library of Congress, www.loc.gov/law/help/refugee-law/kenya.php#_ftn69 (accessed 16 December 2020).

Robertson, Megan. 'Queerying Scholarship on Christianity and Queer Sexuality: Reviewing Nuances and New Directions', *African Journal of Gender and Religion*, 23:2 (2017). 125–144.

Rodriguez, S. M. *The Economies of Queer Inclusion: Transnational Organizing for LGBTI Rights in Uganda* (Lanham: Lexington Books, 2019).

Sadgrove, Joanna, Robert M. Vanderbeck, Johan Andersson, Gill Valentine, and Kevin Ward. 'Morality Plays and Money Matters: Towards a Situated Understanding of the Politics of Homosexuality in Uganda', *Journal of Modern African Studies*, 50:1 (2012), 103–129.

Salhi, Kamal (ed.), *African Theatre for Development: Art for self-determination* (Bristol: Intellect Books, 1998).

Sanneh, Lamin. *Whose Religion in Christianity? The Gospel Beyond the West* (Grand Rapids: William B. Eerdmans, 2003).

Schottroff, Luise. *Lydia's Impatient Sisters: A Feminist Social History of Early Christianity* (Louisville: Westminster John Knox Press, 1995).

Schüssler Fiorenza, Elisabeth. *But She Said: Feminist Practices of Biblical Interpretation* (Boston: Beacon Press, 1992).

Shivute, Namupa. 'UNHCR's Kakuma Camp is No Refuge', 25 February 2020, https://gal-dem.com/kakuma-lgbtqi-refugee-unhcr-kenya-queer-phobia (accessed 22 April 2020).

Shore-Goss, Robert, and Joseph N. Goh (eds). *Unlocking Orthodoxies for Inclusive Theologies: Queer Alternatives* (London and New York: Routledge, 2020).

Spear, Thomas C. 'Introduction: Autobiographical Que(e)ries', *a/b Auto/Biography Studies*, 15:1 (2000), 1–4.

——. 'Introduction: Autobiographical, Queer We's', *a/b Auto/Biography Studies*, 15:2 (2000), 167–170.

Spivak, Gayatry C. 'Can the Subaltern Speak?' in Rosalind Morris (ed.), *Can the Subaltern Speak? Reflections on the History of an Idea* (New York: Columbia University Press, 2010), 21–78.

Stiebert, Johanna. 'Of Borders, Crossings, Colours and Botswana', in Johanna Stiebert and Musa W. Dube (eds), *The Bible, Centres and Margins: Dialogues Between Postcolonial African and British Biblical Scholars* (London: T&T Clark, 2018), 15–23.

Stinton, Diane B. *Jesus of Africa: Voices of Contemporary African Christology* (Nairobi: Paulines, 2004).

Stone, Ken. 'Queer Reading between Bible and Film: Paris is Burning and the "Legendary Houses" of David and Saul', in Teresa J. Hornsby and Ken Stone (eds), *Bible Trouble: Queer Reading at the Boundaries of Biblical Scholarship* (Atlanta: Society of Biblical Literature, 2011), 75–98.

Stone-Mediatore, Shari. *Reading across Borders: Storytelling and Knowledges of Resistance* (New York: Palgrave Macmillan, 2003).

Straubhaar, Rolf. 'The Stark Reality of the "White Saviour" Complex and the Need for Critical Consciousness: A Document Analysis of the Early Journals of a Freirean Educator', *Compare: A Journal of Comparative and International Education*, 45:3 (2015), 381–400.

Stories of Our Lives (Nairobi: The Nest Collective, 2015).

Talvacchia, Kathleen T., Michael F. Pettinger, and Mark Larrimore (eds), *Queer Christianities: Lived Religion in Transgressive Forms* (New York: New York University Press, 2015).

Tamale, Sylvia. 'A Human Rights Impact Assessment of the Ugandan Anti-homosexuality Bill 2009', *The Equal Rights Review*, 4 (2009), 49–57.

Thapa, Saurav J. 'LGBT Uganda Today: Continuing Danger Despite Nullification of Anti-Homosexuality Act', *Human Rights Campaign: Global Spotlights*, September 2015, http://assets2.hrc.org/files/assets/resources/Global_Spotlight_Uganda__designed_version__September_25__2015.pdf (accessed 16 December 2020), 1–5.

The Bible and Homosexuality (Cape Town: Inclusive and Affirming Ministries, 2008), http://iam.org.za/wp-content/uploads/2019/01/IAM-Booklet-The-Bible-Homosexuality-Eng-content-1.pdf (accessed 16 December 2020).

The Nature Network. 'Could This Be The Love You Get From Your Biological Parents?' 29 October 2019, https://thenaturenetworkgroup.blogspot.com/2019/10/could-this-be-love-you-get-from-your.html (accessed 16 December 2020).

——. 'Homosexuality, Religiosity and the Beauty of All Creatures; A Transgender Group's Take', 2 July 2017, https://thenaturenetwork-group.blogspot.com/2017/07/homosexuality-religiosity-and-beauty-of.html (accessed 16 December 2020).

——. 'Nature Network – a Profile', 9 April 2020, https://thenaturenetwork-group.blogspot.com/2020/04/nature-network-profile.html (accessed 16 December 2020).

'The Ujamaa Centre for Biblical and Theological Community Development and Research', http://ujamaa.ukzn.ac.za/Homepage.aspx (accessed 16 December 2020).

Thoreson, Ryan R. 'Troubling the Waters of a "Wave of Homophobia": Political Economies of Anti-queer Animus in Sub-Saharan Africa', *Sexualities*, 17:1–2 (2014), 23–42.

Tofa, Eliot. 'The Bible and the Quest for Democracy and Democratization in Africa: The Zimbabwe Experience', in Masiiwa R. Gunda and Joachim Kügler (eds), *The Bible and Politics in Africa* (Bamberg: Bamberg University Press, 2012), 42–60.

Trible, Phyllis. *Texts of Terror: Literary-Feminist Readings of Biblical Narratives* (Minneapolis: Fortress Press, 1984).

'Uganda Report of Violations Based on Gender Identity and Sexual Orientation', The Consortium on Monitoring Violations Based on Sex Determination, Gender Identity and Sexual Orientation, September 2015, https://outrightinternational.org/sites/default/files/15_02_22_lgbt_violations_report_2015_final.pdf (accessed 16 December 2020).

van der Walt, Charlene. 'Is "Being Right" More Important than "Being Together"? Intercultural Bible Reading and Life-giving Dialogue on Homosexuality in the Dutch Reformed Church, South Africa', in Ezra Chitando and Adriaan van Klinken (eds), *Christianity and Controversies over Homosexuality in Contemporary Africa* (London and New York: Routledge, 2016), 125–140.

van Klinken, Adriaan. 'Autobiographical Storytelling and African Narrative Queer Theology', *Exchange: Journal of Contemporary Christianities in Context*, 47:3 (2018), 211–229.

——. 'Changing the Narrative of Sexuality in African Christianity: Bishop Christopher Senyonjo's LGBT Advocacy', *Theology and Sexuality*, 26:1 (2020), 1–6

——. *Kenyan, Christian, Queer: Religion, LGBT Activism, and Arts of Resistance in Africa* (University Park: Penn State University Press, 2019).

——. *Transforming Masculinities in African Christianity: Gender Controversies in Times of AIDS* (Farnham: Ashgate, 2013).

van Klinken, Adriaan, and Ebenezer Obadare, 'Christianity, Sexuality and Citizenship in Africa: Critical Intersections', *Citizenship Studies*, 22:6 (2018), 557–568.

van Klinken, Adriaan, and Johanna Stiebert. 'Challenging Contexts from the Lions' Den: Reading Daniel with Ugandan LGBT Refugees in Nairobi', in Louise Lawrence, Peter-Ben Smit, Hannah Strømmen, and Charlene van der Walt (eds), *Challenging Contexts: Biblical Texts Beyond Boundaries* (Oxford: Oxford University Press, forthcoming).

van Klinken, Adriaan, and Masiiwa Ragies Gunda. 'Taking Up the Cudgels Against Gay Rights? Trends and Trajectories in African Christian Theologies on Homosexuality', *Journal of Homosexuality*, 59:1 (2012), 114–138.

Wahab, Amar. '"Homosexuality/Homophobia Is Un-African"? Un-Mapping Transnational Discourses in the Context of Uganda's Anti-Homosexuality Bill/Act', *Journal of Homosexuality*, 63:5 (2016), 685–718.

Ward, Kevin. 'Religious Institutions and Actors and Religious Attitudes to Homosexual Rights: South Africa and Uganda', in Matthew Waites and Corinne Lennox (eds), *Human Rights, Sexual Orientation and Gender Identity in The Commonwealth: Struggles for Decriminalisation and Change* (London: Institute of Commonwealth Studies, 2013), 410–428.

Weems, Renita J. *Just a Sister Away: A Womanist Vision of Women's Relationships in the Bible* (Philadelphia: Innisfree Press, 1988).

West, Gerald. 'Negotiating with "the White Man's Book": Early Foundations for Liberation Hermeneutics in Southern Africa', in Emmanuel M. Katongole (ed.), *African Theology Today* (Scranton: University of Scranton Press, 2002), 23–56.

——. 'Reception of the Bible: The Bible in Africa', in J. Riches (ed.), *The New Cambridge History of the Bible* (Cambridge: Cambridge University Press, 2015), 347–390.

——. *The Academy of the Poor: Towards a Dialogical Reading of the Bible* (Sheffield: Continuum, 1999).

——. *The Stolen Bible: From Tool of Imperialism to African Icon* (Leiden: Brill, 2016).

——. 'Towards an African Liberationist Queer Theological Pedagogy', *Journal of Theology for Southern Africa* 155 (2016), 216–224.

West, Gerald, and Charlene van der Walt. 'A Queer (Beginning to the) Bible', *Concilium*, 5 (2019), 109–118.

West, Gerald, and Musa W. Dube (eds). *The Bible in Africa: Transactions, Trajectories, and Trends* (Leiden: Brill, 2010).

West, Gerald, and Phumzile Zondi-Mabizela. 'The Bible Story that Became a Campaign: The Tamar Campaign in South Africa (and Beyond)', *Ministerial Formation*, 103 (2004), 5–13.

West, Gerald, Charlene van der Walt, and Kapya Kaoma. 'When Faith Does Violence: Reimagining Engagement between Churches and LGBTI Groups on Homophobia in Africa', *HTS Theological Studies*, 17:1 (2016), 1–8.

West, Mona. 'Daniel', in Deryn Guest, Robert E. Goss, Mona West, and Thomas Bohache (eds), *The Queer Bible Commentary* (London: SCM, 2006), 427–431.

Weston, Kath. *Families We Choose: Lesbians, Gays, Kinship*, rev. edn (New York: Columbia University Press, 1997).

Wilcox, Melissa M. *Queer Religiosities: An Introduction to Queer and Transgender Studies in Religion* (Lanham: Rowman & Littlefield, 2020).

Williams, Delores S. *Sister in the Wilderness: The Challenge of Womanist God-Talk* (Maryknoll: Orbis, 2013).

Xaba, Makhosazana, and Crystal Biruk (eds). *Proudly Malawian: Life Stories from Lesbian and Gender-Nonconforming Individuals* (Johannesburg: GALA, 2016).

Yafeh-Deigh, Alice. 'Rethinking Paul's Sexual Ethics within the Context of HIV and AIDS: A Postcolonial Afro-Feminist-Womanist Perspective', in Madipoane Masenya (Ngwan'a Mphahlele), and Kenneth N. Ngwa (eds), *Navigating African Biblical Hermeneutics: Trends and Themes from Our Pots and Our Calabashes* (Newcastle: Cambridge Scholar Publishing, 2018), 20–39.

Zomorodi, Gitta. 'Responding to LGBT Forced Migration in East Africa', *Forced Migration Review*, 52 (2016), 91–93, www.fmreview.org/solutions/zomorodi (accessed 16 December 2020).

Index of Names and Subjects

Authors' names are by surname with one first name or initial. For full names, see the Bibliography.

Index of Biblical References

The order of biblical books follows that of the NRSV, New Revised Standard Version

Old Testament

New Testament

Previously published titles in the series

Violent Conversion: Brazilian Pentecostalism and Urban Women in Mozambique, Linda Van de Kamp (2016)

Beyond Religious Tolerance: Muslim, Christian & Traditionalist Encounters in an African Town, edited by Insa Nolte, Olukoya Ogen and Rebecca Jones (2017)

Faith, Power and Family: Christianity and Social Change in French Cameroon, Charlotte Walker-Said (2018)

Contesting Catholics: Benedicto Kiwanuka and the Birth of Postcolonial Uganda, Jonathon L. Earle and J. J. Carney (2021)

Islamic Scholarship in Africa: New Directions and Global Contexts, edited by Ousmane Oumar Kane (2021)

From Rebels to Rulers: Writing Legitimacy in the Early Sokoto State, Paul Naylor (2021)

Sacred Queer Stories: Ugandan LGBTQ+ Refugee Lives and the Bible, Adriaan Van Klinken and Johanna Stiebert, with Sebyala Brian and Fredrick Hudson (2021)

Labour & Christianity in the Mission: African Workers in Tanganyika and Zanzibar, 1864–1926, Michelle Liebst (2021)

The Genocide against the Tutsi, and the Rwandan Churches: Between Grief and Denial, Philippe Denis (2022)

Competing Catholicisms: The Jesuits, the Vatican & the Making of Postcolonial French Africa, Jean Luc Enyegue, SJ (2022)

Islam in Uganda: The Muslim Minority, Nationalism & Political Power, Joseph Kasule (2022)

Spiritual Contestations – The Violence of Peace in South Sudan, Naomi Ruth Pendle (2023)